NATIONAL PAST-TIMES

BODY, COMMODITY, TEXT

Studies of Objectifying Practice

A series edited by

Arjun Appadurai,

Jean Comaroff, and

Judith Farquhar

NATIONAL PAST-TIMES

Narrative, Representation, and Power

in Modern China

ANN ANAGNOST

Duke University Press

Durham & London

1997

© 1997 Duke University Press
All rights reserved
Printed in the United States of America on acid-free paper ∞
Typeset in Minion by Keystone Typesetting, Inc.
Library of Congress Cataloging-in-Publication Data appear on
the last printed page of this book.

CONTENTS

ACKNOWLEDGMENTS

The essays that compose this book were written over a period of ten years and are the product of three research trips to the People's Republic of China. The first in 1981–82 was funded by a Fulbright-Hays Dissertation Research Grant, the second in May and June 1989 was funded by the University of Illinois Research Board, and the third in 1991 was funded by the Committee on Scholarly Communication with China. In addition, I acknowledge the support of the Stanford Humanities Center, where I was a fellow for the 1989–90 academic years. Research support was also provided by the China Program's Fritz Endowment at the University of Washington Jackson School of International Studies. I thank all these institutions for their generous support of this project. Nanjing University provided the institutional locus for all three research trips, and I acknowledge the friendship and support of Zhongqi Lu, Ling Xiao, Xiaoming Zhang, and numerous other friends whose contributions to this project, in the spirit of ethnographic confidentiality, must remain anonymous.

I am indebted to many colleagues and friends who have engaged in innumerable discussions with me or who have tirelessly read and commented on earlier versions of this work. Among my colleagues at the University of Washington, I thank Tani Barlow, Stevan Harrell, Marilyn Ivy, Charles Keyes, John Pemberton, and Lorna Rhodes. Among colleagues at other institutions, I am indebted to Christopher Roberts Davis, Norma Diamond, Prasenjit Duara, Elena Feder, Akhil Gupta, James Hevia, Theodore Huters, Bill Kelleher, Lisa Rofel, Michael Taussig, and Marilyn Young. I also acknowledge Judith Farquhar's elegant amendments to the "Introduction," Ted Huter's close reading and Tani Barlow's editorial help for Chapter 1, Lisa Rofel's comments on Chapter 5, and Kevin O'Brien's careful reading of Chapter 6. I thank Ken Wissoker, acquisitions editor for Duke University Press, for his persistent encouragement, and the two anonymous reviewers for the Press, both of whom contributed greatly to my final revisions.

Earlier versions of some of these essays have been published elsewhere. Parts of Chapter 1 appeared as "Who Is Speaking Here?: Discursive Boundaries and Representation in Post-Mao China," in *Boundaries in Chinese Culture*, ed. John Hay (London: Reaktion, 1995). Chapter 4 appeared as "The Politicized Body," in *Body, Subject, Power in China*, ed. Tani Barlow and Angela Zito (Chicago: University of Chicago Press, 1994), and in the *Stanford Humanities Review* 2, 1 (1991). Chapter 5 appeared as "A Surfeit of Bodies: Population and the Rationality of State in Post-Mao China," in *Conceiving the New World Order: Local/Global Intersections in the Politics of Reproduction*, ed. Faye Ginsburg and Rayna Rapp (Berkeley: University of California Press, 1995). Parts of Chapter 6 will appear as "Constructing the Civilized Community," in *Culture and State in Chinese History: Conventions, Conflicts, and Accommodations*, ed. R. Bin Wong, Theodore Huters, and Pauline Yu (Stanford: Stanford University Press, in press). Chapter 7 first appeared in *positions* 1, 3 (1993). I am grateful for permission to reprint them here.

INTRODUCTION

"Pastime" suggests a state of leisured reverie, the occupation of keeping oneself amused while time passes imperceptibly, surely a paradoxical condition given the bustle of China's economic "takeoff" in the last decade. Even more odd, perhaps, is the idea of making a pastime of the nation, usually thought to be nothing if not eventful. And yet, in the midst of the hurly-burly, boom-and-bust conditions of everyday life in reform-era China, one does occasionally catch sight of sometimes ephemeral ways in which the nation becomes an object of contemplative reflection, whether in the hidden spaces of everyday life or as a commodified space of leisure activity. In the cramped interiors of urban apartments, the constant reorganization of objects stowed away in the recesses of daily life may cause one's hand to come to rest on a small trove of Mao buttons or a diary—mementos of tumultuous political movements in the Mao period. Too precious to throw away but not quite right for public display, they resurface periodically as an uncanny reminder of a very different time of the nation. Or, one might tour to a distant theme park that presumes to encapsulate all the different "times" of the nation in all its deep antiquity, from which the Mao years appear to be curiously absent. At times, this contemplative mood shifts into a more "fevered" activity, as it did in the heated intellectual and political debates of the 1980s, when something called "Chinese culture" was being (re)constructed, assessed, rejected, embraced, and transformed, as China itself, increasingly incorporated into a global economic system, was undergoing a profound economic and social transformation.[1] During this decade, no practice that announced itself as "modern" or "reformed" escaped examination of what its relationship to Chinese "culture" should be. Moreover, Chinese "tradition" was similarly subjected to an intense scrutiny for elements that might either impede or facilitate China's progress toward economic and political modernity.

What is striking about these discourses and practices is how the paradoxical unity of the "nation" in time and space has been fragmented by the accretion of layered temporalities within social memory. These different layerings of time that break up the continuum of the recent past become expressed as modes of nostalgia or lament for moments when the nation had been "imagined" in very different terms. Therefore, the word "pastime" also refers, in one of its more obsolete senses, to "passed time," a temporality alien to the present that none-theless bears its traces in the nostalgic process of "rememoration," a backward glance that reconfigures the past in terms of desire and loss. Therefore, with my theme of "national past-times" I gather up all these meanings in an attempt to capture the very particular temporality of the modern Chinese nation-state, encompassing such a complex stratigraphy of the disparate "times of the na-tion" of the recent past and the nation's propensity for continually looking backward in order to face the future.

In China, these layered temporalities assume their most explicit form in the mass media production in the late 1980s of a set of generational classifications. Generations spanning Chinese history since Liberation are numbered in se-quence and each is attributed with certain kinds of experiences, emotions, moral qualities, modes of nostalgia, and relations to the commodity culture and its explosive emergence in late century. Beginning with the generation of the "old revolutionaries" (*lao geming*), which included Mao and his cohort, and ending with the "fifth generation," who are coming of age in the period follow-ing the 1989 suppression of students in Tiananmen, these generational cohorts have become, in popular discourse, a means of social analysis, a way of posi-tioning individuals, including oneself, in a time of rapid change.[2] As a set of generational identities, they provide the stuff of narration, in which the narra-tor's life is fitted into the larger narrative frame of the nation itself.

In what way are nations "like" narrations? This is the question posed in recent discussions on nationalism which insistently draw our attention to the nation as an "impossible unity" that must be narrated into being in both time and space.[3] Indeed, the very impossibility of the nation as a unified subject means that this narrating activity is never final. For narrative exemplifies the performativity of language itself, disrupting the closure of any totalizing defini-tion of the national community. The gaps bridged by narrative always bear the potential to reappear at moments of crisis, producing a "double time" of the nation whereby the nation's impossible unity in the present rests on its (re)nar-rativization of the past. In the following chapters, I have attempted to capture this doubleness in the narrative practices of the nation as they have unfolded in modern China by noting important disjunctures in its recent history. By focus-ing on a series of moments rather than writing a continuous narrative, I wish to break up a monolithic construction that would see the "nation" as the evolution of a selfsame subject through time. Instead, I wish to note the discontinuities, times at which the national narrative has been radically reorganized at critical moments in China's modern history. My selection of these moments is not arbitrary; rather it is motivated by a need to locate the discourse of the nation within a more global context, for the idea of the nation is never sui generis but is constituted always in relation to an "outside."

This tension between the inside and the outside, between the principles of incorporation and exclusion in defining the national body and its culture, often takes the form of the tension between the universal and the particular.[4] Although the nation almost universally claims to be the transcendental expression of a "modern" political sovereignty, it tends to do so in the name of a cultural essence that distinguishes its particularity from all other nations. Partha Chatterjee suggests that whereas the idea of the nation announces itself as a category of universal history, the postcolonial nations of Africa and Asia are constituted on a principle of difference, founded on a construction of their cultural particularity, rather than a wholesale adaptation of the nation as a universal form.[5] Thought of in this way, the nation situates itself within universal history (as the history of the nation's coming to self-awareness) while preserving its "spiritual essence" as an identification with a primordial (hence timeless) culture that becomes enframed as the national "tradition." And yet the specific ways in which postcolonial nations participate in the universal and particular dimensions of nation-ness are as multiple and varied as the historical contingencies that pull them into the dynamic embrace of an articulated world economic system, in that the sites which become ideologically loaded as central to the national essence may be quite differently located and configured. Insofar as these sites are discursively constructed, they are ordered by symbolic and imaginary figures that cannot be fully assimilated to any unifying logic. Therefore, this apparent split between the universal and the particular—between modernity and national "essence"—cannot in itself be reduced to any uniform "third world" model but is the product of a complex set of exchanges working globally. Certainly, at the turn of the century, Japan's military successes made "in the name of" a newly constructed national "spirit" become the "model" par excellence for attaining national sovereignty not only for China but also in places of the world far removed from East Asia.[6] Indeed, the notion of "dissemination" has been suggested to supplant the mechanical replication of the model, given the varied and uncertain trajectories that the idea of the nation (and the national essence) has taken in its complex global dispersal.[7] Moreover, the tension between the universal and the particular cannot be expressed merely as a tension between East and West but is also a complex and dynamic set of exchanges circulating throughout the non-Western world, exchanges that took quite disparate forms with differing measures of success in realizing national dreams of wealth and power, not to mention the assurance of national sovereignty itself.

Not only does the nation mark its impossible unity in relation to time, but also in space. The nation-space is never unitary but multiple within itself. Communist rhetoric, in its exquisitely detailed language of class analysis, situated subjects in differential positions in relation to the national culture. Moreover, these constructions of class had to overcome the paradoxical enterprise of staging a Communist revolution in what was still overwhelmingly an agrarian country. The image of an insurgent peasantry surrounding the modern social spaces of the treaty ports is a striking image of how this impossible unity was created and sustained, a unity that has fragmented in the dramatic reterritorialization of the post-Mao economic reform in which the rural hinterland seems to become almost a different "time" as well as place. The principles of inclusion and exclusion, however authoritatively stated, are never completely successful but are always subject to contestation by those who have been closed out or, in the case of some of China's ethnic minorities, forcibly included. All these paradoxical sites—the primordiality of the modern nation, the contestation of boundaries defining the national space, the "awakening" to self-awareness through the embrace of global processes—require narrative to do its job, endlessly constructing an apparently seamless story of the nation's place in space and time.

Narrative, however, requires the presence of an enunciating subject. This simple fact directs our attention to the power of a national imaginary to call forth subjects who "speak for" the nation. In the history of modern China, the designation of who or what class represents the agency to propel the nation forward in its historical destiny has been very much at stake in national struggles.[8] Implicit in this contestation has been a "politics of presence" in which the speaking subject claims to or is attributed with the power to speak with the force of history. In this sense, the national subject is made to embody abstract conceptions which are not immediately present to experience (such as History, Nation, Society, People) but which become emblematic of the nation speaking with the voice of history.

Exploring this myth of presence in Chinese revolutionary culture is the project that opens this book. Beginning with the construction of the "oppressed class subject" in the revolutionary practice of "speaking bitterness," I explore how this subject came to define a new reality, how the authority of this speaking imploded in the "chaos" of the Cultural Revolution and was subsequently decentered by the contestation of multiple constructions of the national subject in the post-Mao era. These successive moments of construction and contestation represent different "times" of the nation, the multiple layerings of which rest, sometimes uneasily, within subjective memory.

Not only does this book refuse to offer a continuous narrative, but its relative weight also falls heavily on Deng's reform era, both as the contemporary frame in which national subjectivities are produced and as a particular perspective from which these processes can be viewed as they took place in earlier periods of China's modern history. The discussions that follow, therefore, clearly reflect the premise that one's interest in the past originates out of the concerns of the present. Accordingly, this book addresses issues about power and representation that I feel have presented themselves with particular clarity in the years since the violent crackdown in 1989 on the student movement. The elitism of the student movement and, subsequently, the state's largely successful efforts to justify its actions after the crackdown force us to consider why an alliance between intellectuals and others (politically restive workers, peasants, independent entrepreneurs) appeared to be such a political improbability during and after Tiananmen.

This post-Tiananmen situation plays ironically against the specter of an earlier historical moment when a cross-class alliance between intellectuals and "others" did successfully launch a mighty revolution, one that was to serve globally as a model for political transformation for most of the latter half of the twentieth century. I argue that the difficulty of building a political alliance in the 1980s is due not to an inability on the part of intellectuals to read the revolutionary potential of other classes but to a certain narrative framing of national subjectivity in the context of capitalist transformations specific to the late twentieth century. As a class defined by their ability to deploy modern modes of knowing, intellectuals find themselves in a very ambiguous position in late-twentieth-century China, where knowledge retains a certain power to define elite status but where this status is threatened by the very dynamism of a marketplace that allows uneducated peasants to aspire to unimaginable wealth. The uncivilized bodies of the rural masses present an ambivalent set of possibilities: they heighten the value of educated, civilized, urban cosmopolitan subjects, yet that value is thrown into question by the emergence of those peasant entrepreneurs who prosper despite their relative lack of education. This ambivalence was strikingly portrayed in the 1990s film *Relian* (Hot love), which tells the story of a young intellectual woman's romantic dilemma of choosing to marry a crude, upwardly mobile peasant who had become a wealthy building contractor on Hainan Island instead of her ascetic, idealistic, and intellectual male lover. Most of the film records her profound regret at having made the "wrong" choice in light of her peasant husband's uncouth manners and crass materialistic values.

What is interesting about this ambivalence concerning the rural masses is that it is not new but has its antecedents earlier in this century in negative images of the uncivilized crowd. This ambivalence makes understanding the exaltation of the abject peasant body in revolutionary discourse as a *contingent* historical possibility all the more essential. But, although many of the discursive elements that define the problem of the "people" as an undisciplined mass have long histories in modern China, their uses in the present do not necessarily result from continuous histories of unilinear development. The genealogical approach I prefer insists on tracing the trajectories of discursive elements stemming from unlikely places, deploying transformed meanings in disrupted histories. The genealogist must be sensitive to resonances across time—not to set them into a continuous evolutionary narrative but to "isolate the different scenes where they engaged in different roles."⁹ Therefore, we have to be attentive to the ways in which the present reprise of notions that were current earlier in China's modern history mark a conscious retrieval of the past that is nevertheless fundamentally conditioned by the tumultuous history of the socialist era separating then from now.

The early part of the century represents a moment in China's history when it was being pulled into the orbit of global capitalism. Because of China's semicolonial status, however, this process operated on vastly different terms from those of the present, resulting ultimately in a rejection of capitalism. In contrast, China is now undergoing a "passive revolution" marked by the controlled insertion of capitalist forms by a powerful bureaucratic state, a revolution that is producing unimaginable wealth for those functionaries who can provide a docile, disciplined, and cheap labor force for transnational capital in a globalized marketplace.

These two different moments in China's modern history—the rejection of capitalism and its later controlled insertion into the national economy—could be fitted into Chatterjee's schema defining the development of nationalist thought, in which he distinguishes three "essential" moments: the "moment of departure," which is an elitist project of defining the national essence; the "moment of manoeuvre," in which the people are mobilized by means of a rhetoric of anticapitalism; and the "moment of arrival," when the nation has congealed into a stable power ensuring the "passive revolution" of capitalist transformation, which Chatterjee claims is the general form of the transition from colonial to postcolonial states in the twentieth century. By differentiating these successive moments, Chatterjee hopes to develop a "general theory" of nationalism that can be sensitive to the indeterminate play of ideological forces specific to each national context. Chatterjee cautions against using this schema as an invariant template, arguing instead that the moment of maneuver in particular is one that presents many contradictory possibilities. Although China could be said to fit this "paradigmatic model," one could perhaps also argue that Maoism itself became "paradigmatic" for anticolonial struggles elsewhere and therefore must be counted as one of those ideological forces that disseminated globally to play a role in diverse national contexts.[10]

Moreover, in observing some of the cultural fixations in 1990s China that seem to echo similar obsessions of the 1920s, such as population quality and eugenics or the disciplining of "the people" into a modern citizenry, one must carefully note their occurrence in relation to the dramatic reorganization of capitalism in the past two decades, an era that has been characterized as "the age of flexible accumulation," "post-Fordism," or "late capitalism."[11] One cannot help but note the timely conjuncture between global economic restructuring and Deng's economic reforms mandating China's progressive opening to global flows of capital and labor. These two events, so neatly contemporaneous, suggest the "just in time" provision of a cheap and docile labor force, as if the entire socialist era was, in retrospect, destined to function merely as a temporary holding pattern for a heterogeneous economic formation capable of giving capitalism its second wind—just as it was about to be overwhelmed by its own contradictions. In the dialectic of history (in its most ironic mode), socialism would seem to have become the necessary antithesis for capitalism to evolve to its next stage. And yet the triumphalist narrative of the victory of capitalism over socialism, in the context of China especially, tends to be told as the universal unfolding of a unitary logic; and socialism itself is depicted as an irrational disruption of the "normal" progression of history toward a capitalism that must ultimately triumph.[12] Indeed, Maoist strategies of mass mobilization and tactical plays on time in schemes of accelerated socialist transformation once offered an alternative to the passive revolution of capitalist development. The Great Leap Forward is the most striking example of this play on time, one that substituted the brute power of laboring bodies in place of advances in material development to play the game of catch-up, but with catastrophic results. The odds were against success, but the stakes were high. The logic of the game is essential to understanding Mao's motivation to risk all in a desperate face-off between East and West. Such tactics are now seen as not just foolhardy but also evidence of a monstrously overweening will to power that ultimately resulted in a historically unprecedented magnitude of mass starvation and deprivation. But more important to the obsessions of the present, these tactics are also blamed for having led to the actual *devolution* of the Chinese people, who must now be disciplined anew for an intensely competitive global labor market. Therefore, the present reprise of discourses that first emerged early in the twentieth century can be contextualized as a nostalgic reaching back to another historical moment when China was, under quite different conditions, being pulled into the global expansion of a capitalist economy, whether it is to salvage socialism by uncovering its fatal flaws or to retrieve a moment when China was still "on track" in the universal progression of history.

At both these moments, we see an urgency to find Chinese referents for the categories of universal history. In this book I therefore seek to contribute to a history of "presencing" in the sense that I consider how "modern" categories of understanding are made present in discourse, powerfully enframing new realities and new political possibilities. What happens when a metaphysics of presence inherent in a universalizing Western social theory becomes disseminated to fertile ground in quite a different social and historical context? Claude Lefort has noted how categories fundamental to the emergence of bourgeois society in Europe were inextricably part of Marx's theorization of radical social transformation. Concepts such as History, Nation, Society, Man, Individual, and so on (all those which announced their timeless universality with capital letters) had to be made palpably present for Marxism to work in China as the theoretical underpinning of social revolution.[13] For leftist intellectuals of the 1920s, these abstractions had to be filled with a Chinese referent so that China could be positioned within the metanarrative of Enlightenment History as a subject progressively realizing its self-awareness and agency. These enframing categories generated new kinds of subjectivities—a socially conscious intellectual elite as well as emerging categories of gender and class that were to produce the agents for social revolution. With the collapse of a Marxist vision of history, we see a "fevered" search for a national subjectivity that can restore a sense of historical agency to China in terms which are in some ways a striking departure from the Maoist era but which are in other ways strangely continuous with it.[14]

One intellectual strategy that appears throughout the modern era is the figure of prolepsis—the representation of a thing as already existing, as if the process of representation itself could magically effect its emergence in reality. Chapter 1 therefore traces a genealogy of the "class subject" in Chinese revolutionary discourse—the oppressed worker/peasant/woman—who made present in speech the larger historical forces of capitalism and imperialism bearing down on the nation. Indeed, the "speaking out" of the class subject became emblematic for China's own emergent consciousness of a subaltern identity in the global community of nations. Yet the possibility for this subject to emerge as one who can make history "speak itself" required certain discursive preconditions to be set into place. This part of my argument is indebted to Marston Anderson's important book *The Limits of Realism*, in which he explored the literary experiments with social realism as inspired by a wish for political agency on the part of China's intellectuals during the 1920s and 1930s.[15] I want to push Anderson's argument further, however, to suggest that these literary efforts, which apparently ended in disillusionment, had a much more far-reaching effect. They helped to establish the discursive apparatus for the narrative practices of the Chinese Revolution—practices that were no longer "literary" in the sense of a self-conscious literary project but appeared in the form of spontaneously "erupting" speech. The literature of China's May Fourth realists helped to install a new metaphysics, a radically different way of looking at the world, that literally inscribed people's bodies with a rhetoric of suffering and retribution. By tracing the discursive linkages between literary representation and revolutionary practice, I hope to pose the problem of the Chinese Revolution as a problem of colonial modernity in which an alien metaphysics attains great power to write its reality on the world, resulting in the practice of "speaking bitterness" as the emergent product of a specific historical conjuncture in China's resistance to imperialism.[16]

Therefore, my concern is not necessarily with the immediate political effects of literature itself but with its more indirect contributions to a broader discursive frame in which literature becomes a theater for the display of a dispersed social evil, ungraspable except by way of narrative, that must be redressed through revolutionary action. These literary representations mobilized the subjectivities of a certain class of leftist intellectuals who indeed became agents of social revolution, often abandoning literary pursuits to engage directly with the "wheels of history."[17] Indeed, even those literary productions that expressed the most radical doubt about the gulf between intellectuals and their "others" eventually became subsumed within the narrative production of speaking bitterness, in which the literary "thing" itself disappears in the representational machinery of the socialist party-state. Such was the fate of "New Year's Sacrifice," Lu Xun's short story exploring the unbridgeable paradoxes of elite desire for social change and real social misery, in its post-Liberation cinematic recasting as an operatic melodrama in the southern *yueju* style. In this retelling, the figure of the narrator disappears completely, so that the story fits unproblematically into the conventions of "speaking bitterness" (*suku*) narrative. Lu Xun's story is set up as a transparent reflection of a reality that comes to speak itself, effacing entirely the problematic role of the intellectual in the act of representation.[18] This was especially apparent in the congealed form that the subaltern class subject was to take in post-Liberation political culture.

In Chapter 2, I explore the creative deployments of class identities in a moment when these congealed categories had already begun to deconstruct themselves in the wake of the Cultural Revolution. The true story of a young imposter who in 1979 claimed to be the son of a high-ranking military official was transformed into subversive theater and provided a public frame for critiquing the arbitrary system of class statuses. The young man set in motion a gift of a bottle of mao-tai that completed a circuit of exchange powered "in the name of the father" and returned to his hands as confirmation of his identity as an "empty signifier." I consider how oppositional modes of practice colonized the rigid categories of identity in the Maoist class-status system. In this instance, an "economy of pleasure" in the passage of the gift undermined the discursive spaces of a "regime of truth." At the end of this chapter I suggest that this young man's creative deployment of identity presaged the post-Maoist emergence of a multiplicity of new identities, some emanating from the marketplace, that insistently contest and disturb the maintenance of any monolithic official order.

Indeed, the new kinds of subjectivities made possible by the economic reforms have led to new problems for the party-state in representing itself as a unified agent that exerts a palpable force in society. The next four chapters of this book all deal with different aspects of this problem of political agency in a period of tremendous economic growth and dislocation. With the "muting" of the class subject in the post-Mao era, however, the party-state has had to devise modes of self-representation different from those of the Maoist period. Although at times these may resonate with nationalist themes from earlier in this century, they must nevertheless be placed in contexts specific to China's vigorous reinsertion into a global economy.

In Chapter 3, then, I argue that a discourse of "civilization" (*wenming*) has taken the place of an emphasis on class struggle in defining national subjects and the strategies of transcending China's subaltern position in the global community. Wenming has a complex history heavily implicated with the history of Chinese nationalism beginning in the late nineteenth century. I examine how and why present constructions of the nation and debates about the national culture in the 1980s invoked discourses from the turn of the century. I then focus on representations that feature the quiescent peasant body stimulated by the party-state and its disciplinary practices to new heights of productivity. Peasant bodies have become the medium on which the party-state inscribes its civilizing rhetoric, in terms of the body's productivity and re-productivity, and its discipline (or lack thereof) to consume appropriately. These discourses on the body as a consuming/producing machine have much to tell us about the microtechnologies of power that have developed in Chinese society along with its rapid incorporation of the rural economy into a global system of capitalist production.

The unreadiness of peasant bodies for full participation as a modern citizenry has been a recurring figure in the discourse of Chinese nationalism—from the *xinmin* (new citizen) of the early-twentieth-century modernizer Liang Qichao to the prolonged project of political tutelage under the Guomindang. The problem of "the people" centers precisely on whether they can be trusted with participation in the political process. Mao critiqued fearful representations of the masses in his famous "Hunan Report," arguing that whether one sees peas-ant insurgency as "terrible" or "fine" has everything to do with one's particular class perspective.[19] But even Mao, who rested his revolutionary strategy on the explosive energy of the masses, envisioned the pedagogical project of the state to be the creation of a new socialist person upon the "blank sheet" of the peasant masses. Within the discourse of wenming from its inception in reform projects at the turn of the century, the question was, How is the inert mass to be made into a modern citizenry? At what point do "the people" make the transition from pedagogical object to performative subject?[20] In China, the language of modern social analysis used by reform intellectuals captured this emergence of "the people" in its differentiation between the inscription of the relatively inert *nongmin* (the peasantry), a Japanese loanword, and *qunzhong* (the masses), a mobilized political force.[21] The tension between these two defines what Prasenjit Duara has called the "split time" of the nation—caught between its past and its future, it is both of primordial antiquity and quintessentially modern. In 1920s China, this split was transferred to the discursive construction of "the people" to create a division within the very foundation of the political legitimacy of the modern nation-state. Intrinsic to the idea of the nation as an identity that is deeply historical, "the people" likewise retain an identity that is primordial in character. Yet to constitute a popular sovereignty that is proper to the modern state, "the people" have to be remade as part of a massive pedagogical project to rid them of the contamination of their "feudal" past. This project includes not just the formal educational apparatus but also, as Duara suggests, the creation of a modern literature and the emergence of folklore as a motivated recuperation of the national essence.[22]

I argue in this and subsequent chapters that this "indeterminacy of the people," caught between their past and future, continues to be a fundamental aporia in the discursive economy of the Chinese party-state that can be explored at the level of its attempts to subject the population to new modes of discipline, inscribed as "civilized." At its base lies the question of whether the Chinese people can really be trusted with full political sovereignty. Will true civility emerge by way of the tutelage of the state, or will it be generated spontaneously by the emergent sphere of the market? Or does the answer lie somewhere in the complex dialectic between the two? Posing the question in this way suggests a dynamic tension between the state discourse of "civility" (*wenming*) and the international debate about the transition of "formerly" socialist societies toward a "civil" society by way of a newly liberated economic sphere.

Chapter 4 continues the discussion of the disciplinary practices of the party-state through examination of how individuals become stitched into subject positions within the state's socialist realist modes of representation, which have had to be radically refigured in the years since Mao's death. However, my argument is not limited to exploring the production of docile political subjects but looks at how the ritualized forms of subject production project representations of the party-state as a subject written large, as the unified voice of the "people as one"—a projection that conceals the internal fragmentation and diversity within not only the national community but also the party organization itself. This chapter therefore deals with the issue of subjectivity at two levels: at the level of individual bodies and at that of the body politic. My intent is to demonstrate that politicizing the body is not merely a manipulative project of the state to ensure social control and ideological domination but that it is essential to the party-state's own self-identity, its creation of a self-referential reality that is in itself an ideological effect.

Chapter 5 focuses on the notion of China as a nation that is "excessively populous" (*renkou guoduo*), exploring how the discourse of the Chinese socialist party-state constructs China's population as "too large" and mobilizes images of the body as being consuming or producing. These images are intrinsic to the pedagogical imperatives and disciplinary practices of the Chinese socialist state in ways that serve to displace political critique of the internal contradictions of Chinese socialism. Yet the party-state's own discourse on population intersects with the language of everyday life in common expressions of hope or despair about China's development in the international order. Population has become central to post-Mao obsessions about China's failure to progress in History. These dimensions of China's population policy have been almost entirely ignored in the massive Western-language literature devoted to it in the last ten years; and yet the issues they raise are crucially important in understanding the tremendous power that this policy carries in post-Mao Chinese political discourse. No policy is more resisted at the level of popular practices; nevertheless, no other policy has greater power to reinvigorate the imperative for party leadership. In Chapter 5 I examine a number of discursive domains in their relationship to the issue of population—the culture debates of the 1980s, the discourse of social disorder, the party-state's modes of self-representation, and the global proliferation of a neo-Malthusian rationality in the context of late capitalism.

Chapter 6 counterposes the party-state's rhetoric of political reform with its radical reworking in a cultural production made outside the party-state's apparatus. Zhang Yimou's film *Qiu Ju da guansi* (The story of Qiu Ju) is the story of a young peasant woman's search for redress for the wrongful exercise of power. By playing with the conventions of socialist propaganda, the film produces quite different readings and thereby offers the possibility of contrasting the "narrative address" of the civilizing practices of the state with other sorts of political possibilities. In particular, I explore the film's depiction of the process of conflict resolution within the context of the post-Mao "village compacts" (*xianggui minyue*) as the model for ordering social relationships under the economic reforms. Promoted by the party propaganda apparatus, this model imaginatively positions the rural masses as both its author and its object. The "masses" are in effect subjected to a pedagogical practice of which they, as active subjects, are said to be the authors. This confusion between subject and object restores to the party apparatus its claim as being the only legitimate source of political agency. The film, however, disturbs this representational economy by rejecting the supposition that the masses are still unready for political reform, and it does so by suggesting that even a semiliterate woman from an isolated rural village is capable of political agency. Whether we can state unequivocally that Qiu Ju's politics derive entirely from the marketplace or are in a complex dialectic with the state's own conventions of its moral role in society is made more complex here. Her actions are not necessarily inimical to the ideals expressed through the compact but instead raise questions about the inability of an authoritarian system of governance to set limits to its own power. In her search for an explanation of where these limits might lie, she refuses the passive subject position scripted for her within the institutions of power.

The figure of Qiu Ju challenges the ambivalent construction of the people on the part of national elites. As was argued above, this ambivalence is at the very heart of constituting "the people" as the source of legitimate power in the modern state. As Prasenjit Duara has suggested, the source of this power must be removed from the unruly mess of a popular politics "in the streets" to a more abstract and impersonal mechanism: the written constitution. "The people," in a very real sense, are "written into being."[23] This emphasis on writing "the people" into being suggests to me Jacques Derrida's critique of assumptions that writing "supplements" speech, in that it is ambiguously regarded as both a "substitution for" and a "filling in" for "what is missing," a maneuver that he suggests is a cover that obscures the limits of any totalizing claim. The supplementary nature of the village compacts covers over the hidden violence of a system that represents itself as a power that knows its proper limits." The supplement has not only the power of procuring an absent presence through its image, procuring it for us through the proxy of the sign, it holds it at a distance and masters it. For this presence is at the same time desired and feared."[24] The figure of "the people" in Chinese political rhetoric exemplifies this ambivalence toward an imagined presence that is both desired and feared, one that must be held at a distance by a consistent disavowal of their exclusion from the political process. Qiu Ju seeks to close this distance and make power answer directly to her, a project that takes her on epic journeys to confront power's elusive "face." At the same time, however, although the marketplace is viewed in the film as a domain of magic and transformation that enables her to act in pursuit of her goals, its effects may not be read as purely liberatory but rather as suggestive of new kinds of discipline through the commodity form.

In Chapter 7 I depart from state rhetoric to look at how the market has become another venue for narrating the nation. This chapter presents successive readings of a series of material representations that, beginning in the late 1980s, convey how the desire and ambivalence for a national past are becoming displaced onto commodified forms along with the expansion of a market economy. Splendid China, a theme park in Shenzhen, represents famous historical sites in a construction of the nation-space in miniature as a timeless, essentialized identity, a copy that "makes real" its original. China's "old towns" too compose a set of variations on a theme, reconstructing the antiquity of the nation in the very process of its commodification. They are at once a re-creation of the "color and flavor" (*guse guxiang*) of the past and a marketplace, enclosed within a modern urban space. I explore the tension between the inside and the outside of these spaces of representation while also carefully noting the tension between what lies inside and outside the circuit of commodity exchange into which these spaces of representation are so tightly bound.

As should be apparent from the summary above, this book is not an ethnography in the traditional sense: it is not a detailed description of life in a localized setting. And yet it draws freely from ethnographic methods of participant observation and interviews, combined with close readings of cultural productions, both textual and otherwise—oral narrative, official documents and propaganda materials, popular media, theme parks, domestic interiors. In particular, a number of the chapters rely heavily on a detailed reading of what might be referred to as the *petits récits* of the propaganda machine: the brief stories that actively seek to construct a socialist realism which is not confined to the space of literary fiction but which in a certain political sense spills over into the realm of lived reality. The petits récits of the late 1980s and 1990s suggest a narrative practice increasingly desperate to convince itself of its own reality, challenged as it was by the increasingly commodified realities of a burgeoning consumer culture. The chapters have been written over a period of ten years, thus defying any attempt to characterize the book as an up-to-the-minute account of life in China. Indeed, some of the chapters written earlier in the project reflect realities that have already transformed into something else. Nonetheless, I hope they will prove of value in capturing the vertiginous sense of imbalance that the rapid pace of change induces in those most caught up in its embrace as well as in the researcher who wishes to capture it in the prolonged labor of scholarly production.

1 MAKING HISTORY SPEAK

> During a great revolution, literature disappears without a sound.
> —Lu Xun, "geming shidai de wenxue"[1]

Lu Xun's prediction must, in retrospect, be read ironically. Revolution in China may have meant, for many, the silencing of literature, but this "silence" was surely filled by the embodied voice of the oppressed peasant subject. Was this relationship merely adventitious? The suggestion that literature leaves no trace in revolutionary action belies the power of narrative to construct subjects who act. If literary realism did not have the power to effect social change, as many May Fourth writers had hoped, it had perhaps a different kind of power already implicit in the project to make "literature speak with the voice of history."[2] Revolutions, especially great ones, are seldom silent, but filled with words—words that have the power to perform new worlds into being.

What I argue below is that the failed project to make literature translate directly into political action was completed in a profound sense by the narrative practices of the revolution. "Speaking bitterness" (*suku*) provided a narrative structure in which oppressed members of the "old society" took center stage to vent their rage in a compelling performance that made the working of history palpably "real."[3] To link literary experiments in social realism to the practice of speaking bitterness is not to suggest a linear relationship of cause and effect but to explore the contingent process of history itself, in which the origin of a thing and the ultimate uses to which it is put may indeed lie "worlds apart."[4] My objective is to trace a genealogy for the politics of representation in Maoist political ritual that invests the body with the ability to make physically present the theoretical abstractions of Marxist discourse. I argue that this "myth of presence" that focuses so intensely on the body ultimately led to the physical violence of the Cultural Revolution and that it continues to have its effects on the narrative practices of the post-Mao era.

In exploring this uncertain trajectory, I focus on three specific moments. The literary experiments of the 1920s were a powerful means of translating the categories of bourgeois ideology inherent in Marxist social analysis into Chinese contexts through the adaptation of social realism as a tool of social critique. Transcendental categories—such as Society, Class, History—took on local referents in literary explorations of society and its ills in a process that Tani Barlow has referred to as the "localization of the sign."[5] Alongside these literary explorations, the party's narrativization of class injury as a spoken performance gave these transcendental categories flesh and blood form in the retributive justice of class struggle, which ultimately overtook literature as a strategy for revolutionary change. In the development of a postrevolutionary political culture, however, the ritualized drama of class struggle during land reform ultimately took on a more congealed form as writing.[6] To summarize the argument: What was first written as fiction came to be spoken as the unmediated truth of History speaking itself and was then written again as inscribed speech in the forging of a revolutionary culture.

In negotiating these shifts between writing and speech, the distinction between them implodes. "Speaking bitterness" was not possible without a prior writing, and yet its status as "unmediated speech" enabled a later writing to secure the institutionalized violence of the class-status system of the socialist era. I use "writing" here in the expanded sense suggested by Derrida, who would collapse into it all systems of social inscription through which persons are made subject to the order of the symbolic. In the Chinese Revolution, the symbolic order was often cruelly written on the bodies of class enemies as a physical enactment of a new regime of truth. Speaking bitterness was elevated to the status of "history speaking itself," but the body provided the material ground through which this history was made real. The speaking voice and the body became tied in the labor of making present the abstracted circulation of a dispersed social evil. The spoken pain of the oppressed class subject was posed against the Confucian order identified with the authority of the written word. While this privileging of speech over writing suggests a myth of presence already inherent in Marxism, in China this was to take a historically specific form. Given the power of this narrative strategy to fuel a massive revolutionary movement, we might well ask what the attendant costs were of founding a new socialist reality so heavily on a notion of "presence" that was to engender repeated cycles of violence literally inscribed on the bodies of its victims.

In this circulation of violence through narrative, a politics of representation realizes its concrete materiality through spectacularizing the body in pain. As Marston Anderson has argued, the spontaneous cry of the body became a privileged signifier of the "real" for May Fourth intellectuals, providing them with the means by which the "wheels of history" could be actively grasped through literary practice. But this literary appropriation of the body was only the first of a series in which the body and its pain are made to speak a kind of truth.[7] In revolutionary practice, a poetics of the body and its insults moved from literary representation to the spoken words of uneducated peasants. This eruption into speech of the peasant subject must therefore be placed within a whole system of representations in which new conceptions of the social and historical became "real-ized" through the visceral experience of the speaking subject. The physical body itself became the medium for registering the collision of material forces in history.[8] The old order was narrativized as a violence that seizes hold of the body. What was spoken became identified with the release of bodily anguish, a speaking that carried narrative to the very limits of language and beyond—to the materiality of the body and the immediacy of tears and blood. However, this use of the body did not end with the establishment of a new social order but was reprised in the postrevolutionary period, most viciously during the Cultural Revolution. This physical writing upon the body was again transcribed into literature in the "literature of the wounded" (*shanghen wenxue*) of the early post-Mao period, which displayed insults to the bodies of intellectuals, who then turned to writing as a means to redress the injuries of the past.

This circulation of violence between writing, the spoken word, and the body is central to understanding how class subjects were constructed in revolutionary China. Marston Anderson noted in the literature of the 1920s and 1930s a profound shift in literary representations of the subaltern from a passive object of "pity" (*tongqing*), who must be represented by others, to a subject who speaks.[9] This "coming to voice" of the subaltern subject in literary realism is eerily doubled by the party's early experiments in peasant mobilization. Therefore, rather than claiming a directly causal relationship between the two, we need to theorize one that is more subtly dialectical in character, placing both within the larger project of making the categories of Marxist social analysis manifestly real.

The literary explorations of subaltern speech must therefore be read not merely as reflecting the political struggles of the time but also as actively constituting the subjectivities "unleashed" in those struggles—most important, the reciprocal constitution of a modernizing intellectual elite and the subaltern subject as its "other."[10] Rey Chow has suggested that the predominant subjectivity of the May Fourth period was not just the densely portrayed center of the bourgeois subject but also a tripartite figure in which the relationship between intellectuals and "the people" becomes triangulated with an emerging concept of the nation itself.[11] Chow appeals to the image of *zhao duixiang*, a phrase that condenses the meanings of mating and mirroring (in the psychoanalytic sense of mirror image), to characterize the specular pleasure of Chinese intellectuals in the pain of the subaltern.[12] In this light, we must read speaking bitterness narratives not as an explosive sounding of voices silenced in history but as having emerged from a historically specific politics of representation.[13] If intellectuals sought their *duixiang* in subaltern bodies, they later found themselves cast into the position of *douzheng duixiang* (struggle objects), including many of those writing realist literature in the 1920s and 1930s. Indeed, the word "duixiang" also gathers into itself the meaning of "target," the arrow finding its mark.

In exploring these particular issues, what follows could therefore be considered a contribution to a "history of presencing" that traces how the transcendental categories of bourgeois ideology came to define the "real" in modern China.[14] Such a project entails a theory of narrativity that spills across the usual disciplinary boundaries between literary scholarship, history, and ethnography.[15] Thus I must acknowledge my debt to all these fields of scholarship, each of which in turn has provided the intellectual inspiration for the three sections of my argument as presented below.[16]

Writing upon the "Real"

[Sociology is] the science of a society which speaks, which is a society *precisely because it speaks.*—Roland Barthes, "Why I Love Benveniste"

The construct of colonial modernity has been suggested as a way of noting the colonizing power of modernizing discourse among Chinese intellectuals and the local trajectories of what declared themselves as universal categories.[17] Notions such as Society, Nation, Individual, History, and so forth, all belong to the language of colonial modernity, as the categories of a bourgeois ideology that come from elsewhere to operate as signs of what China "lacked"—its inability to access the "real" because of its literary ties to an older metaphysics. And yet, despite their presence as "lack," they offered a powerful source of agency for a modernizing elite intent on the project of constituting a modern nation, a project made compelling by the unequal exchanges of China's semicolonial status. This imperative seemed to confirm the transcendental nature of their "truth" as necessary for the progressive movement of history with the nation as its proper subject.[18] Therefore, these categories had to be filled with local

referents in order to operate effectively as the tools of social analysis and transformation. This necessity perhaps explains why literary realism became so
important to Chinese intellectuals as a sign of the modern, even as realism was
being superseded by modernism in the West.[19]

These categories were transplanted to China through the literal process of
translating European literature and political philosophy into Chinese. They
formed a constellation of elements whose individual functions in local sign
systems are difficult to isolate because of the complex relationships among
them. Here, however, I focus specifically on the notion of "society" (*shehui*)
because its denotation as the ordered heterogeneity of a complex social totality
was fundamental to a concept of "class" (*jieji*), and it is the discursive determi-
nations of the latter that I wish to move toward. The phrase translated into
English as "class status" (*jieji chengfen*) includes the Chinese term "chengfen,"
for which the literal meaning is "component part."[20] The Chinese term therefore explicitly embodies the objective language of scientific analysis that breaks
down a larger totality ("society" itself) into its constituent elements. A concept
of society was the necessary ground for the discursive constitution of the abstracted categories of social analysis—gender as well as class—that could mobilize new kinds of actors for the project of national salvation.

For Chinese intellectuals, shehui defined an object unaware of itself because
it lacked representation. Its unknown contours had to be delineated as a necessary precondition for a "modern" social critique. It was the sign of a novel
desire to map the contours of a social totality, to hold it within the grasp of
language from an imaginary space "outside."[21] Literary realism was accorded
great power as a tool of social critique, as indeed a form of social science, a
means of making society "present" to itself as a self-conscious national community. The close association of realist literature with the high tide of nationalist
movements in Europe attributed it with great powers for social transformation.
Yet despite the novelty of this conception, the very inscription of society as
shehui betrays an ambivalence about its foreign origin. Shehui was not so much
a neologism as a reinscription of an older term by way of an "innovative
classicism" not by Chinese, initially, but by Meiji modernizers in Japan eager to
fill a void in their conceptual vocabulary to facilitate the appropriation of
Western political theory.[22] This genealogical link offered a reassurance that the
resources necessary to achieve modernity were hidden somewhere within the
cultural repository of "East Asian" tradition. Its movement as a "back translation" from Japan to China would seem to affirm its status as a category of
universal history that recognizes no single point of origin.

Therefore, we see in this history how shehui emerges as a category that defines the nation. The definition of this national community perhaps begins with Liang Qichao's notion of *qun*, a word whose root meaning is "group" or "crowd"; its later inflection as *qunzhong* gave rise to the revolutionary usage of "the masses" to mean the social collectivity that stands for the nation. Indeed, Liang's use of "qun" approximates Hegel's idea of "nation" as a historical subject, which in Liang's formulation progresses through history via a Darwinian competition for survival *among* nations. Therefore "qun," in Liang's sense of the word, denotes an undifferentiated social collectivity as a homogeneous national community.[23]

The notion of "society," on the other hand, refers to a heterogeneous totality, in which the Darwinian struggle for existence, in the light of Marxist discourse, as we shall see, becomes internalized as the struggle between warring classes. However, as I explore below, this conception of class as the marker of *intra*-national heterogeneity is made by metonymic extension to be continuous with forces operating *internationally* through the economic and political processes of imperialism and semicolonialism.

Indeed, as a marker of China's semicolonized status, shehui marks another heterogeneity in the body of the nation that becomes closely bound with the discursive construction of "class" in Maoist revolutionary practice. Shehui came to mark an imaginary space "outside" the Chinese feudal order, a space of relative autonomy, an escape or exit from the oppressiveness of the "old" society, in which individuals were free to interact anonymously in a shared symbolic universe, in which Confucian hierarchies and kin ties could become displaced by an imagined community of individuals not necessarily known to one another, a space made possible by the intrusion of imperialism into the body of the nation, hence its characterization as a "colonial modernity." Barlow suggests that the concept of shehui allowed intellectuals to occupy a new social field, one that "acquired concrete referents" in the context of the treaty ports, a new modern mode of existence that defined itself against more established hierarchies and kin relations subsequently designated as "tradition."[24] In this sense society represented a new ordered collectivity prepared to receive and contextualize new kinds of subjects liberated from earlier forms of identity.

This new social space provided a platform for cultural critique in which the objectivity of its gaze depended on the distance between this new urban social field and the rural hinterland as its "other" that was still rooted within the horizons of a Confucian world.[25] The urgency of constructing society as an object of knowledge was to reorient the social order away from an imperial "high center" and a kin-inflected universe toward a horizontally defined democratic national community that could respond to the aggressive challenge of imperialism.[26]

"Society," therefore, marked a discontinuity in the time and space of the national community—the division between "modernity" and "tradition," a territorialization between city and country.[27] Therefore "society" bears within its sign an interesting oscillation of meanings referring both to the social totality and to the discontinuities that made this totality problematic. The very heterogeneity of the social landscape made compelling the desire to grasp hold of the totality in representation. The figure that bridged this indeterminacy was, of course, the notion of a shared national destiny that made the literary display of modernity's other a "call to arms," a mobilization for national self-determination. Therefore, a "modern" literature had to seek its proper object in this other, so that subaltern bodies became the medium through which the exhaustion of the "traditional" culture could be exposed in its failure to support even a minimal human existence. Lu Xun perhaps best captured this aspect of social realism in his characterization of it as a literature that "speaks mostly of others" (*duojiang bieren*).[28] In this sense, then, the conditions of possibility for the subaltern's coming to voice are precisely the conditions of its impossibility in that this absence becomes the compelling imperative for a "making present" in literature.

Through the body of the oppressed peasant subject, the inequities internal to Chinese society were made continuous with China's subaltern status in a world system of nation-states. By this logic the peasant body became the physical medium through which larger forces could be registered, a link to the "real" that hovers beyond the grasp of language. The materiality of the body is made to bear witness to the abstract categories of social critique wresting them from the domain of "just writing" to that of the "really real." The spontaneous truth of the body in its pain, speaking a "language" of blood and tears, intensifies the metaphysical privileging of speech over writing to a heightened degree. This effect of presence is perhaps the quintessential linkage between immediate experience and the ungraspable effects of a dispersed global economic system. Such a linkage rests on the possibility of "a telescopic vision," in which the multiple levels of extralocal circuits of economic exchanges become (sometimes violently) collapsed into highly localized dimensions of experience.[29]

As many scholars have suggested, the problem is how the enlightened social critic was to relate to his *duixiang*. How would it be possible for the two, living in separate social spheres with no common language, to translate effectively across the barrier between them? No one was more able to appreciate this paradox than was Lu Xun. Here, I presume to tread upon the territory of literary criticism and do yet another reading of his story "New Year's Sacrifice."[30]

During a New Year's visit to his home village, the story's narrator is suddenly confronted by Xianglin Sao, a minor figure from his past who seeks him out as a well-traveled scholar "who knows." She appears prematurely aged and wraith-like to him: "Her face was fearfully thin and dark in its sallowness, and had moreover lost its former expression of sadness, looking as if carved out of wood. Only an occasional flicker of her eyes showed she was still a living creature."[31] She is a spectral presence, and her ghostly aspect is entirely in keeping with her purpose for seeking him out—not for a handout, as the narrator expects, but for certainty about knowledge of the afterlife. The narrator finds himself unsettled by his inability to answer her questions. He stumbles for an answer that will do her the least harm and absolve himself of any responsibility for whatever events might follow. He finally takes comfort in the answer, "I am not sure," covering over his indecision about a question that he, as a "modern man of science," should know with certainty. The value of scientific knowledge in this context is doubtful here, feared as perhaps doing more harm than good. Because of the undecidability of how to answer her questions about the supernatural, Xianglin Sao becomes an uncanny presence haunting him until, on the morning after learning of her death, he hears the explosions of demon-dispelling firecrackers announcing the New Year and sweeping his mind clear of the doubts that had assailed him since their encounter.[32]

Chow asks the question, "Why is the narrator so terrified?"[33] My own answer to this question is suggested by Chow's use of duixiang to refer to the psychoanalytic concept of the mirror image. In this story, we experience the narrator's horror of being confronted with Xianglin Sao as his unlikely double. When he overhears his uncle's exclamations at the news of her death—"Not earlier or later, but just at this time—sure sign of a bad character!"—he assumes that it is he to whom his uncle refers, recognizing that his presence in his uncle's household is as unwanted and embarrassing as Xianglin Sao's death.[34]

If the widow's ghostly presence in life portends her impending death, the narrator is confronted with his own tenuous identity as an agent of social change. His encounter with Xianglin Sao forces him to face his inability to negotiate between the social space of his urban milieu with its modern modes of knowledge and what he experiences as a claustrophobic conservative backwater. This woman has already become a hungry ghost, an unredeemable presence. Her questions suggest a death wish that hangs on his answer, a burden that weighs heavily on him—hence his "relief" on hearing that the cause of her death was only "poverty, of course," absolving him from responsibility. But his fear of responsibility is compounded by the narrator's terror of his own annihilation as a subject, of having no agency, forced, as he is here, to face his own inadequacies in implementing any kind of meaningful social change, making his presence in Luchen, his hometown, as superfluous as that of his spectral other. The effect of her death produces a cathartic evacuation of the self-doubt and incriminations assailing the narrator in the night. As her light flickers and goes out, his terror is superseded by the compulsion to narrate her life, to hold it at a remove—he vicariously appropriates the surplus value of her death as a means of restoring his solidity as a subject.[35]

In his discussion about the spread of nationalism, Benedict Anderson has suggested the importance of the realist novel in constructing the homogeneous time of an imagined national community.[36] Lu Xun's story exemplifies how the discontinuities within that desired community become an obsessive point of return, worrying the refractory stubbornness of two worlds for failing to acknowledge their paradoxical simultaneity with each other. The narrator looks with jaundiced eye on the collection of Confucian classics among his uncle's books and notes with irritation that he can't take his uncle's ranting about revolutionaries too personally because he was referring to Kang Youwei, the late Qing reformer. This becomes yet another sign of the "backwardness" of this place and its refusal to recognize the modern social space from which the narrator draws his identity. His irritation arises from his having to recognize his own lack of consequence (not to mention the failure of the literary revolution to penetrate very far into rural society). This "hometown" is no longer home to him but only the place from which he launches his escape into the "modern" spaces of the city, as if to a different temporality. Lu Xun's story in a sense problematizes the whole project of colonial modernity in its cosmopolitan condescension to its other. At the same time, the story demonstrates Lu Xun's faith in the power of writing to "draw" (in the dual sense of "pulling" and "depicting") these radically different "times" of the nation together in a single temporality, to force their contemporaneity as a place of disjuncture reflecting back onto the narrator himself as the object of literary scrutiny.[37]

If the imagining of a homogeneous time-space is essential for a national awareness to emerge, then Lu Xun's story signifies the ghostly presence of the nation form apparently stuck in a state of incomplete manifestation. Nation, as well as History, Society, and so on—insofar as they are invested with a transcendental reality—has a power to announce *proleptically* (as a category of "universal" history) presences that must be narrated into being.[38] These concepts thereby become "citations" in which the sign "carries with it a force of breaking with its context" to be "grafted" onto other signifying chains. The global dissemination of signs explodes them from one context to scatter them anew on fertile ground. This characteristic of the sign—formally accorded by a European philosophical tradition to "writing," in the strict sense of the word—Derrida would extend not only to spoken language but also to the totality of "experience" itself.[39] These abstractions are therefore in themselves a kind of "writing," in the general sense, that share with speech acts a perlocutionary force, a force that propels events in the name of a subject which emerges through its articulation in discourse.[40]

It should not surprise us, then, that literature was seen as a means of making these presences visible—a writing, however, that breaks from the classical language of Chinese "tradition" and moves closer to the transparency of a spoken language, as if these presences could be invoked only through a writing that "claims" a closer proximity to speech more directly connected to the "real," claiming not just transparency but a transitivity as well, so that its effects are no longer merely effects of writing but an incitement for these categories to manifest themselves through the power of representation itself. Indeed, in discussions of May Fourth realism, it is the concentrated attention on literature as a speech act intended to engage the hearts and minds of its readers actively that is often used to distinguish Chinese realism from a "Western" obsession with mimesis. But there is perhaps a sense of the mimetic in Chinese realism as well, in its attempts to give flesh and blood form to the abstractions that promise to be the very "wheels of history" which must be grasped so that revolution may be its outcome. I would suggest that Chinese literary realism shared with other mimetic literary practices the fundamental impossibility of its project to capture the "fullness" of an external reality. And, yet, what is perhaps not sufficiently acknowledged is the performative effects of even failed attempts to make these abstractions "fully" present.

If literary realism did indeed become a force for social change in East Asia, its impact goes beyond mere propaganda to the exploration of a new metaphysics in which abstract entities such as Society, Nation, and History can be given concrete literary referents that attest to their autonomous reality.[41] As Timothy Mitchell has argued in the context of colonial Egypt, the "reality or objectivity of the social resided entirely in its representational nature"; it was an effect that was "more and more to be built into things," thereby constituting a self-confirming system of representations.[42] In 1920s China realist literature did in fact have a performativity, more profound than the one consciously sought for it and yet unnoticed because of the self-confirming nature of its "truth." Indeed, the "failure" of literary attempts to encompass the totality of the social whole helped to confirm the reality of this abstraction *as so immense as to defy attempts to represent it fully.* This failure may have been the precondition for enabling History to speak itself as an evocation of a presence *apparently unmediated* by effects of writing.

The work of Mao Dun, in particular, best exemplifies the ambition to represent the social totality and the limitations encountered in the attempt. Mao

Dun saw literature as a superior mode of social science, especially suited for constructing a new kind of "ob-jectivity," the root meaning of which in Latin is a "casting before" through which objects "come into view." This reading of the word activates the transitivity of the observer in the act of "making object." The idea of society comes before, but the need to fill this abstraction with a Chinese referent is what makes Mao Dun's project so urgent for him—to make a diffuse and fragmented reality into a representable whole.

Although his novel *Midnight* has been widely acclaimed as a masterpiece of social realism, it nonetheless disappointed its author, who found himself forced to resort to a kind of shorthand as a way of representing abstract forces operating globally. Specific characters are made to "embody" social and economic processes, a strategy that lay at the very heart of the "speaking bitterness" narrative, in which local conflicts were made to stand metonymically for the historical collision of warring classes rendered in an idiom of known personalities.[43] This metonymic reduction enabled a "telescopic vision" that collapsed abstract forces into adversaries who can be identified in local sites of struggle. While global forces did undeniably have their local agents, we must nonetheless note the way in which this process of metonymic reduction carries with it a particular urgency "to fill" these abstractions with local referents. This act of identification itself became a process of "abstracting" individuals out of the complex fabric of social life and rendering them as the material embodiment of a dispersed social evil.

However, the sheer complexity of the task Mao Dun set for himself—to display with all its paradoxical interconnections the relationship between treaty port society and its rural hinterland—became too overwhelming, causing him to limit the spread of his novel to the urban milieu of Shanghai. On the other hand, his short story trilogy, "Spring Silkworms," "Autumn Harvest," and "Winter Ruin," could perhaps be recognized as providing the missing rural component of the novel.[44] The figure of metonymic reduction is multiply registered in this work—the incursions of imperialism and the capitalist world system via the presence of modern industrial artifacts such as the silk filature and the water pump, but also through the generational characterization of peasant consciousness and its transformation. Tong Pao is the elderly patriarch whose understanding of the world is constantly put into crisis by the external forces transforming rural society. And yet he is bound within a traditional mind-set that lacks the power of telescopic vision to see the true source of his misery, except as a malign form of magic. His youngest son, by contrast, recognizes the supralocal dynamic that causes the family's repeated failure to secure a livelihood. He has the vision to reorganize his social world along horizontal lines of class solidarity and to eschew vertical ties of patronage to class superiors. Tong Pao is far from silent, being a great complainer—perhaps the greatest in the history of Chinese social realism—but his "speaking bitterness," unlinked as it is to the larger forces bearing down on peasant society, carries no power whatsoever to alter his social condition, except to carry him down the path toward physical annihilation.

Indeed, the trilogy dramatizes in highly condensed form how the lone figure of the subaltern subject shifts over time, from being a mute and passive object to its eruption as a crowd, as a force of nature in the ineluctable working out of History as a history of struggle.[45] However, Mao Dun's narrative fails to register fully the agency that grants to the peasant subject the ability to see the telescoping circuits of abstracted economic exchange that impinge on their phenomenal world. As will be explored in the following section, the speech of the subaltern subject is not the spontaneous flow of pent-up sorrow but the careful reworking of perception and experience into the narrative frame of Marxist class struggle as the specific lens that renders this vision. This new frame was put into place via a complex dialogical exchange between a political vanguard and the rural masses. And yet this painstaking labor of translation that renders the categories of Marxist social analysis into more immediately graspable form is a process that must always be backgrounded, in a closed space apart from the public scene of struggle, to lend to subaltern speech itself the irresistible force of History itself.

As Theodore Huters has argued, Mao Dun's trilogy problematizes the project of realist narrative as a "making" of presence, a getting of "something for nothing," akin to the capitalist market itself as an "all-or-nothing speculation" that may lead to the incurring of "crushing unexpected costs."[46] I would argue that crushing costs were indeed the result of an "overinvestment" in the myth of presence, a myth that extended far beyond the scope of literature into the making of a "socialist reality" that came to be written again, not just as a literary document, but on the body itself.

Who Is Speaking Here?

> Every revolution creates new words. The Chinese Revolution
> created a whole new vocabulary.—William Hinton, *Fanshen*

> Violence implies a language of violence.
> —Roland Barthes, "Writing the Event"

Fanshen, William Hinton's eyewitness account of revolution and land reform, was perhaps the book that most changed American cold war perceptions of the

Chinese Revolution.[47] It reads as if it were written in a preindustrial time-space in its representation of a complete world, just as the great nineteenth-century novels presumed to do. It dwells lovingly on the agrarian rhythms of peasant life and evokes through all the senses the sounds, smells, and sights of Long Bow Village on the eve of national liberation. I tell my students, as they slog through its more than six hundred pages, that this book was not written for the frenetic rhythms of postindustrial society (not to mention the academic quarter system). Hinton himself noted that the events that he recorded—the torturous working through of the revolutionary process in Long Bow Village—could never have taken place in a society governed by industrial production. Nevertheless, I insist that my students read the book in its entirety, for *Fanshen* offers more than the sensory evocation of another time: it reminds us how knowing must be situated in its historical moment. In weaving together local narratives of oppression and survival, it embraces them within broader national narratives of struggle and liberation, thereby rendering meaningful the revolutionary process itself, not excluding the episodes of occasional violence that disrupt Hinton's text.[48] Despite its characterization as an "eyewitness" account, much of what Hinton recorded was not directly observed by him but narrated to him by others. Therefore, Hinton's text demands that we attend to the power of narrative in shaping the course of events and in fixing their meaning.

Intrinsic to this argument is the role of narrative in a revolutionary consciousness. Mao saw the problem of consciousness as central to his revolutionary strategy not just in terms of creating support for the Communist Party but also as an expression of his belief in the ability of revolutionary activity to create the conditions for its own fulfillment. This was considered as necessary, given the immature conditions for revolutionary transformation in what was still fundamentally an agrarian society. As Arif Dirlik argues, Mao was posing the power of revolutionary consciousness not against social and material reality but against consciousness in general, the outlook on life and society that guides people in their everyday activity, shaped both by immediate social and material circumstances and by inherited cultural traditions. These are just as much a part of social existence as are the material conditions of life. This consciousness in general is "what goes without saying," the unquestioned premises of social existence.[49] The narrative structure of "speaking bitterness" provides a new frame for the reworking of consciousness in which the speaker comes to recognize himself or herself as a victim of an immoral system rather than a bearer of bad fate or personal shortcoming. In other words, one had to recognize one's conditions of existence in terms of class antagonism.

In prerevolutionary China, outside of the Western-influenced intellectual discourse in the treaty ports, there was no concept of "class," just as there was no concept of "society." They were alien categories, "discursively unavailable" for addressing one's social reality, bound by the vertical integration of primordial loyalties of patron clientage and the hierarchies of the Confucian family structure.[50] The older categories of status of the Confucian moral order were not defined in terms of antagonistic relations. The job of a revolutionary vanguard was to present to the peasantry its image in history to help it achieve its historic destiny. The speaking bitterness narratives provided this representational function. They worked on people's ideology not as a process of conscious intellection but as a system of representations or images that encouraged people to "see their specific place in a historically peculiar social formation" in a way which was entirely new to them but which still articulated with their sense of social reality.[51] As suggested by my very language, our theorization of the ideological is very much figured by the metaphor of vision and seeing, a specular logic. And yet here we must direct our attention to the power of the word as both spoken and heard. Indeed, Louis Althusser's famous theory of the interpellation function of ideology is dependent on the spoken, a calling out or "hailing" of the subject who recognizes herself or himself as the addressee. Likewise, the narrative structure of speaking bitterness hailed the peasant subject as its speaker, as an "I" victimized in the context of "enchanted relationships" with those who in the process become identified as class enemies.[52]

Narrative was essential to Mao's adaptation of Marx's theory of revolution to the essentially agrarian context of China in which peasants became the privileged revolutionary actors. Marxian categories of class and exploitation had to be radically reworked to address the complexity of interpersonal relationships in social contexts not yet subsumed by capitalism. Dirlik has drawn our attention to Mao's political conceptualization of class, which located actors within hierarchies of power, "especially in terms of relations of exploitation," rather than in their relationship to the means of production.[53] It is no wonder that the speaking bitterness narrative focused so much on the *experience* of exploitation and powerlessness. *Fanshen* recorded the complex discussions of how exploitation was to be defined, how to locate and measure it, but, above all, how to situate individual actors with respect to it—a discussion that took into account many factors other than the purely economic, including factors of religion, sexuality, personality, social status, and power. Maoism, therefore, constituted the class subject in terms of relative powerlessness rather than in terms of relations of production in and of themselves. These antagonisms experienced in the context of village life were consciously linked to abstract and impersonal macrolevel forces giving them a recognizable face by personifying them with a cast of local characters. Although the process may have started with the abstract categories of Marxism, these in turn had to be linked to the concrete experience of village life, and in so doing they were realized within a local politics that compromised any pure logic of class.

Moreover, speaking bitterness as an oral performance may have had indigenous antecedents from within Chinese village culture. The public venting of injured feelings is a familiar enough event in daily life in both China and Taiwan. In a public space, outside the walls of a compound or in a residential alley, the injured party, usually a woman, will wail and loudly proclaim the injuries inflicted by husband or kin. A crowd gathers and acts as a "court of public opinion" that affirms or contests the woman's sense of injury. The crowd of listeners actively participate in assessing the moral liability of the accused and may be moved to intervene as mediators in the conflict.[54] If this sort of public remonstrance was a pervasive feature of prerevolutionary village life, then the genius of the party's revolutionary practice was to give this venting of complaint an undeniably antagonistic character as proof of class-based inequity, creating a breach that cannot be redressed except through revolutionary action.[55]

Joseph Esherick and Jeffrey Wasserstrom have suggested more recently that the Confucians of the imperial period "mistrusted clever speech," preferring instead the authority of the written word.[56] If Confucian thinking was indeed graphocentric, privileging the written word as more "truthful" than the spoken word, then the privileging of oral performance in the context of revolution would suggest a reversal of the established hierarchy of writing over speech. The identification of speech as a more transparent conveyance of truth with the subaltern subject (allowing women and low-status men to speak their anger) certainly represents a turning over of Confucian social and familial relationships. And yet implicit within this signifying order is the link between subaltern speech with the language of the body, as if speech alone were not enough. A repeating trope of speaking bitterness narrative was the muting or silencing of subaltern speech by more powerful voices. It was through the language of the body and its pain that the truth of class antagonism achieved its undeniable presence through the materiality of the body, in which the different classes cease to be merely theoretical but take on an embodied form as the subjects of history. This myth of presence cannot be attributed entirely to its local context but was already inherent in Marxism itself. Mao and his followers were not merely manipulating a politics of representation: they were themselves caught up in the cogs of the Marxian master narrative.[57] If class, as a Marxian concept, was alien to Chinese discourse, did not this phonocentrism (the location of truth in the spoken word as opposed to writing) speak to the ontological reality of class as a universally valid category of social analysis? By giving "voice" to the subaltern class subject, the party engaged in a myth of presence, one that authenticated its leadership as representing the constituencies its own discourse had constituted.[58]

Thus speaking bitterness was not simply an imposition of a narrative structure on the speaking subject. It represented for the party the process of merging the consciousness of the party with that of "the people," which legitimated its claim to represent the voice of the masses.[59] This reworking of memory into a narrative of class antagonism occurred not in solitude, but was very much a dialogical process initiated by a very specific interlocutor (the party and its agents). Jack Belden describes this process in the case of a peasant named Ma who required twenty-four sessions with the cadres to rework his memory into narrative form. From understanding his ill fortune in terms of his personal shortcomings or bad fate, he learned, in his encounter with the cadres, to reinterpret his experience in terms of class and to attribute his misery to the landlord as the agent of a corrupt economic system. The familiar elements of his personal experience were reassembled into a new narratival form, in which he slowly came to recognize himself.[60] But, as Hinton notes, this process was a dialogical one, requiring the constant rethinking and redefinition of class categories by cadres faced with bringing them into accord with peasant experience.

Moreover, by suggesting that narratives were simply interposed onto the speaking subject, one fails to note their deeply emotional content. Indeed, it was precisely the evocation of sorrow and loss that made these narratives so powerful in eliciting an identification among class peers. Weeping is an intrinsic part of the structure of these narratives. In *Chen Village* we find a description of speaking bitterness as public performance, in which at a certain moment—such as the death of a parent—the story is suspended by a breaking through of deep emotions that render the speaker momentarily speechless.[61] Indeed, it is this momentary rendering mute of the speaking subject—going beyond mere words to weeping as a sign that points, once again, to the "spontaneous truth" of the body—that gives these narratives their power to hail the subjectivity of the hearer. This is not to suggest that tears were merely part of a script and were therefore "inauthentic" but rather that these narratives were made to express what Raymond Williams refers to as a "structure of feeling" in which meanings and values are "actively lived and felt . . . defining a social experience which is . . . not yet recognized as social but taken to be private, idiosyncratic, and even isolating." As these emotional expressions become institutionalized within the hegemonic structures of everyday life, a new structure of feeling will arise that better captures the "true social present" in place of the already formed practices of social life.[62] Likewise, speaking bitterness solidified an authorized structure of feeling as a means of making individual experience socially available for the launching of revolutionary subjects defined by class. But with its routinization within postrevolutionary political culture, it ultimately lost its power to articulate with subjective experience in its failure to reflect sufficiently the "true social present."

The memory of personal sorrow is central to the speaking bitterness narrative.[63] It constructs the old order as oppressive, inherently violent, and immoral by recalling instances of social antagonism between individuals who occupy very different positions within hierarchies of power in Chinese society. Within this narrative structure, the moral vision of the Confucian order, in which human relationships are ordered in terms of reciprocity and hierarchy, appears bankrupted by the struggle for existence. The old society is haunted by the specter of necessity and need that reduces people to an almost animal existence, making them powerless against class enemies with whom they are pitted in a duel to the death, a metonymy of the larger struggle for national sovereignty. This history was mythic in the sense that it entered into the space of the imaginary. It did not convey the past as it really was but as the negation of everything the new society promised to deliver. This is not to deny the misery of a society shattered by political disintegration and the tragedies of war but rather to point to the constructed nature of how the contrast between old and new had to be rendered absolutely black and white, unequivocally a moral drama between the forces of good and evil.

The narratives of class struggle dramatize these ruptures in the social fabric. Recalling social injustice led not just to the release of sorrow but also to a sense of violation, unleashing a wild fury. This wave of violence reached epic proportions in Long Bow Village and resulted in a dozen deaths, which represented far more than a symbolic catharsis or the purging of those identified as the natural enemies of the new order. This unfolding of events had the quality of ritual drama in literally performing a new world into being. In suggesting that class struggle was a kind of performance, I do not mean that it was "scripted" in the sense of a scenario that was fully worked out in moving toward an already determined denouement. The masses were, for the party, still an indeterminate object whose capacity to leap from the position of pedagogical object to performative subject had yet to be fully demonstrated. The process had a certain logic and dynamic of its own not fully controlled by the cadres who had unleashed these powerful forces. Indeed the very fury of the masses became, in a sense, an affirmation of the Marxist theory of history and its insistence on the necessity and inevitability of revolution and class struggle. For the work team cadres, the violence fulfilled the function of the imaginary completion of their self-identity as the vanguard of a revolutionary force. As Roland Barthes has suggested, violence is linked within our modern mythology with spontaneity, "the site of released speech," and is therefore linked to the truth of the subject, whereas writing is "what is invented."[64] Therefore, it is important for us to note the "scripted" (that is, "written") nature of this performance in the sense of its hanging on a system of representations that is its enabling condition to present itself as a historical inevitability.

Whether conditions in China had deteriorated to the extent to which a revolution was inevitable is perhaps beside the point, although this issue animates an impressive body of Western as well as Chinese scholarship. It takes more than oppression and misery to make a revolution, as Hinton makes very clear in his text. The undeniable fact is that a revolution took place in China and that it was not just the result of the objective miseries of existence. There is no threshold of human endurance beyond which human beings automatically become revolutionary. A revolution is the product of the human ability to reflect on one's conditions of existence and to work those reflections through a system of ideas that provides a vision of a more hopeful future, a social vision that exists at the level of the imaginary in that it conceives of something that does not yet exist.

The history of class struggle as a political strategy in the Chinese Revolution is important for those who wish to rethink the parameters of a radical politics in the late twentieth century. In mapping out a post-Marxian political strategy, Ernesto Laclau has made an important attempt to identify the flaws of the Marxian narrative that have led to its present impasse. For Laclau, the fatal error in Marxist theory was its misapplication of the Hegelian concept of "contradiction" to the notion of class struggle. Class struggle is not inherent to the contradiction sensu stricto between the relations of production and the development of the forces of production, which, Laclau suggests, is an abstract and impersonal process of history that bears no human face. A Marxist conception of the relations of production is not between fully fleshed social actors but between their abstractions as buyers and sellers of labor power. Class struggle arises from social antagonisms embedded in historically specific processes external to the economic field, what Laclau refers to as the "constitutive outside." The supposed contradiction in the relations of production depends on Marx's "reduction of concrete social agents to the economic categories of buyer and seller of labor power." But concrete social agents are much more than this abstraction when viewed in the totality of their social being, and antagonisms between them and their relations of production arise from contingent factors external to the relations of production themselves, that is, "the contingent power relations between forces that cannot be reduced to any kind of unified logic."[65]

As suggested earlier, Maoist theory of class struggle attempted to incorporate this "constitutive outside" into its theory of history. But class struggle is a contingent and not a necessary event. We see this in Mao's political strategy, in his emphasis on the role of revolutionary consciousness not as something inherent to the process of the working through of contradictions, but as something that had to be quite carefully constructed by a revolutionary vanguard. Yet in the unleashing of a politics of class resentment, social antagonisms were given the force of historical inevitability, rendering the bodies and property of "class enemies" into the raw material through which social transformation could be represented. This linkage of Marx's vision of history, as the ineluctable working out of contradictions, with the social antagonisms historically specific to the conditions of village life captures the sense in which Mao's conceptualization of class was a political one. The speaking bitterness narratives gave voice to the total social being of an actor situated within hierarchies of power and not just as a seller of labor power, for the experience of exploitation did not take that abstract form but was embedded in the face-to-face context of village life. These social relations were then made to stand in a metonymic relationship to the impersonal and abstract forces bearing down on the nation. The categories of class thereby operated by way of a catachresis, a "misapplication of the term," in which the social antagonisms of village life were identified with macroforces understood to be historically inevitable.

A recent critique of ethnographic writing has cited *Fanshen*'s conscious representation of world-historical forces as they work themselves out at the local level as a model for what ethnographers should do. For George Marcus, *Fanshen* succeeds in transcending the dichotomizing categories of local and global processes that threaten to blunt the critical power of an ethnography defined by its special focus on "local knowledge."[66] But Marcus may not have fully recognized that this intersection between the global and local was already part of a narrative process intrinsic to what Hinton was recording. The revolutionary praxis forged by the party in the crucible of class struggle was precisely to render the abstract world-historical forces of imperialism and capitalism into a highly embodied form identifiable within a local cast of characters. The power of this personification was amply demonstrated in the text by the periodic explosions of mass violence.

Writing the Spoken of History

Speaking bitterness did not end with liberation, but reappeared as a genre of oral performance enshrined in postrevolutionary political culture, eventually recorded in writing. Indeed, our present access to these narratives is primarily through this later writing that inscribed what had already congealed in spoken culture. In *Fanshen*, we see these narratives as a recognizable genre already embedded in Hinton's text as personal testimony. Indeed, it is this personal testimony that makes the drama of *Fanshen* so immediate for its readers. Yet we can recognize the traces of writing already present in their narrative structure (indeed as the very conditions of their enunciation). Why then, years later, must these spoken texts be literally inscribed as part of a massive political mobilization that suggests an obsessiveness concerning the act of writing in excess of any intention merely to preserve them "for the archive"?

Throughout the Maoist period, the same materials were worked and re-worked both as written narrative and as oral performance in the context of successive political campaigns. More than a simple act of rendering oral history into written form, the task of writing itself completely refracted the very process it was recording. If speaking bitterness had its uses as a pedagogical process in revolution in the constitution of a class as a revolutionary force, then this later act of writing is an inversion of the roles of pedagogical subject and object. The revolutionary subject speaks as the voice of history, and it is the role of the hearer to record the spoken of history as if it were something alien, a "truth" external to the writing subject that must be internalized through the act of writing.

The writing of these narratives was not a singular event. Sidney Greenblatt has described it as a "sporadic and recurrent mobilization of Chinese historical consciousness and historical resources."[67] It was not truly coordinated on a national scale, however, until the Four Histories Movement (*sishi yundong*), which began in the shadow of the Anti-Rightist Campaign in 1957. This project was later absorbed into the Socialist Education Campaign of 1962–66 as a gloss on Mao's dictum, "Never forget class struggle."[68] Its purpose was to preserve China's revolutionary heritage for those generations who would never directly experience the old society. But the exhortation for historians, students, and other intellectuals to leave the academy to write local histories coincided strikingly with the rustication (*xiafang*) policies of the late 1950s.[69] This emphasis on spoken narrative reflected the anti-intellectual political atmosphere of the time, which advocated getting intellectuals out of the libraries and into the factories and fields so that they might reform their class outlook by learning from workers and peasants.

The Four Histories Movement was first and foremost a pedagogical practice intended to inscribe profoundly the subjectivities of those engaged in the task of writing. This becomes patently obvious in the foreword to Sidney Green-blatt's *People of Taihang*, in which the local party secretary informs us that the work teams of young people sent into the Taihang Mountains to record family histories from poor and lower-middle-class peasants collected altogether seventy thousand narratives, of which only seventeen were selected for publication. Such a monumental effort can be understood only in terms of its value in the actual process of inscribing speech and secondarily in terms of producing a text to be read.

The materials resulting from this mobilization were often selected and compiled for local distribution in mimeographed form. The method of reproduction was frequently unmechanized—a film was inscribed by hand with a stylus and printed by hand using a flexible scraper to draw the ink over the text onto crude paper. Earlier texts were later reworked into new forms as local histories were written and rewritten, thus reflecting shifts in the national political culture.[70] Authorship of these texts was for the most part attributed to the work of anonymous compilation committees, except for first-person narratives in which the speaker was identified by name. In the process of writing and rewriting, what had begun as oral performance passed into the realm of mythos. Speaking bitterness was institutionalized within an emerging socialist culture that continued to inscribe powerfully the subjectivity of the "revolutionary successors" (*geming houdai*) for whom the old society could be known only in its narrativization.

In the escalating political mobilization of the Maoist period, the process of recording the past had a specifically ideological function: to establish a socialist revolutionary culture that set local memories of struggle into the larger national narrative. These narratives were to work on the consciousness of those doing the recording. Once recorded, they would also work on the consciousness of those who were to read them (just as the narratives in *Fanshen* work on our consciousness as we read them). In their written form, they became an integral part of a system of representations that not only structured memories of the old society but also defined identities in the present. Many of the narratives included in the published selections from Taihang record the personal histories of individuals who became active revolutionaries and attained positions of importance in the new society.[71] The emergence of a "class-status system" positioned individuals within the new society according to a logic of entitlement determined by their prerevolutionary class status or that of their parents. These representations operated at the level of a national culture, in which the basic narrative became reworked into a vast array of different cultural forms: revolutionary opera, school textbooks, exhibits, and fiction.[72] These representations had an undeniable effect in the production of political subjects long after the revolution was over.

As written documents, the structure of these narratives was reorganized around the moment of Liberation as a point of rupture. And yet that rupture in historical time failed to deflect a radical uncertainty intrinsic to all revolutionary narrative that recognizes that they are continuous with the past and yet radically other. As a "natural" outcome of a continuous evolution, revolutionary society is linked to the past while defining itself against it as a profound break. In the Chinese postrevolutionary political culture, speaking bitterness no longer stood alone but became temporally split by the double trope of "recalling past bitterness" to "savor the sweetness of the present" (*yiku sitian*). The narrative re-presents all that was presumably swept away by the cataclysm of the revolution, and yet its obsessive reprise betrays an uncertainty that what came before has not been completely erased, not entirely swept clean. The narrative is obsessed with the death of the old, but this obsessive retrieval of the past betrays a sort of terror that there might be a return from the dead. The past has to be represented so that it can be annihilated again and again by the present. This temporal split is a profound discursive reorganization of the narrative in terms of what it can be understood to be "making present." The past is rematerialized (through tears, through remembered pain) so that it unsettles the present as a sweetness continually under threat, requiring vigilance, self-sacrifice, a will to follow the party's lead to obtain a surer purchase on the future. To those who were in their young adulthood in the 1950s, yiku sitian is associated with the unified purchase of grain instituted by the state in 1956, producing willed consent for a policy that was sure to encounter popular resistance. An extensive propaganda campaign actively deployed historical memory through the public performance of yiku sitian as personal testimony, inaugurating in the process a new configuration of power that permitted the state to extract more agricultural surpluses for investment in heavy industry and to exert a tighter control over the movement of population through its grain-rationing system to a degree unprecedented by any previous Chinese state.

If the performance of speaking bitterness in the context of revolution is considered as a speech act on the order of "j'accuse," then we must place it within the category of speech acts that J. L. Austin has called the category of verdicts that display the exercise of judgment.[73] These narratives therefore enact a judgment on and the termination of an entire social order. Yet this act is never singular but is always already one in a series that multiplies its effects in each local context and indeed becomes disciplining by holding the specter of its unfulfilled performativity as a threat. Indeed, the force of speaking bitterness in post-Liberation political culture rests on its ability to "make present" what has presumably been made to vanish. Its performativity, what the postrevolutionary narrative is intended "to do," has become quite different in terms of what it is making present.

Discourse is forever haunted by the notion of presence. Emile Benveniste's theory of language and subjectivity focuses on how pronouns locate the subject in the social field by its positioning in language. According to Benveniste, language always includes an "ensemble of 'empty' signs that are nonreferential with respect to reality." These signs are filled as soon as a speaker introduces them into each unique instance of actualized speech, when language becomes discourse. Pronouns in particular are implicated in producing the effect of presence by means of a system of internal reference (a "here" and a "now") that circulates around the "I" of discourse as a "unique but mobile sign."[74]

In the context of revolution, this "I" is the mute body that is made to speak, standing metonymically for the nation coming into its self-presence in history. In its later inscription, this "I," as the site of both a "now" and a "then," gives witness to the spoken of history and its uncertain ability to deliver its telos. The speech act has already been spoken, its perlocutionary force has become history, but it is now spoken again for the express purpose of an "other" (a rather significant other) to write it down. Once again, the bodily register is accorded a priority over the intellect. Having suffered physical pain, the subaltern body can "never forget" class injury but can be made to speak it again and again. The body that has not had the suffering of the old society inscribed directly on it must internalize history in a different way, through the act of writing. Writing as the sign of the scholar's traditional privilege thus becomes the means of her or his own subjection, just as writing itself must be made subject to the laws of history by becoming, simply, inscribed speech.

If bodies reprise the spoken of history, so do inanimate objects come to stand metonymically for it as ghostly presences that can speak the past—the millstone shoes, the wheelbarrow, the miner's lamp from the narratives collected in *The People of Taihang* are transformed from silent witnesses of suffering and death to congealed representations of the oppressiveness of the past.[75] These congealed objects of representation were satirized by Gu Hua in his novel *A Small Town Called Hibiscus*, when a quilt grown worn and tattered since Liberation is seized upon for a local exhibit to remember the bitter past. We see in this instance how the contradictions of post-Liberation society are continually being displaced by evocations of the old society, a process of disavowal or deferral. Likewise, the parade of bad elements before the educated youth sent to Chen Village appear to them as physically repulsive. They are, in fact, wraiths, their social identities imploded into "ghosts and monsters," haunting the present from the grave of the past in a way calculated never to disappear, a living dead, as mute as any object. But despite their visibly abject status, their haunting presence testifies that the past is never really dead but must always be guarded against.

Of course, the congealed nature of these narratives did much more than merely reprise the past. These narratives were fundamental to the system of representations that structured an entire social order in which class status determined not only personal identity but also one's entitlement to the "sweetness" of the present, and it did so in a way that seemed strangely frozen, fixed in an arbitrary order that violently proscribed any mobility across categories. What did this system of representations actively produce in the postrevolutionary society that sustained its power to inscribe social reality for so long? Can it simply be reduced to a convergence of newly entrenched interests on the part of those who benefit from the new order, or were there historically overdetermined forces working on the national imaginary that sustained a sense of threat from within?

In Jean-François Billeter's brilliant discussion of the operation of the Chinese class-status system during the Maoist era, he insists on referring to the categories of class division as a *misrecognition* of the real nature of Chinese agrarian society, suggesting a willful perversion of Marx's original concept.[76] To do Billeter justice, rather than dwelling on the failure of this discourse to approximate the pure logic of Marxist categories, he seeks to determine what it actively produced in Chinese socialist society—namely, a highly elaborated system of defined statuses that determined one's place in a postrevolutionary redistributive economy according to a moral logic that inverted the status hierarchy of traditional society. For Billeter, it was in its operation as a set of moral statuses that the system betrayed its lack of scientificity and hence its deviation from a pure notion of class. After all, by the late 1970s the system incorporated more than just economic categories to embrace over sixty heterogeneous designations that could embrace the social totality so that "no individual could escape it."[77]

Billeter seems to assume that there is a purer, more true conception of class as an empirical category that the Chinese class system simply failed to achieve, in no small part, through a process of ideological distortion. His conception of ideology is still very much bound up with the idea of its being a mystification of the *real* conditions of existence rather than the instituting moment for a social imaginary that is not simply the arbitrary ordering of culture but one that is historically overdetermined! If the language of class appears to us now as "absurd, mad, divorced from the facts," then we must make some attempt to understand why it carried such power despite all the internal contradictions that Billeter so helpfully lays out for us.[78] After all, the system, despite its apparent anachronism, did not remain fixed over time but accumulated over successive political campaigns new categories of bad elements, until the "enemy within" seemed to be everywhere. It is perhaps not possible to understand fully this obsessive concern for the "recrudescence of evil" in terms internal to China itself; it must be placed in the context of China's increasing isolation from the rest of the world and its defensiveness in the face of significant threats from without.[79] Just as class enemies provided the human face of the impersonal forces of imperialism and capitalism in the context of revolutionary struggle, this myth of presence lingered into the cold war era as a means of binding the nation together to face off external threats as they were projected inward.

The continuing evocation of class struggle thereby suggests that the tactics of guerrilla war extended into the postrevolutionary era. The Communist Party may well have won its status as "the proper locus" of power within the nation, but it was still very much operating according to the tactics of guerrilla warfare that "play upon time" on the global stage to make up for its material weakness in relation to the Soviet Union and the United States.[80] Speaking bitterness not only mobilized increased vigilance against the return of class society but also ushered in accelerated schedules for agricultural collectivization that greatly increased the grip of state power over its population. In the personal narratives of the Cultural Revolution period, we get a clear sense of the degree of urgency felt by ordinary people which may appear to our present consciousness as overwrought or misplaced in finding the enemy so close to home but which, nonetheless, reflected real threats to national sovereignty projected inward. Therefore, to suggest that the class-status system developed sui generis in China as a hybrid monster born of an ancient tradition of "rectifying names" (*zheng-ming*) and the imported luster of Marxist science is perhaps being a little disingenuous in its very denial of China's isolation in the context of cold war politics and the importance of class in the coalescence of a national subjectivity that was no less salient for the postrevolutionary period.

As already suggested by Laclau, the misapplication of class to categorizing specific persons, rather than abstractions, was already inherent in Marxist theory and not specific to China. Claude Lefort's powerful critique of Marxism elaborates this further by suggesting that there is no pure concept of class. He urges us to no longer "confuse social division with the empirical distribution of individuals in the process of production." There is no objective space that preexists mediation of the symbolic to name it. The differentiation of the social space is inseparable from "the deployment of a discourse [already] at a distance from the supposed real."[81] It is impossible to grasp the totality of social relations, just as it is impossible to grasp the totality of historical development, because such an attempt conceals one's own insertion within the domain of discourse. Thus Billeter suggests, in the tradition of French structuralism, that the Chinese class-status system demonstrates the arbitrary working of culture (*arbitraire culture*) that renders social relations into an intelligible order with specific practical functions. This arbitrariness, therefore, is supposed to explain the otherwise incomprehensible features of the system—its heterogeneity, its hereditary nature, its anachronism, and so on. But what he fails to emphasize is how this apparently arbitrary arrangement did not arise as one of convenience, as a means by which a redistributive economy can be ordered, but was one that was historically overdetermined by China's position in a global system of colonizing powers that operated as imaginary and symbolic orders. Indeed, Billeter's presentation of the differentiated functions of the class-status system betrays a rather vulgar priority for the economic and political functions of distribution, concealment, and exclusion, putting representation last as the least concrete of its many functions. And yet the order should perhaps be reversed, representation being the instituting moment on which all other functions depend!

If we can no longer presume to examine ideological discourse with reference to a reality derived from positive knowledge (because of the way that reality reveals itself as a failure of the ideological to conceal its traces through the operation of the imaginary), Lefort suggests that the project then becomes how the dominant discourse is organized to generate a social space. Every cultural arbitrary seeks its foundational moment that covers over its arbitrariness, its appeal to a transcendent order. For Marxism, it is its scientificity, and Billeter faults Maoist constructions of class for failure to be science. This judgment, I would suggest, fails to see, or refuses to acknowledge fully, the power of bourgeois ideology to imagine a national subjectivity into being; it obscures the very real problem of colonial modernity. As my discussion of Laclau's critique of Marx has perhaps already suggested, the movement of class from an abstract theoretical category to the historically located subject of revolutionary praxis already invests it with a myth of presence—a myth, moreover, that exerted a brute material force in the Chinese Revolution. In the wake of the revolution, this myth lingered on in the uncanny reappearance of class antagonism, reanimating national subjects with a sense of urgency and national mission.

Billeter attributes the determination of the Maoist discourse of class in the orchestration of interests without perhaps examining how those interests are already constituted within the symbolic order. Perhaps more useful here than Pierre Bourdieu is Michel Foucault, in which we can see a construction of class as becoming a "dense transfer point of power" rather than an "orchestration of interests," which in Billeter's application reduces the latter to the premise of a bourgeois subject.[82] Marxism was invested with the power to displace the system of social ascription already in place, to institute a radically new order of social division, severing the bonds understood as natural and moral and replacing them with new modes of affiliation according to one's identity in the new order. What Billeter fails to examine is how the Chinese discourse on class presents itself as "an anonymous discourse in which the universal speaks of itself" and seeks its foundation in the transcendence of ideas such as Society and Nation. He fails to recognize its power in the simultaneous construction of Nation and Subject. According to Lefort, "The determination of an order of appearances is asserted or assumed by virtue of the transcendence of the idea."[83] The categories of bourgeois ideology thereby have a "double nature" as both representation and norm. This is particularly true in a colonial context in which the inability of society to represent itself subjugates colonial subjects at many levels at once to the rule of the norm, as a failure to achieve the objectivity of positive knowledge, an inability to access the real.

Finally, we must note the ultimate exhaustion of speaking bitterness narrative and its transmutation into post-Maoist narratives that legitimate an intellectual class with high stakes in the modernization effort of the Deng era. Here I appeal once again to Lu Xun's "New Year's Sacrifice," this time as an allegorical figure of the performative power of narrative to produce strong emotions *and* the limits to that power. Xianglin Sao's story of her son's capture by wolves first moves her audience to tears. Elderly women would seek her out, wishing to hear her tale, waiting for the moment when words would fail and weeping began, so they too could weep and go away "satisfied." We have a dramatization of the power of narrative to solicit this pleasure and its exhaustion through obsessive return. This masochistic pleasure has its sadistic side. Lu Xun suggests its cannibalistic nature in his characterization of how this narrative loses its emotive power having been "tasted by people for so many days, [it] had long since become stale, only exciting disgust and contempt."[84] We have in this story an eerie anticipation of the fate of speaking bitterness narrative in post-Maoist political culture when young people in Chen Village mock what is supposed to be a moving account of sorrow and loss.[85] Speaking bitterness narratives possessed a performative power with far greater transformative effect than the one claimed by Xianglin Sao, but this power had its limits and the capacity to exhaust itself, to create the distaste of having been heard too many times. The presence invoked by these narratives became too jarring in its inability to address new subjectivities emerging in the wake of the Cultural Revolution. They had become merely a manipulative tool, yet we can see that the essential contours of these narratives are reawakened in certain modes of nostalgia well into the 1990s.[86]

The intent of my argument in this chapter has been twofold. In highlighting the myth of presence that inheres in Chinese revolutionary narrative, I question the claim that the socialist revolution was merely the product of a cynical "will to power" from the very beginning, noting carefully the specific historical conditions that overdetermined the power of this narrative to articulate a national identity in the face of political disintegration.[87] At the same time, I wish to explore what the implications of displacing History as the progressive working toward a predetermined telos might have for rethinking the strategies of a politically engaged scholarly practice. In particular, I wish to foreground the discursive preconditions that made a cross-class alliance possible in the making of a socialist revolution in China and why that possibility seems so unlikely today. And I do this in hopes of redirecting our critique of the 1989 student movement away from the students' lack of savvy in articulating their politics with other class elements toward a clearer understanding of how their subjectivities are formed by processes specific to China's integration with the capitalist system in the late twentieth century. Whereas in the period leading to the revolution the figure of the subaltern became the mirror image of the intellectual's own sense of powerlessness and pain, while also promising a connection to the "real forces of history," the image of the great unwashed masses has now reemerged on the other side of a great divide as a tumorous growth on the body of the nation, sapping its strength and slowing its course toward its historic destiny. Given this profound division, what sorts of articulatory practices are possible in reimagining a more democratic national community? Partha Chatterjee has suggested that it is precisely this problem of community that is most pressing in postcolonial nations in the late twentieth century, and one might add that it is equally pressing for the increasingly diverse populations of the metropole.[88]

2 THE MIMESIS OF POWER

We could very well wonder whether it is not precisely the fact that *everyone is fooled* which constitutes the source of our pleasure.—Lacan, "Séminaire sur 'La Lettre Volée' "

In the fall of 1979, the exploits of a young man named Zhang Longquan became a cause célèbre in Shanghai, China's most sophisticated and cynical city. He had impersonated the son of Li Da, the deputy chief of staff of the People's Liberation Army, an old and revered revolutionary cadre, for a period lasting several months until his exposure the previous spring. His imposture had begun one evening when, frustrated at not being able to get tickets to the theater, he had spontaneously hit on the idea of pretending to be the son of a ranking Communist Party member, thereby appropriating for himself the special privilege (*te-quan*) accorded the children of high-ranking cadres. The success of his ruse did not stop there. He was soon pulled into a social network of influence and obligation that sought to capitalize on the status of his putative father. Assuming an unworldly persona, the imposter appeared willing to obligate himself to others indiscriminately. Gifts and special favors flowed toward this young man from people eager to obligate him for their own ends. One by one, letters asking for "backdoor" requests accumulated in his pockets.[1] After a period of several months, his true identity was revealed, and he was arrested.

In September, a full five months after his arrest, detailed reports of his exploits appeared in at least two Shanghai newspapers in anticipation of his upcoming trial. In these official accounts, the young man's imposture was described as a criminal act, a trick played by an unscrupulous character on innocent but wrongheaded people. A group of young Shanghai playwrights wrote, almost overnight, a play called *Jiaru wo shi zhende* (If only I were real), which offered an alternative reading. The play clearly pointed a finger at the entrenched practices of *guanxixue*, the calculated exchange of influence and obligation, which enabled this imposter to succeed in his skillful manipulation of other peoples' desires.[2] The play was staged for a brief period in Shanghai until it was unofficially suppressed, but not without considerable debate in the cultural organs of the party and in Shanghai literary circles. Despite the fact that certain prominent literary figures spoke up in its defense, the play was not "rehabilitated." Its authors, however, appear not to have been punished and continued to write for the stage.[3] The suppressed play was smuggled out of China to Hong Kong and from there to Taiwan, where it was made into a film.[4]

I have opened my discussion with an account of this history as a way of showing how this particular example of the art of imposture has generated so many readings—by party officials, artist-intellectuals, the media, and, as we shall see, ordinary people as well. The multiplicity of these readings suggests a certain playfulness reflected in the young man's own imposture in which the meaning of events was unhinged from the official order to become a commentary on the workings of power in Chinese society in the early reform period. The imposter's mimesis of power unmasks the ways in which power spins its own fictions. This unmasking provided a source of great delight to the discussions of ordinary people despite the efforts by the party-state to impose its own reading.

In exploring these multiple readings, I consider the dynamic of imposture itself. How is the economy of desire so constituted in Chinese society to enable such an imposture to crystallize? How does the play of seduction and desire embodied in the figure of this young man rest on the creation of a self-referential reality through the passage of the gift?[5] In the context of these questions, I want to explore how the passage of the gift duplicates in practice some of the performative aspects of certain speech acts, such as the act of "promising." In China, accepting a gift, especially from someone inferior in status, is a form of promise of an often unspecified return. In the case of our imposter, this promise is given "in the name of that which one does not have"—that is, position and power.[6] The flow of gifts toward the imposter is "empowered" by the "name of the father," whose power to reciprocate is constantly deferred or given an alibi by playing off one obligation against the other. The informal structure of power, which rests on the arbitrary definition of statuses, is thereby unmasked by this lack, this play around an empty center, because it demonstrates how the charisma of the party itself, whose morality excludes it, powers the gift through a network of social relations created in its passage.[7]

However, I go beyond the event itself to explore the play of readings opened up by this imposture in the light of its exposure. The official representation of the imposter's story does not forestall subversive readings that then produce effects in the domain of popular practices, namely, a proliferation of imposters who continue to improvise on the themes of this well-publicized case. New imposters appear to subvert the foreclosure of meaning; the repressed continually returns to deliver the message of how deeply the formal and informal structures of power are implicated in each other.

Finally, I also consider how identities are created in the wake of the chaotic years of the Cultural Revolution and its aftermath when the stable categories of the Maoist class-status system began to unravel, undermined by the constantly shifting ground of signification in a context of political terror. In pursuing this theme, I focus on the experience of a "duality of being" in which the subject is forced to play a role or occupy a status imposed by the spinning of power's own fictions so that it is experienced by the subject as alien or "inauthentic." I do not mean to suggest that this inauthenticity must be measured against any idealized notion of an "authentic" self. Rather, I want to focus on how the power to name, to fix persons into a moral category, came to be experienced as a form of alienation, as something imposed from outside. What I suggest is that the manipulation of identity, which became necessary as a survival tactic in the upheaval of the Cultural Revolution, has led to a certain self-consciousness of this as an artful process and therefore enabled the creative elaboration of identities that poach on the existing relations of power. In this sense, then, the imposture of this particular young man was an early precursor of the explosion of self-fashioned identities unleashed, in no small part, by the economic reforms of the 1980s.

The readiness of official voices to attribute this young man's actions to the maximizing rationality of the self-interested individual evades the question of the multiplicity of discourses that transect the subject and the tremendous social momentum propelling his imposture onto a rapidly expanding stage. In this sense, the theoretical trajectory of this chapter comes full circle in its discussion of a multiplicity of readings. By questioning the assertion by official voices that the motivation of the imposter was entirely for self-interested reasons and therefore can have *no other meaning*, one can perhaps question the more universal issue of the rational actor as a self-determining individual as well as the performative dimensions of even the most totalizing symbolic order. In this sense, then, we can see the young man's imposture as enacting a complex structure of seduction and desire, an economy of pleasure which derives from the felicity of its outcomes and which can therefore become "detached" from the regime of "truth."

I begin with a narrative account based on the newspaper stories of the "true" events on which rests the subsequent play of readings. I then examine various modes of the "imposture" of power, the fictions that it must spin to sustain the effect of its own reality. Next, I discuss the gift as a language, constitutive of identity, that can be ventriloquized and how the gift structures the informal relations of power to provide a space in which imposture can be effected. I then suggest an alternative logic of practice that seeks to reverse the relations of power, if only momentarily, or to force them to yield a certain "pleasure" that can be understood only as a performative excess to the calculus of ends in themselves. Finally, I discuss the conflict of readings and how official voices, in their very attempt to fix the meaning of the event, produce the very means with which the event itself can multiply its effects.

The narrative that follows is constructed from accounts that appeared in two major daily Shanghai newspapers, the *Jiefang ribao* and the *Wenhui bao*, on September 11, 1979. I have taken the more interesting details of each to patch together a single narrative. To this extent, the story as it appears below is an artifact of my own manufacture. In any case, these are the "originals" on which the play was based, although they are themselves already several times removed from the event. While the play, although based on a factual case, is framed as a fiction, the newspaper stories, although intended as factual accounts, are perhaps fictions of another order, doing much more than merely reporting the "facts" of the case. They are highly structured narratives; dialogue is quite freely reconstructed; and specific motivations are ascribed to the actors. Despite these caveats, these accounts allow us to follow the working of the gift as it moves through a network of social relations that it creates in its passage.

"A Trickster Tricks Himself into the Net"

On the evening of January 31, a youth named Zhang Longquan was in Shanghai visiting his family for the New Year's holiday. Although he was originally from Shanghai, he had been sent down to the countryside to the East Wind Farm in Chongming.[8] Unable to obtain tickets to the theater, he pretended to be a department head (*buzhang*) of the municipal party committee and telephoned the Shanghai Arts Theater. He told them that the son of an old revolutionary cadre, an official in the headquarters of the general staff in Beijing, wanted to see the performance and asked if they would receive him. The assistant administrative head of the theatrical group immediately responded with enthusiasm and ordered a comrade to wait at the door for the unexpected guest.

Not long after, Zhang Longquan appeared wearing a faded and patched army uniform. Such humble garb is seldom seen among the youth of Shanghai.[9] He swaggered up to the door, and curling his tongue to affect a Beijing accent, he introduced himself as Li Xiaoyong. After an exchange of greetings, he was ushered into the theater and given an excellent seat in the sixth row, displacing a cadre from the municipal cultural bureau.

A phone call comes from a department head—the son of a senior officer wants a ticket. What can you say? Zhang Longquan had every assurance of success in this venture. He already knew from a previous experience of posing as a high-ranking cadre that high position engendered respect. He was also aware that this special regard extended to the children of such persons.

After the play, Zhang made his way backstage where he was greeted with smiles by the assistant administrative head, who promised him a seat whenever he wished in the future. The two had a pleasant chat, and then, as Zhang prepared to take his leave, he was approached by the director of the play who asked if he could visit Zhang the next day. To forestall a risk of exposure through this proposed visit to a hotel where, in fact, he was not a guest, Zhang encouraged the man to tell him what he wanted. The director, overjoyed, said in a low voice that his living quarters were very cramped and he was hoping Zhang would pass on a housing request to the department head (who had presumably made the call introducing Zhang earlier that evening). Playing along, Zhang replied that housing in Shanghai was very tight and difficult to arrange but that he would see to it. At six the next afternoon, Zhang returned to the theater to pick up the director's written request. He was then happily greeted by the assistant administrative head who chatted with him over tea and boiled eggs. Finally he too unburdened himself with his innermost problems. He was ailing and wanted his son who worked in a coal mine to be transferred home to take care of him. Would Zhang pass on the request?

One request after another found its way into his pocket. People who were good at heart but muddled in their methods had found an improper pathway to their desires. They cast their vigilance to the winds. Secretly the imposter had a good laugh; everything had been smooth sailing up to now, and he grew even bolder.

One evening a few days later, Zhang used the same ploy to gain entry to the Xuhui Theater, where he made the acquaintance of a certain actress who was currently performing there. This actress took a fancy to this stranger who was so obviously well connected. A few days later, he was a guest in her home. The conversation naturally got around to Department Head X. Zhang claimed that this man had been an old subordinate of his father's and that they were very close. This time he already had the experience behind him of dealing with his other friends, so he didn't bother to wait for her to approach him but said, "If you have any problems, you can just ask me to help get his assistance." Delighted, she requested that he ask the department head or the district party secretary to expedite her housing problems. She also asked if he would help her husband in the competition for theatrical roles.

The next time he went to visit, he brought her a bottle of mao-tai. But this gift was just as bogus as his assumed name and status. He had bought an empty mao-tai bottle for two *mao* (twenty cents), filling it with one catty of ordinary liquor and sticking some red cellophane on the neck of the bottle to make it look authentic. On this visit, he wangled an invitation to accompany her to the spring tea at the Municipal Cultural Liaison Bureau the next day at which the highest-level personages in the literary and arts world of Shanghai would be present. To ensure his reception he took the extra precaution of again impersonating Department Head X and telephoned the Cultural Liaison Bureau to tell them that they could expect Zhang's attendance at the affair. His friend the actress introduced him to famous writers and actors. They shook hands and nodded at each other. What a putting on of airs!

At this affair, the imposter made friends with a leading cadre from a Shanghai cultural unit. He was especially cordial to Zhang, giving him theater tickets and offering him the use of his car. His motive was to use Zhang's influence to get his daughter transferred back to Shanghai. Zhang "dutifully " made a call to this new friend, this time posing as the municipal party secretary to inform him that he had been told of the matter and that it would be difficult to arrange. The improbability of a personal call from such a high personage never occurred to this man, who was convinced that Zhang had a lot of pull, and so he ignored the "difficult to arrange" part and was satisfied that things were being taken care of. When the demands of this man became too importunate, Zhang merely made another phone call, again assuming the identity of the party secretary, asking him to refrain from more requests as it was getting too "risky." Moments earlier he had made another phone call to the same man, only this time posing as his putative father, asking him to take good care of his "son" while the latter was in Shanghai.

At the same tea party, Zhang had also sought an introduction to a very illustrious party secretary of a university. As Zhang chatted with him, the photographer who was recording the event snapped their picture. This further elevated the imposter in the eyes of everyone there. At first this old gentleman was somewhat perfunctory in his attentions to Zhang, perhaps even a little wary, especially when Zhang asked to use his car. Again the imposter had only to pose as his father in another call to get this man's complete cooperation. Before long the old comrade's car was at Zhang's disposal in his daily jaunts around the city.

Meanwhile, Zhang had asked his actress friend to help him find a "girl-friend." She took him on a tour of all leading dancing schools and entertainment troupes around the city, looking over every studio and classroom to survey the available talent. None of them suited Zhang. Finally he settled on an actress in an amateur theatrical troupe attached to a neighborhood cultural station. Zhang and his go-between told this candidate that the Beijing general staff was about to establish a new cultural troupe and if she wanted to work for them, they would give her an introduction. Boundless gratitude quickly turned into love at first sight. The girl's father, who had been a capitalist in the old society, was ecstatic at this unexpected happiness. The parents of the girl insisted that Zhang move in with them to save money at the expensive hotel, where they assumed he was staying. Zhang's New Year's holiday from his unit was drawing to an end, and he could no longer stay at home, so this invitation fit in beautifully with his plans. The whole family was delighted with this sweet-talking, filial fiancé of their daughter who was also the son of a high-ranking cadre. His future mother-in-law noticed that he lacked a wristwatch, so she gave him her own imported one as a token of her regard.[10]

By this time, Zhang had everything he needed to fill his role: the use of private cars and money for expensive restaurants and new clothes. Some of the money was pressed on him by the relatives and neighbors of his future in-laws, many of whom had bad class backgrounds, in hopes that Zhang could help them recover confiscated property or other favors. Some of the money was given to him to act as an agent in procuring certain material goods.[11] Zhang's girlfriend had two older brothers: one worked in a factory and the other in a school. Zhang made personal appearances at both their work units to improve their position in the eyes of their superiors.[12]

On March 18, Zhang decided he wanted to tour Suzhou (about one hour's drive from Shanghai). He borrowed his usual limousine and added a jeep from the Shanghai Song and Dance Troupe so that he could take all his new friends, including his girlfriend and her father. There were ten people altogether. They drove to Suzhou, where they were met by the section chief of the municipal government, who greeted them warmly and provided them with a tour guide to accompany them on their sightseeing. This scene was truly one of "bustling people and honking horns."[13]

Zhang finally "fell into the net" of the legal system of the dictatorship of the proletariat while trying to arrange a work reassignment for his girlfriend. This was a difficult undertaking, for he was trying to get her transferred from a small collective to a state-owned unit.[14] When Zhang approached the neighborhood party committee on this matter, they began to suspect this stranger whose origins were not clear but who came and went every day by car in grand style. An investigation revealed the true identity of the imposter, and he was arrested on April 6, 1979.

The Impostures of Power

Stephen Greenblatt has suggested that the quintessential sign of power is the ability to "impose one's fictions upon the world." Surely, this aspect of power must have been experienced most acutely by those caught up in competing constructions of reality in the factional fighting of the Cultural Revolution.[15] The insulation of the self from the dangers of a shifting political reality has led, it would seem, to the creation of a curious duality in which an outer surface is artfully manipulated to sail with the prevailing political "wind." Yet it is perhaps too easy to collapse this dualism into the pat dichotomies of social science— between state and society, inner and outer selves, public and private, surface and depth, duplicitous and authentic selves. Our inquiry must examine more carefully how identity is constituted in Chinese society and how these identities become located within the historical narrativizations of the Chinese socialist state discussed in the previous chapter.

Recent discussions of the concept of "face" (*lian* and *mianzi*), which attempt to go beyond the colonial constructions of a "national character" narrative of Chinese culture, perhaps suggest some lines of inquiry.[16] Chinese conceptions of face usually draw the distinction between *lian*, roughly understood as moral respectability, and *mianzi*, as social prestige and power.[17] Indeed, it is this problem of translation in which these two senses are collapsed in English that Andrew Kipnis has taken care to disentangle. I am primarily interested here in the concept of mianzi and the subtle practices that can cause it to expand or shrink. Unlike lian, which, once lost, can never be regained, mianzi is conceptualized as a two-dimensional surface which measures the scope of one's power and influence and which is therefore potentially limitless in size. Mianzi has therefore been described as "a site from which hierarchical communication is possible."[18] The larger this surface, the more potential one has in initiating social relationships. Mianzi is a surface on which social relationships are activated; it is not a mask for some deeper reality. Concern for one's "face" is not fear of exposure but concern for the very basis of one's social identity. Kipnis suggests that mianzi is *constitutive* of social identity in its very visibility to the social gaze. "The performances that create or destroy *mianzi* constitute identity, selfhood and social hierarchy. They are neither reflections of a pregiven reality nor (worse yet) illusions."[19]

He illustrates the constitutive character of face by citing Mao's "Report on an Investigation of the Peasant Movement in Hunan," in which Mao describes the crowning of evil gentry with dunce caps as a practice that strips them of their "face" (*yanmian*) so that they can no longer "be regarded as human" (*zuobuqi ren*).[20] This crowning, which is really an "uncrowning," goes beyond the exposure of a person to public ridicule that is merely temporary in its effects; it is nothing less than a stripping away of someone's social identity, a violent act of expulsion from the community that not uncommonly led to suicide. The importance of the social gaze here, Kipnis suggests, is registered in the phrase of being "unable to get off the stage" (*xiaobuliao tai*) once one has lost one's mianzi or lian. As Kipnis suggests, the theatrical metaphor does not refer to a surface level of artifice but an intensity of the social gaze focused on the person in the ritualized dramaturgy of struggle. This fate of being unable to get off the stage was all too literally experienced by individuals who found themselves stuck in the role of struggle object in the obsessive repetition of successive political movements.

Ironically, the theatrical metaphor as an image of surface effect over a deeper reality returns to haunt us in such cases where the only identity left to the subject was precisely this total absence of yanmian, which could then be deployed as a negotiable currency. Several accounts of the Cultural Revolution period mention how seasoned struggle objects worked out a tacit accommodation with local officials in "playing" their "role" in struggle sessions so that others might have their mianzi spared. Gu Hua's novel *Furongzhen* (*A Small Town Called Hibiscus*) offers a moving story of how a young woman learns to play her role as a struggle object under the tutelage of a "bad element" more experienced than she. She learns to perform her role as a way of rendering the repeated struggle sessions pro forma, a mode of resistance to a power which denies her a social identity and which would otherwise drive her to suicide or madness were she to resist more openly. On the surface, she is complicit with power in spinning its fictions, but her complicity also provides her with a means to buy herself a respite from the stage without being broken in spirit. Power produces the very means by which its own impostures are undermined when the actors are aware that they are playing a role imposed from "outside" as a violence of writing inscribed within the categories of the class-status system.

This self-conscious manipulation of identity in relation to power arose as a tactical adaptation of individuals to a totally new organization of power that beginning in the 1950s and early 1960s became firmly entrenched within a shifting political reality. *Shenfan*, William Hinton's sequel to *Fanshen*, which carries the history of Long Bow Village through the period of socialist transformation, is richly illustrated with examples of what Lowell Dittmer describes as "communicational adaptation" that emerged with the increased pace of the socialist transition in the middle to late 1950s. Mark Selden dates it from the high tide of collectivization, a period that he sees as having "reinforced the arbitrary and manipulative tendencies in the Party and the state, and [as having] undermined the democratic possibilities inherent in the cooperative form."[21] Judging from Hinton's description of the Great Leap in Long Bow Village, the gap that opened between local communities and the higher-ups became a space in which fictions of power and its effects could be spun.[22] What may be new in the post-Mao context is the degree to which the manipulation of identity has become a self-conscious and artful process. This elaboration of new identities is not solely a product of a cynical relationship to power, however, but has been propelled by a dramatic reorganization of power in the post-Mao period.

In the period since 1978, the relations of power between the state and new kinds of economic actors have been caught up in a complex process of negotiation. This is perhaps most observable on the local level; local officials are often the most active agents in the new enterprise economies, where it becomes impossible to draw a line between state and society or between public and private ownership, thus enabling new kinds of enterprise structures. The reforms enabled the explosive expansion of new forms of enterprise economies, creating newly consolidated constructions of identity in terms of credit worthiness (*xinyong*) and market savvy which emanate from the new market economy but which are still not totally detached from state discourses of power.[23] Indeed, the party-state continues to want to order and classify these new economic actors, seeking to absorb them into its own officially defined morality by improvising new models.

Therefore, whether we are talking about the Maoist period or the Dengist reforms, the shaping of identity in relation to power is best observed in the ways in which the boundaries blur between art and life in the representational practices of the state. This blurring of boundaries between truth and fiction is very much akin to "socialist realism," which, as a protocol for artistic production, dictates that art and literature must have a didactic function to represent ideal behavior for emulation rather than to focus critically on the negative aspects of society. It therefore specifies a literature that represents the way things are supposed to be in a socialist society, not the way they "really are." Socialist realism is a strong statement about the power of representation to "write" upon the "real." What this means in practice is a mode of censorship that closes down any attempts in art and literature to represent directly the contradictions, ambiguities, or social costs of socialist development. In the post-Mao period, the censor has relaxed enough to allow the development of an "exposure literature" and a literary journalism that examines specific kinds of social problems that become marked as signs of social disorder. Despite this apparent liberalization of the reform era, the representational machine of socialist realism continues to extend itself beyond the confines of art and literature to the domain of lived reality itself. Socialist realism therefore bridges the line that divides art and life in the production of "hegemonic fictions," in which individuals find themselves re-created as little "fictions," as objects through which the larger fiction achieves its material reality.

Fundamental to this process is the designation of individuals or, in certain cases, whole communities as models for emulation, who are themselves conscious of the fact that they do not fulfill what may at times be an impossible ideal, a "bogus" reality, a "false model." This dynamic is not restricted to the model alone but extends itself along a much wider ground in the guise of the "apparently reformed individual," one who is forced to take on the appearance of conforming to the model in order to "get off the stage," the cost of which is to play a role in the fictions of power.[24] The state, in this way, spins a fiction about the efficacy of its own power, and survival depends in no small degree on one's ability to step into this fiction and improvise a role in it. At the same time, those who are caught up in the fiction are very aware of their imposture and need to build a buffer of secrecy to sustain the illusion. In some of the literature written since 1978, this process has been quite graphically described for the Maoist era in, once again, the work of Gu Hua. His novella *Pagoda Ridge* describes the efforts of members of an entire community to enact the form of the Dazhai model as a cover for their own heterodox economic practices that give them the material means to display the markers of economic success.[25]

This re-creation of the self as part of a larger hegemonic fiction is nicely countered by the opposite move—namely, the elaboration of an identity that poaches on the existing structures of power. It is with this later realm of practice that the story of Zhang Longquan must be identified. In interpreting his act of imposture, I seek to elude a logic of utility so that I can explore other logics that may lie within practice. This ambition may seem especially quixotic in that contemporary Chinese society appears to be so much one of cynical, hardened individualists, ostensibly unassimilable to any register outside of naked self-interest, blinded by the obsessive reduction of all social relations to the pursuit of wealth as captured in the phrase *xiang qian kan* (look only toward money). This phrase began as a pun on *xiang qian kan* (look toward the future), a party directive delivered in response to the tumultuous release in the late 1970s of suppressed grieving over the disastrous events of the Cultural Revolution. This "play" on words compressing the whole history of the transition from Mao to Deng must be added as a powerful example of *ji* (stratagem) as the mutually implicated play of language and practice explored below. However, I would like to consider this story of imposture as being among those forms of practice that invoke "a return of the repressed," a reclaiming of something that has been "lost," reconstituting a sociality severed by the disjunctures of bureaucratic order, using a tactics of the everyday that can restore a measure of control over the powerful but arbitrary forces that intensify the struggles of daily life. But beyond the merely practical ends that these means inscribe, such tactics yield a certain "excess" of effect that suggests an economy of pleasure which circulates within a wider social field—the imposter and his dupes—constituted by this very circulation. Moreover, even when it is summarily truncated by the state security apparatus, this circulation of pleasure continues in narrative and in the reduplication of its effects in practice. But, as we will also explore below, this pleasure carries with it specific dangers that may result in madness.

The tactics of everyday life, therefore, can be creatively extended to enact extraordinary forms of imposture, scams, and ruses in contemporary society, and these events have their specific modes of representation in the form of literary reportage, legal pictorials, social commentary, and so on, that render them visible as "scandals," but scandals that are readily "consumable" as a popular literature.[26] The idea of mimesis is taken from Aristotle's *Poetics*, in which art is seen as deriving its power through its imitation of life, but in this case of imposture, mimesis is the seizing upon the "appearance" of things to appropriate their power. Mimesis lies at the heart of a representational economy currently undergoing deconstruction, in which representation is understood to have a certain power to write on the real, to evoke its referent through the process of representation itself, rather than to reflect an external reality directly. In Chapter 1 we saw this process in the political imperative to represent in literature concepts such as Society and Nation so that they might be seized on as the "wheels of History," as the very means of historical agency. Here, however, mimesis becomes a means of play, "an end in itself that takes one into the magical power of the signifier to act as if it were indeed the real, to live in a different way with the understanding that artifice is natural," according to Michael Taussig.[27] It is precisely this aspect of mimesis that I wish to explore in this chapter, in which a regime of "truth" is made to reveal its self-referential nature, yielding a certain pleasure for those who are outside its privilege. The hero's deployment of a putative status and the gift mimics the informal structure of power in contemporary China, but the state's own representations of his "crimes" make the impostures of power accessible not only to public discussion but also to an endless reduplication of the scandal in narrative and in practice.

The art of imposture in this context subverts the objectifying language that had, throughout the Maoist era, fixed individuals according to class status, household registration, and occupation, determining one's access to the "goods," both tangible and intangible, of the new society. Imposture then becomes the play of the signifier over the signified. It not only deconstructs the arbitrary nature of the system but also reveals the degree to which the prestige of the party itself supplies the imposter with the means to effect a self-referential reality.

The Language of the Gift

In the imposter's story, the passage of the gift is an important figure in the creation of identity. The identity that it creates, however, is one that is self-referential, in which the scandal of imposture is deferred by a hall of mirrors reflecting back to its "victims" the image of their own desire. In this sense the passage of the gift shares the performative power of speech acts such as "promising."[28] Shoshona Felman notes how in speech act theory "promising" has become the exemplary model of speech acts in general. But she extends her analysis into a philosophical realm that sees an irreducible scandal in the possibility of a promise made in bad faith, a scandal that is, as Nietzsche suggested, part of the paradox of being human. To Felman, this paradox suggests a linkage between speech act theory and psychoanalysis that allows us to look at how the effects of speech acts, such as promising, construct an economy of pleasure. She demonstrates this by showing how the confrontation of two opposing models of language plays itself out in the myth of Don Juan. Don Juan's promising to marry (to more than one) is a performative model of language that is premised on the felicity or infelicity of his speech acts in obtaining his desire, whereas the model of language espoused by the other actors is a cognitive one that demands to know the "truth" as somehow transparent to language.[29] This encounter is strikingly parallel to the tale of our imposter, who plays with the language of the gift to effect the felicity of obtaining his desire. The state is what anchors a cognitive model of meaning; it stands for "the name of the father," which fixes language (and identity) into a regime of truth while denying how the play of desire threads itself throughout its official order. The imposter's play on the "name of the father" therefore unmasks the state's regime of truth as founded on a performative logic on which it must depend to spin its own fictions.

Felman's intervention is important here in reclaiming the subversive potential of the performative in language. This move counters attempts made by Emile Benveniste and others to strengthen the distinction in language between the performative and the constative, which in J. L. Austin's hands is always threatening to collapse, by specifying that the performative utterance "has existence only as an act of authority."[30] Pierre Bourdieu's work on language also echoes this notion that the illocutionary force of the speech act derives from its context of speaking, its institutional authority and the power of the speaker to insure reception.[31] In other words, by enforcing the distinction between the performative and the constative in language, the performative is put into the domain of the "proper," "the law of the father," which has the power to fix meaning in language, the emblematic act of which is the act of naming! In this sense then, Jacques Derrida's discussion of Austin, read as a virulent attack by Austin's own disciples, may be read as an incitement to Austin's own contradictory proclivity to erase the very distinction he raises between the performative and the constative, suggesting that language is always already irreducibly performative (and perhaps especially so when it announces itself as a fixed order of truth).[32]

In the specific case at hand, we see the performative power of language (and the gift) to contaminate any pure foundation of truth. If power is performative in spinning its own fictions, then resistance to that totalizing project is equally so. In the play of power and resistance, the performative is never unambiguously one or the other but marks for each the absolute limit of the other. In Austin's own classification of speech acts, we can therefore position the category of orders (including naming) that fix meaning into a regime of truth against the category of commitments (including acts of promising, contracting, espousing, enrolling, swearing, betting, and so forth) that hold the "promise" of being executed in bad faith, of being insincere, of misfiring, and therefore reintroducing the slippage of meaning into the order of language.[33] The category of promises returns the play of desire into language, enabling both seduction and imposture to achieve its effects. This is why for Felman the act of promising constitutes the essential paradox not just of language itself but also of being human, which in our specific context is posed as an irreducibly paradoxical question of identity. The imposter subverts the meaning of identity, the positioning in language of a unique location, by reproducing its effects through a mimicry of the power to name; he does this by naming himself and thereby undermining not the performance of language (the state's power to name) but its very *authority* to do so.[34] In naming himself, the imposter unsettles the "promise of paternal meaning" as a basis for identity, "the promise of a *proper meaning* and of a *proper name.*"[35] This authority is shaken by the conditional "were I but real" in the popular judgment that the young man committed no crime other than the one of not being who he said he was, so that all the felicitous outcomes of his whole network of obligation, which operates as a constant deferral of the absolute "presence" of the father, quite suddenly crash against the authority of the "legal system of the dictatorship of the proletariat." The legal apparatus reimposes its truth in a "rectification of names" (*zheng ming*), the imperative of rule once identified with Confucius, to readjust behavior in accord with the individual's place in society: "Let the ruler rule, the subject be subject, the father be a father, the son be a son."[36]

As Felman suggests, the seducer does not lie, the promise is made whether it misfires or not, whether it is sincere or not. What makes the imposter seductive, what gives his promise its force, is the way in which he produces a specular image of the other's narcissistic desire, so that the other is eager to induce obligation in this figure who seems to obligate himself in such a profligate manner. Therefore, the act of giving is displaced onto those who expect a return so that the generosity of one can be played against the demands of another. This ability to defer endlessly any direct appeal to the father allows the imposter "to elude the status of referent" in the creation of a "reflexive, self-referential debt" that can circulate endlessly without coming to rest on its supposed point of origin—a circulation that suggests the specular structure of language itself.[37]

One of the distinctions in language that is put into crisis here is that between the self-referential quality of the performative and the referential quality of the constative. As Felman suggests, the performative reintroduces the problem of the referent into linguistics, but what has gone unnoticed is how the referent in Austin's theory has changed its status in ways analogous to Lacanian psychoanalytic theory. If all language is at some level performative, then the referent is itself "produced by language as its own effect." The referent is "no longer simply a pre-existing substance, but an act, that is, a dynamic movement of modification of reality."[38] This language effect is an action that exceeds language and modifies the real; it leaves its traces on the real. Felman cites Mallarmé: "To act . . . [is] to produce on many a movement that gives you in return the feeling that you were its cause, thus that you exist: of which no one believes himself, at the outset, sure . . . to determine a force in some direction, any whatsoever contradicted by several."[39]

To understand the power of the gift to constitute a promise, we must first turn to a discussion of its importance in contemporary Chinese society for creating networks of influence and obligation. We shall see that the act of giving is often a counterprestation in advance for a favor which may as yet be unspecified and which may never be delivered. In this sense, accepting the gift is analogous to the speech act of promising in that it always contains within it the possibility of a misfire or an abuse.[40]

The language of the gift has its own vocabulary and ritual forms. An exchange can be initiated with an offering of a *jianmian li* (roughly, "a gift on first meeting face to face"); the form it takes is usually that of a less accessible item of high "ritual" significance.[41] The etiquette of the opening gambit is based on ancient principles. The sage Laozi is attributed with the expression, "What will be taken is first bestowed." The presentation requires a certain amount of tact, a careful judgment of character, as well as indirectness (the offering must not look like a bribe), or it may bring unfortunate results.[42] Many of the exchanges represented in the imposter's story are precisely of this nature. Indeed, the imposter touches off the flow of gifts toward himself by his own proffering of a gift: the refilled bottle of mao-tai that becomes, in the play, a metaphoric image of his false identity, a play of surfaces that obscure the "bogus" substance within.

What is promised in the passage of the gift is an invitation on the part of the imposter for the gift giver to *incorporate* access to a power that the imposter does not have.[43] What is performed here is an identity that is "bogus" because it poaches on the official power of "naming," also a speech act that is the quintessential exercise of power which fixes (incarcerates) individuals within a system of status categories.[44]

The narrative of the newspaper accounts shows the imposter as always in full mastery of events; he manipulates the desires of others to get what he wants, without ever delivering to others their expected return. And yet one cannot help but suspect that there is a moment in this series of events in which the imposter finds himself no longer in control of a chain of obligations that begin to propel him from behind. This possibility is not limited to the extraordinary case of imposture explored here but is implicit in any figure who takes up the role of the "able person" (*nengren*) in the art of exchange. Consider the two cases below, which are transcribed from a television documentary.[45]

The camera rests on a young man who had been an inmate for three months in what was called the male "schizophrenic ward" of a Harbin "mental hospital." The nurse reads out his case history. He had been admitted after a quarrel with his wife and then with the leader of his production team. He had become moody and couldn't sleep. He had abnormal conversations. He beat up his parents and his wife. In his abnormal conversations, he would brag about how capable he was, how he was acquainted with this cadre and that person. Because of what he said, people thought he could be trusted to get this and that. He conned about 350 yuan from these people. But he spent it wining and dining and socializing and then couldn't pay them back. He could go into a shop and ask for things. When they wouldn't give them to him, he would get angry and smash up the shop.

Doctor: You didn't hear voices? You didn't hear voices telling you things?
Patient: No, no voices. I smashed up the shop six times. I stuck posters all over the place. Writing, printing, smashing things. [These are all ac-

tivities suggestive of the political struggles of the Cultural Revolution.] It was all my own doing.

Doctor: Why don't you recite one of the poems you composed? How about the one about eating and drinking and becoming an official? (Hands him his notebook.)

Patient: I don't need that. (Begins to recite from memory.)

He toils all day because of hunger.
But when his stomach is full, he wants a wife.
So he marries a wonderful woman.
But then, he desires a carriage and horse.
His horses multiply, and his donkeys as well.
But now he lacks an official title.
Every title he gets, he finds is not grand enough.
Until he becomes Prime Minister.
But then, he wants to rule beyond his term.
But even after he is sitting on the throne of the Son of Heaven,
He longs for immortality.
It means people are never satisfied. . . . I can read another for you.

Doctor: No, that's enough.

They approach another patient.

Orderly: Meng Qinglin, we've come to visit you. (He gently pushes the patient to sit on the bed and then intones:) Meng Qinglin, 40 years old. Worked with Dongwang Machinery Company in Harbin. This patient since admission hasn't had any fits. His symptoms developed slowly. After he became ill, he wandered all over the place. He was continually starting things. Sometimes he would even damage things. He has had tranquillizer treatment. After more than two weeks, he does appear to have markedly improved. Will the doctor say something?

Doctor: How do you feel?

Patient: Quite good. . . . I hope my four modernizations will be carried out soon.

Doctor: Your four modernizations. *Your* four modernizations?

Patient: Yes, meals, feasticized. Clothes, woolenized. Housing, high-rised. Transportation, motorcyclized. (He repeats these, modified somewhat, but also taking on the public speaking voice of a ranking party member—the voice of authority.) *Eating, banquetized! Clothes, westernized! The whole country, high-rised! Transport, limousinized!*

Doctor: Okay, okay. (Standing over Meng and talking down to his upturned face.) You've been here a number of times. This time, we must cure you. You'll be discharged when you are recovered.

Patient: (Getting to his feet, speaking loudly, he has not yet relinquished his public persona.) *After my cure, I will start my second life!*
Nurse: Rest now, you must rest.
The doctor and nurse pat him repeatedly about the shoulder, sitting him down again. Meng looks confused, then raises his hand and says, "I salute you!" Then he says [in English, presumably to the foreign camera operator?] "Good-bye."

Both these cases suggest delusions of power that resemble the mimetic behavior of the imposter. The question that lies unanswered in the documentary is precisely why these two men were selected as representative of those with mental disorders. Do such delusions of power say something more generally about the self-referential illusions of power in the Maoist era?[46] The first case above clearly suggests the dangers of accumulating a large amount of "abuses," so that the circulation of debt does come finally to rest on its central figure as a mounting series of misfirings and infelicities, unsettling the "capable person's" identity as master of the situation. Felicitous outcomes draw the social expectation of more, propelling the capable person to promise more than it is possible to deliver or creating in himself or herself an illusion of a mastery that may be wildly in excess of reality. The second case is more obviously mimetic: through posture and voice, the patient casts himself into the recognizable demeanor of a political leader, a "polymorphic simulation" that Michel de Certeau suggests is an almost instinctual response to power, reminiscent of the ruses of primitive animals like the cuttlefish. This patient's particular take on power identifies itself with a potentially subversive project of "modernization" that extends certain highly visible privileges of party officials to all the people—in a generalized festive excess—banqueting, and unrestricted access to private transportation, the latter especially being, as we learned from the imposter's story, the sine qua non of official status. His final declamation concerning his cure and a second life vibrates in strange harmony with rehabilitations of a more political character, the public aspect of the "apparently reformed," perhaps suggesting an obsessive return to a prior scene when power inscribed itself on his person.

A Self-Referential Reality

Before we can deal properly with the folkloric aspects of the tale of the imposter, this discussion of the gift allows us to see the social dynamic that enabled him to create a self-referential reality. First, consider his practice of ventriloquism. The imposter appropriated a language of power that was not entirely his own. That language is that of the gift and its power to create networks of influence and obligation among individuals of power and position. Through the gift, one can build a self-validating network of social relations that constitutes identity. The more gifts and favors flowed toward the imposter, the more he not only appeared as a figure of power but also became one in fact. His careful manipulation of obligation enabled the imposter to get people to do things for others that he otherwise would have been powerless to do. And yet the symbolic capital for all these accomplishments still accrued in himself. His power was structured like a Ponzi scheme in which investors pay off one another. But the felicity of these exchanges, their success in supporting the fiction of power, was dependent on the imposter's mastery of the code, the language of the gift.

I have already suggested above that the practice of the gift is akin to a language in its resemblance to the speech act of "promising." De Certeau would take this further in his suggestion that the study of rhetoric, the science of the different "ways of speaking," offers a model for how the " 'turns' and tropes" of everyday practices resemble the performative play of language.[47] He elaborates a taxonomy of "situational logics," which he locates in games (games of strategy, practices of divination), tales and legends, and stylistic effects of language. In particular, he notes the importance of narrative in communicating these kinds of logics. The tactics of the game linger as narratives of actual hands played, a paradigmatic repertoire that records "the rules and the moves simultaneously," preserving them in their particularity along with the twists and surprises of the fortunes of this idealized mode of "warfare." Likewise, tales and legends remove the stakes outside of daily struggles and clothe them in the guise of gods or heroes, which become "models of good or bad ruses," providing a repertoire of tactics in the everyday. Finally, the stylistic devices of language itself, displayed in the very act of narrating the fortunes of gamesmanship, the tales of gods and heroes, provide models of the "ruses, displacements, ellipses, etc." that models of rationality (whether scientific or bureaucratic) have eliminated from the system.[48]

How does our tale of imposture illustrate these alternative logics of practice? The practice of the gift, which embodies a complex tactical field that centers on a highly evolved "art of social relationships" (*guanxixue*, literally, "the 'study' of *guanxi*," or social relationships), is negatively figured in narratives of corruption. However, it would be foolish to dismiss it as merely that, a gesture that marks the practice as a failure of political modernity, a mark of Chinese otherness. Rather, the gift also needs to be put into the tactics of the everyday as a way of restoring a sociality torn asunder by the impersonal disjunctures of a bureaucratic rationality. But I wish to go beyond the capacity of the gift to attain merely utilitarian ends to explore how it is also a means of "scoring" against the domain of the "proper" that fixes everything down to an official order of operations. The gift, in its performative "excess," *gives* pleasure. This was made patently clear to me one day in 1991, when I enlisted a friend's help in untangling what seemed to me to be a hopeless bureaucratic problem about a very minor matter concerning a magazine subscription. We rode our bikes to the district post office, where my friend began to work through the postal personnel systematically until he was able to locate someone with whom he had guanxi and who promised to help us. Biking our way home, my friend's face radiated a delight that seemed wildly in excess of the somewhat doubtful practical ends achieved. But I found myself strangely untroubled by this, reflecting on the vicarious pleasure I had received in listening to my friend's humorous banter with the postal employee in the process of negotiating a possible relationship between them. It is not unusual to hear people, on meeting in any official capacity, explore the multiple connections that may already tie them together, mutually absorbed in the task of finding a pathway to the other. The "promise" of help may or may not have its felicitous outcome, the debt may or may not be recalled, but what was obvious was that a new element had been added to my friend's universe of connections that could then be activated in future for some, as yet unspecified, end.

My friend's skill at the art of social relationships is not equally shared by everyone, and I had numerous occasions to note how sought after he was by friends and kin anxious to secure his help in mediating their own everyday dilemmas. In my strict accounting as to what was owed in our relationship, I had to resort to a deviousness of my own in attempting to reciprocate his open generosity of time and trouble on my behalf, until I discovered the wider social stage of his practice, in which his many applications to me on behalf of others in his circle were, in effect, the only way in which a return from me would be accepted. It was a sign of my heteronomy, my enclosure within a circuit of exchange of which I was not master. Yet he never abused his tactical superiority, as others who were less skilled might have done (and, in fact, did); he never asked me for anything that I was not happy to give! In time I recognized that my exoticism was in itself a resource—in effect, all I had to give in return. One day, for instance, he brought his sister-in-law to my room for a visit. She was a peasant from his home county who had come to the city and was awaiting entry to the hospital for a mastectomy. He had spent the entire day taking her to see the sights of Nanjing, trying to lift her spirits. I was the final stop on their itinerary, and we sat grinning at each other in mutual fascination. Later, in the fashion of my highly commodified notions of sentimental exchange, I sent her a get-well card, a practice that became re-exoticized for me in its reception. How curious a custom to send this alienated expression of my concern for her instead of actually appearing in person with a bag of fruit. This card was passed around the entire ward and wondered over. My fascination with the gift has everything to do with how badly I play the game! Merely laying out the rules of the system is clearly never sufficient without the sense of tact that produces felicitous results.

These little triumphs yield a certain measure of pleasure in their narration. Here the experience of everyday life is linked to the heroes of old through a metonymic retelling that connects mythic battles with the struggles of the everyday by way of set phrases that evoke popular historical narrative. The narratives of *banshi* (the successful accomplishment of bureaucratic matters) follow the chain of relationships activated in pursuit of a specific end, a trajectory that threads itself across the bureaucratic divisions that fix identity within official categories of workplace, occupation, and class status. These narratives are a repository of tactics and maneuvers useful in plotting one's own approach to an arbitrary and sometimes unpredictable power. A friend, planning a visit to the United States, canvasses her circle of acquaintances, gathering narratives of both felicitous outcomes and misfires, planning carefully her strategy to procure first a passport and then her visa. Another friend, wishing to study abroad, was refused her request for a visa numerous times until she hit on the tactic of appearing before the U.S. consul in national minority dress, a play of appearances that proved instantaneously successful. Therefore, guanxixue is never revealed as an abstracted set of rules but as a corpus of narratives which are shared as valuable information but which also have a certain entertainment value that can be "subversive" to the proper locus, communicating the pleasures of negotiating successfully around the constraints of a system.

The language of the gift and the "study" of guanxi must be placed within a larger field of play that is filled with legendary and historical reference. Therefore we must place the imposter's story in the context of an ancient wisdom that predates socialism in China. In popular discussion of this young man's exploits, he was much admired for his skillful use of *ji* (stratagem). The concept of ji pertains to a whole literature of cunning intelligence from the historical and literary past. As a corpus of practices, it composes a situational ethics that not only counsels how to act but also how to interpret the actions of others. In fact, the theoretical underpinnings of the system as a whole are based on a series of binary pairings, such as the one between self and other. These pairings are coded into the trigrams of the *Yijing* (Book of changes), the originary text of divination in Chinese culture.

In this sense, the concept of ji is not unlike the concept of *métis* in ancient

Greece, the shape of which Marcel Detienne and Jean-Pierre Vernant attempt to trace in *Cunning Intelligence in Greek Culture and Society*. Although absent from the idealization of Greek culture, métis permeates everything. Lisa Raphals has explored the analogous relationship between Greek métis and Chinese modes of cunning intelligence, which she equates with the Chinese ideograph *zhi*, whose semantic field covers knowledge, intelligence, skill, cleverness, or cunning. Zhi has a range of associated concepts, such as *mou* (plan), *qiao* (skill), and *ji* (calculation); this last concept is extensively associated with zhi in the *Romance of the Three Kingdoms*, a popular novel that exemplifies the use of wile in warfare.[49] In particular, as a domain of cunning in the context of warfare, ji is embodied in a text called the *Sanshiliu ji* (Thirty-six stratagems), a catalogue of tactics whose referents are taken from the *Romance* and other historical novels. The pertinence of this text for the socialist era arose in Deng Tuo's *Yanshan ye hua* (Evening chats at Mount Yan), a series of brief essays that appeared in the *Beijing Wanbao* (Beijing evening news), the fifth and final of which was called "Thirty-Six Stratagems" and appeared on September 2, 1962. The titles of some of the others—for example, "Empty Talk" and "Stories about Bragging"—suggest that Deng Tuo's targets were precisely the exposure of the party's own impostures of power. Much of the final essay was composed of simply listing all thirty-six stratagems. However, the interpretation of the essay's meaning focused on the final item on the list. Indeed, in popular discourse, the thirty-six stratagems are most commonly named in reference to this last, most desperate move, given in the phrase "Thirty-six stratagems, when all else fails, run away" (*sanshiliu ji, zou wei shang ji*), which evokes Mao's own tactic of the long march to evade Jiang Jieshi's encirclement campaign. Deng Tuo's essay, which was undoubtedly a tactical political retreat ending his series of critical essays, was interpreted during the Cultural Revolution as a call to his fellow anti-party conspirators to disband.[50] As a young student, Gao Yuan first acquainted himself with Deng Tuo's essay in the context of the 1966 campaign to criticize the essay series called *San jia cun* (Three-family village), in which Deng Tuo was implicated as one of three authors.[51] Gao Yuan, in his personal narrative of the political struggles in his rural middle school, meticulously lists all thirty-six stratagems for us in his text, disingenuously adding: "I wondered whether I would ever find a use for any of them. Then I thought up another I could use right away: 'Wait and see.'"[52] Indeed, the stratagems are evident not only in the events he recounts but in the written ploys of his narrative itself.

Like métis, ji is a kind of intelligence so "submerged in practice" that it can be communicated only in the form of narrative, the practice of storytelling. According to de Certeau: "A narrative does have content, but that content is also part of the art of 'scoring': it makes a detour through the past ('the other,' 'in former times'), or by the way of a quotation (a 'saying' or a proverb), in order to seize an occasion and make an unexpected modification in the precarious balance of things."[53] Métis and similar types of practices play on time; they wait for the right moment. They "perpetuate their own masks and metaphors" subversive to the proper locus.[54] And (like discourse itself) these practices vanish into their performance, leaving no image of themselves except through their narrativization. Reserved in memory, they become a hermeneutic of everyday life, awaiting opportunities to tip the balance against overwhelming odds to reverse the relations of power. The grasping of an opportunity creates a new world, however minute.

In China, these practices are memorialized in the form of four-character "set phrases" (*chengyu*) that are metonymic retellings of much longer tales, stories of wile in which the predominant image is warfare. De Certeau marks a division within the performative between the "strategies" of the proper locus, a subject of will and power that circumscribes a "space" that it occupies, and the "tactics" of the powerless, which has no locus but must play instead on time in the "seizing" of an opportunity.[55] However, this distinction does not define fixed positions but must be made relative to its context. While the Chinese state defines the proper locus for its subjects, its positioning within the mythic confrontation between socialism and capitalism gives it a history and a present that is replete with the tactics of guerrilla warfare and a "fugitive state."[56] The Chinese road to socialism was in a sense defined by its exclusion from the proper locus of the capitalist world order using a "tactics" of development that played against time (in the urgent mobilization of a massive people) and with appearances (for example, the impostures of power). Therefore, these tactics are not reserved for the Chinese "everyperson" alone but are integral to the identity of the Chinese state as representing a subaltern national subjectivity in a global struggle. This identification accounts for the multiple editions of the *Sanshiliu ji* published by the People's Liberation Army Press, which periodically compiles the stories from the traditional corpus with examples from modern military history to illustrate their perennial applicability.[57] But these tales of wile take struggles within the Communist leadership itself as their popular referents. Just as gods and heroes populate traditional stories, so do the mythic plays of "palace politics" among the party leadership exemplify these tactics of war and cunning in the "small-street talk" (*xiaodao xiaoxi*) of the common people. Here they truly become a "hermeneutic of the everyday" as a means of reading the signs of an uncertain political atmosphere through the power plays going on "up top" (*shangmian*).

Our interest is in the use of ji as a logic that subverts the proper locus in ways that remain invisible. By using the *sanshiliu ji* as a heuristic device to elicit narratives about the Cultural Revolution, one is able to locate the little resistances of daily life that are so infinitesimal as to escape notice. For instance, the first of the stratagems, "cross the sea under cover" (*mantian guohai*), delivers one person's account of the practice of deliberately selecting out newsprint bearing Mao's image for use as toilet paper, a solitary act of desecration that produces a curiously intimate pleasure. In this context, ji is seized on by the ethnographer to wrest practices that are not only invisible but may also be unable to "be spoken of" by any other means. This possibility must redirect our inquiry to the relationship between language and practice as parallel domains of the performative that "elicit" each other.

Ji is at once an act, a "doing," that is also a "speaking," the turns and figures of which are relative to their situation, the conditions of discourse itself. Therefore, these practices can be deployed only through narrative or metonymic expressions that evoke mythic encounters, because the felicity of the act is not captured directly through signification but only as a history of felicitous outcomes that are also capable of misfiring.[58] At the same time, ji is a resource through which one can devise the rhetorical strategies that generate laughter: the laughter that not only helps one to endure the effects of power and its impostures but can, at the same time, reveal power's limit.

As a constellation of practices, ji has been subjected to myriad attempts at cataloguing and ordering. The *Yijing* (Book of changes) is composed of 380 possible permutations. Most catalogues number far fewer. The anthropologist Chiao Chien made a list of 58 of the "better known" ones and was able to condense these down to 24 essential stratagems named by single ideographs. Among these are the concept of *hun* (to confuse, to pass off as), creating an instability in language that confuses identity and the "transparent" correspondence between language and reality. This instability is epitomized by the saying "to put Zhang's hat on Li's head" (*Zhang guan Li dai*), which provides an ironic comment on the imposter, a man named Zhang wearing Li's "hat." Surely, we can read this "play" on a play as a suggestion that ji has the power to reduplicate its effects in ways that comment on its own maneuvers. Another highly condensed concept is *jia* (fictive borrowing). What is borrowed is usually another person's name, influence, or authority to gain the favor of a third party, the principle that allows the imposter to widen the circulation of the gift within a self-referential system. This ruse is illustrated in the Chinese saying "the fox borrows the tiger's terror" (*hu jia hu wei*), meaning to bully people by flaunting one's powerful connections.[59] One more example that relates closely to our story is the concept of *zuan* (to drill), which refers figuratively to the cultivation of guanxi—that is, the seeking out of relationships with persons of influence.[60] This is perhaps best captured in the expression *wukong buru* (There is no hole through which one will not go). A final example, *ren* (to endure), serves as a figure for those during the Cultural Revolution who suffered the impostures of power to be enacted on their persons without having their spirit to resist broken; this is perhaps the most resilient response of the powerless to power.

Zhang's identity—his "value" in a signifying economy—derived ostensibly from a powerful father who was constructed through a series of ruses. His apparent promiscuity in obligating himself made him irresistible, drawing to him people anxious to obligate him for their own ends. The persona he adopted was that of a spoiled and yet "unworldly" son of a high-ranking father. His "father" became a resource used to play one individual against another, without having to draw directly on his "capital"—that is, by a direct application to his "father." The "name of the father" functions as a "caption point" (the uphol-sterer's term for those little buttons) that ultimately promises to anchor the sign to its referent and bring a halt to the constant deferral of meaning. Only when someone hesitated did Zhang stage a telephone call from the "father" or from other powerful figures. The ruse of the telephone call simulated the "presence" of power, but it also enabled Zhang to be the imposter of both an individual and an entire social network. In that sense, the telephone represented the role of the third party in the structure of social exchange, in which favors are never requested directly but are always channeled through an intermediary. The hy-pothetical third party reinforced the imposter's identity by giving it a wider social "reality." As the intermediary to an entire social network of powerful persons, the imposter was able to keep the ball in the air by juggling his obligations against those who wanted to obligate him further. His identity was an "inflated" currency that succeeded in effecting real results as long as its validity remained unquestioned, only to crash when its fictional character was revealed.

Moreover, the imposter was a social creation whose identity became elabo-rated by those who called themselves his "victims." He was the essence of the seducer in that he embodied the desires of his followers. He represented not only power to these people but also power that had wonderfully and voluntarily obligated itself to them. As a focus of their desires, he promised to redeem them from the negative status categories deriving from bad class backgrounds or to help them transcend the bureaucratic controls that intrude into every aspect of daily life. The imposter embodied the desires of all and thus was a collective product. Desire provided the improvisatory space, and the gift provided the

Figure 1.   The fox. (*Wenhui gao*, September 11, 1979)

means for imposture to take its form.[61] This circulation of desire toward the imposter was depicted quite vividly in a cartoon that accompanied the story of his arrest in the *Wenhui bao* (Figure 1). The drawing shows a fox dressed in a People's Liberation Army uniform toward whom gifts are flowing from extended hands. To call someone an "old fox" (*lao huli*) is to imply great craftiness. There is also the image of the "fox spirit" (*huli jing*), an often malevolent supernatural being that can take on the form of another's desire, usually the form of a beautiful young woman. To the anthropologist, the image also evokes the figure of the Polynesian chief in his feathered cloak to whom all riches flow.

The Art of Imposture

This tale of imposture has a folkloric quality to the extent that the impersonation of high-ranking officials appears to have become somewhat of an established tradition in Chinese socialist society. In fact, in its account of the event, the Shanghai newspaper *Wenhui bao* situated it firmly in this tradition with an opening reference to a famous case that dates from the early 1950s. Recent literature on China also offers us several cases of similar impostures that are effected within more localized contexts and not on as grand a scale as the one described above. Yet these other cases are no less remarkable for their daring, despite the relatively narrow limits of their effect. Moreover, in the popular imagination, these imposters attain for themselves something of the quality of trickster figures celebrated in myth and fable.

Hinton, in his account of Long Bow Village during the Great Leap Forward, describes an older man known as "Whiskers" Shen who had a character so adaptable that he was constantly effecting various impostures for immediate ends in the short term. He would pass himself off as a People's Liberation Army officer, a party cadre, or a retired veteran for whatever advantages it could bring him: a free meal, a ride home, or success in courting women. The most he ever paid for his deception was a sound thrashing. He became somewhat notorious for this behavior, and yet he was regarded, so it would seem from Hinton's tone, with a certain laughing tolerance. One of the more common forms of this sort of imposture is based on the calculus of marriage strategies in contemporary China, where marriage to the child of a high-ranking official (*gaogan zidi*) carries with it distinct advantages. The media have publicized cases in which women have fallen prey to the wooing of such bogus personages.[62]

In the midst of this popular tradition, the case of Zhang Longquan is unique not so much in form as in the level at which it was carried out. Not only did he choose to impersonate the son of a ranking party member at the very center of official power, but he had also toyed with the prestige of a wide number of prominent individuals in the political and artistic circles of Shanghai. And yet the relatively unsympathetic accounts of him in the press stimulated a popular response which was much more sympathetic and in which he appeared not so much as an unscrupulous trickster as he did a person forced to use indirect means to reclaim what had been lost.

Imposture of this kind, therefore, can become imbued with a certain romanticism. Of growing up during the Cultural Revolution, Liang Heng recalls his acquisition of street wisdom as a teenager in the midst of the bitter factional fighting of that period. He is able to put this knowledge to good use to right a wrong by impersonating the son of a local military official. He goes to the home of a girlfriend, whose younger brother is being bullied by their older step-brother to be sent down to the countryside in his place. Frustration over the rustication policy that restricted the freedom of urban youth to remain at home has here erupted into violence against an innocent (and even more powerless) party. In his disguise as the son of a powerful father, Liang Heng is able to intimidate the bully and to effect a reversal of power relations between the stepbrothers. Imposture becomes a means for appropriating power by the ordinary individual motivated by a sense of righteousness to correct a wrong, although, here, the oppressor is indirectly the state.

This sort of event, which takes righteousness as a motivation for action, would seem to be modeled on the stories of the *Shuihu zhuan* (Outlaws of the marsh), the popular vernacular novel of late imperial China, which describes the falling out of honorable men into social banditry because of oppressive government. This novel is strongly connected with the sworn brotherhood, which espouses the sentiments of honor among thieves, a form of organization that regained its salience in the chaos of the Cultural Revolution. Closely linked to this tradition but one that in some ways is in a dialectical relationship with it is that of folktales about certain emperors, notably the Qianglong emperor. The emperor in these tales, obviously a personage of great distinction and power, assumes the guise of an ordinary person to scout out oppressive officials and right the wrongs done by them to ordinary people. These two groups of stories are the mirror images of each other, both of them providing commentary on the legitimacy of power.

As a folktale, therefore, the imposter's tale in its many retellings becomes part of a popular repertoire of practices. Since 1979, with the increased economic and social mobilities unleashed by the economic reforms, new forms of the imposter have emerged that poach on the power of enterprise capital itself as a new charismatic locus of desire for those anxious to entice its magic home. No longer does the imposter exclusively take the form of the high-ranking official's offspring but might just as easily mimic a Hong Kong capitalist looking for investment opportunities in China.[63]

The Conflict of Interpretations

> There is a good deal of freedom in "structuring" the history of someone's activities by means of words like "intention."—J. L. Austin, *Philosophical Papers*

In the elaboration of the imposter's identity as a social creation, the significance of his action became more than he had perhaps intended. What I would like to suggest is that his imposture was in itself a form of interpretation through its mimesis of the informal structure of power in contemporary China. This was made possible in large part through the interpretation of his followers as to who he was and what he could bring them. The sense in which the event constitutes an interpretation through mimesis was actualized, however, only by exposure. In this light, Zhang's mimesis carried a message subversive to the prestige of the party. It is no wonder, then, that its exposure engendered a contest of interpretations.

Interestingly enough, the decision to suppress the play based on our hero's adventures was not justified on the basis of suppressing its explicit criticism of the special privilege enjoyed by those in positions of power. Criticism of such behavior, after all, is certainly within the official ideology. The avowed intention was to inhibit a potentially harmful "echo" effect that the play might inspire in others. Suppression was not meant to forestall the interpretation of the event intended by the authors of the play but to forestall the spread of mimetic behavior. In suppressing the play, however, the party has essentially attempted to impose an official interpretation on the event and to effect a foreclosure of competing interpretations. Perhaps the most subversive of these carries the message that the "spirit of the gift" (in the sense put forward by Marcel Mauss, "the *hau* of the gift") which propels it through a system of social relations that it creates in its passage is the prestige of the party itself.[64]

Perhaps it would be useful to summarize the play of interpretations that the event engendered both before and after its exposure.

1. *The act of imposture itself.* Art imitates the real. The imposture is a mimesis of the informal structure of power.

2. *The newspaper accounts.* The act of imposture is identified as abuse. An unscrupulous individual dupes innocent but wrongheaded people for base motives.

3. *The comic drama.* Abuse is elsewhere, not only in the practice of the actor, but in the practice of the duped as well. The imposter exposes the larger imposture—the special privilege of a cadre class in what is supposed to be a classless society.

4. *Popular sentiment.* Abuse is not abuse. Insofar as bureaucratic organization is intrusive to social being, the gift is a means to reconstitute what has been lost. Furthermore, the imposter's poaching on special privilege is the appropriation of something (privilege) which is ostensibly denied to everybody but which in fact is unequally distributed in society.

5. *The anthropologist's deconstruction.* Official morality and its abuse are embedded in each other. The official order itself provides the means that propels the gift through a system of social relations that it creates in its passage.

Power is also dependent in no small part on improvisation, the seizing upon the desires of its subjects to colonize there.

The point with which I would like to finish is simply that in its very attempt to fix the meaningfulness of this young man's imposture, the official order cannot control subversive readings of the event. The newspaper accounts generated alternative interpretations in the streets. As texts, they became transformed in the popular domain into tales that reverse the relations of power and that "offer their audience a repertory of tactics for future use."[65] They have become a catalogue of ruses and tactics that can be used to escape the violence of the letter.

3 CONSTRUCTIONS
OF CIVILITY IN THE AGE OF
FLEXIBLE ACCUMULATION

> What is the image of authority if it is civility's supplement and democracy's despotic
> double? How is it exercised if . . . it must be read between the lines, within the
> interdictory borders of civility itself?—Homi K. Bhabha, "Sly Civility"

If, as suggested in the previous chapter, the discourse of class has been laid to rest in the context of China's economic reforms, what has taken its place as the central organizing figure of a post-Mao national imaginary? Surely it must be the discourse of "civilization," or *wenming*. No other discursive site exceeds the power of wenming to focus the complex emotions about China's past and future captured by the phrase *youhuan yishi* (a sense of sorrow and worry).[1] Barely recovered from the internal political cataclysms of the Maoist period, China now finds itself entering into a new era of increasing integration with a rapidly changing global economy. With this opening out to the world, wenming has become a potent signifier that has enabled both a critical reflection on the national past and an imaginary projection into the future. It is a densely figured site that articulates statist projects of national pedagogy, intellectual critiques of Chinese national character, and popular concerns about the social order.

Wenming is a complex word that signifies many things—"modernity" (*xiandaihua*), "Westernization" (*xifanghua*), as well as "civilization" as an advanced stage of historical development. But it also refers to international standards of labor discipline and orderly behavior in public places. In this sense, it approaches the notion of "civility" or "civil behavior" appropriate to the expanded public sphere of a modern polity. Underlying these themes is a pervasive concern with the "quality" of China's vast population (*renmin de suzhi*). In 1991, this concern with quality was clearly evident in my interviews with a range of party functionaries engaged in "civilization work" (*wenming gongzuo*) as well as in more casual social exchanges with a wider range of people. It was a structure of feeling so pervasive that I found its articulation in the most general terms by the party's propaganda apparatus elaborated to an exquisitely refined degree in the episodic fragmentation of everyday life and talk. Wenming discourse is a discourse of lack, referring to the failure of the Chinese people to embody international standards of modernity, civility, and discipline. All these translate into a construction of the Chinese people as being of "low quality" (*suzhi cha*), which has perhaps become the reigning explanation for all manner of contradictions encountered in the flow of everyday life.[2]

And yet the complexity of wenming discourse cannot be fully understood as a process internal to national borders; its sites of production are also global. China's national identity has become increasingly bound up with its rapid integration into a transnational economy in the reorganization of capitalism that has been characterized as the "age of flexible accumulation."[3] China's rapidly expanding entrepreneurial economy, in which myriad township industries operate on a contract basis, represents a cheap source of labor still partially tied to agriculture that fits well into the compressed time-space of a post-Fordist economy with its transnational flows of capital and labor.

The linkage between wenming and foreign investment was revealed in an epiphanic moment when my field research into the wenming practices of the state had brought me to Jiangdong Township, where I had just received a preliminary briefing on its status as a nationally recognized "civilized township" (*wenming xiang*). During a brief break before lunch, the party secretary took my official escort aside to ask not so sotto voce as to whether I was bringing capital to invest in Jiangdong's local enterprises or whether I was "representing" some third party with enterprising intentions.[4] Clearly, my interest in the wenming status of the township could only mark an entrepreneurial interest in a cheap but well-disciplined and docile labor force ready to be delivered up for the employ of global capital. Subsequent encounters with those engaged in civilization work in the Jiangnan made abundantly clear how constructions of civility in post-Mao China had come to signify the readiness of rural communities to become integrated into global flows of capital and labor. As a "Westerner" interested in problems of civility, I represented close at hand that larger mirror reflecting back to these local officials the evaluative gaze of foreign capital into which they so earnestly hoped to become absorbed.

Located just beyond the outside perimeter of Nanjing City, the township had accomplished much in its development of local enterprise and was justifiably proud of its local status as an "advanced" unit, but when compared with townships closer to Shanghai, it lagged far behind.[5] As one approaches Shanghai, the countryside begins to look less and less like an agricultural landscape and more like one vast, extended industrial park. In the last decade, one third of the agricultural population of large areas of the densely populated Yangzi River delta have made the transition from agricultural to industrial labor, a transition that is perhaps unprecedented in world history in its sheer magnitude and speed. Much of this industry has been funded by joint ventures with capital from overseas Chinese, Japan, and Europe as well as from the United States.[6] But the differences between Jiangdong and the immediate hinterland of Shanghai, in terms of economic growth and, presumably, in graduated degrees of "civility," are minor compared with the dramatic gap opening up between the prosperous Jiangnan region (and other coastal areas) and the poorer provinces of the interior, a territorialization that figures largely in the political imaginary of the 1990s in which the underdeveloped periphery becomes the defining other of "civility" within the nation-space itself.

The speculative gaze of foreign capital becomes translated into the party's obsessive concern with a new architectonics of disciplinary practices regulating work and leisure—inciting greater productivity with the lure of an emerging mass commodity culture and arousing the "latent potential" of the Chinese worker to produce more and to produce better. Indeed, metaphors of arousal from a state of sleep or inactivity are replete in this discourse, as will be demonstrated below. These disciplinary impulses operate at the level of political signification in a welter of official injunctions and incitements: don't gamble, don't banquet, be a "civilized" worker, aspire to a "comfortable standard of living" (*xiaokang shenghuo*). These exhortations from the party communicate a sense of civility as an absence, as something lacking among the Chinese people that needs to be induced into being.

Increasingly in the last half-dozen years, the issue of low quality has come to signify the root cause of China's "*historic failure of the nation to come to its own.*"[7] As such it betrays a curious doubleness, in which an elite subject somehow becomes detached from the mass to view the "inappropriate other" critically, as from a distance. This detached objectification of the other within the nation-space is what Gyan Prakash, in the context of colonial India, has called "second sight," the articulation of class difference within a colonial frame.[8] Prakash uses the "inappropriate other" in the sense of the subaltern as both the other of modernity (a "necessary but embarrassing presence") and that which eludes appropriation into the project of modernity and thus engenders anxiety about the very constitution of this binary. In China today, a number of speaking positions allow this distanced gaze, as Communist Party member, urban resident, intellectual elite. This distance is also expressed in terms of a dramatic territorialization of the national space (second site?) between the developed (*fada*), wealthy (*fuyu*), civilized (wenming) regions of the littoral and the backward (*luohou*), poverty-ridden (*pinkun*) regions of the periphery (*pianpi*).

All these words are symbolically loaded in Chinese political and cultural discourse. As a total assemblage they express the tensions of being caught between the primordial past of the nation and the modernity of the nation-state. Moreover, these territorializations and temporalities span the divide between dissident intellectuals and the party establishment within elite discourse, although they can be made to mean different things. What is common to both is the concerted construction of "the people" in terms of lack, unready for political sovereignty but, as we shall see, being disciplined and rendered docile for the employ of global capital.

This concern with low quality constructs the necessity for a national pedagogy, echoing themes from the May Fourth period. How is the crowd, the unwashed masses, to be made into a modern citizenry? Constructions of low quality reanimate a party apparatus that has willingly ceded much of its control over the economy with a new sense of mission to remodel the Chinese people from a state of backwardness and ignorance. Likewise, the heated debates among intellectuals in the 1980s about Chinese culture—the "culture craze" (wenhua re)—that culminated in the making of the television series Heshang (River elegy) refocused these concerns on constructions of the national character, thus shifting the focus from wenming to wenhua (culture) in an anguished search for the cultural impediments to an unequivocal transcendence of China's "backward" status in the global community of nation-states.

As Timothy Mitchell has shown for colonial Egypt, constructions of national character are often the products of a colonial history. Likewise, Chinese constructions of the national character beginning in the mid-1980s echoed Western missionary discourse of a century earlier but now internalized as an agonized self-critique. The defects catalogued in this critique are the same as those that had earlier constructed a Chinese "other" in need of Christian pedagogy to become receptive to modernization, phrased in terms of a characteristically "Chinese" slavish submission to power, the sly civility of "face" (mianzi) and political passivity.[9] In the late twentieth century, these defects are raised once more as the explanation for the failure of Chinese socialism not just in terms of economic development but also in terms of the failed development of a politically responsible modern citizenry. How else to account for the Chinese people's blind faith in Maoism, which led to the cataclysm of the Cultural Revolution? Does this not demonstrate their primordial desire for an emperor, an "oriental despot" to relieve them of any political responsibility for themselves? This was the message of Heshang, articulated by a group of dissident intellectuals, who used this construction of national character to critique the "premodern" aspects of Chinese socialism.

Therefore, although the state and dissident intellectuals may meet on the ground of wenming, their projects enunciate very different kinds of projects. The state addresses the masses as incapable of political responsibility, thereby in need of a strong party organization to subject them to the disciplinary practices of the state's symbolic order. The project of some intellectuals, at least, addresses the masses directly as a "call to arms," a plea to aspire to political agency.[10] And yet intellectuals do not always share this faith in the people but often view the masses ambivalently, not unlike the way party discourse constructs them as unready for political sovereignty, thus elevating their own educational attainments as essential to the task of modernity, a project that expresses tremendous anxiety over the proper role intellectuals are to play in China's modernizing process and the state's recognition of that role.[11]

How do we situate this discourse of "lack" in the present historical moment, and why does it echo discourses active earlier in the century in the context of a newly emerging Chinese nationalism? Both moments seem to share the need to articulate a construction of Chinese modernity with its past. The "people," or the "masses," figure importantly in the working out of this problematic. Intrinsic to the idea of the nation as deeply historical is the concept of the people as embodying the primordial character of the nation.[12] In contemporary China, this tension is readily apparent in the complex relationship between wenhua and wenming. As suggested above, wenhua is the highly contested ground on which a national culture must be reconstituted in the project of moving toward wenming, a state of civility that is closely identified with the advanced industrial cultures of Asia and the West. And yet the notion of wenming itself is split, for it can also refer to the glory of China's imperial past. Clearly wenming carries with it a sense of being more advanced, rather than simply "modern," at any stage of world-historical development, a distinction that many contemporary Chinese feel China once possessed but is now lacking. This complicates any evaluation of the past, in that what was once highly developed in terms of "Chinese tradition" ultimately became a barrier to further development and was superseded.[13]

Therefore, to constitute a modern nation, the "people" have to be subject to a pedagogical process. To reprise the passage from Homi Bhabha quoted at the beginning of the chapter, the Dengist state sees itself as "civility's supplement" in its pedagogical role of raising the quality of the people, but it acts as capitalism's "despotic double," a socialism with "Chinese characteristics" that invites the imposition of capital logic while suppressing any expression of a popular sovereignty.[14] By means of this project, the party seeks the completion of its own identity as the authority necessary for a polity not yet ready for self-representation. The party sees itself as filling in "what is missing" to cover over those aporetic divides between China's problematic past and its imagined future, but at the same time its rhetoric covers over the articulation between a socialist imaginary and its uncanny compatibility with global capitalism— which must be read, in effect, "between the lines."

This project of radically refashioning the people is perhaps among the most legitimating dimensions of the party's post-Tiananmen practice that has intensified the pace of economic reform while continuing to suppress popular political activity. Here we see the notion of civility appropriated into a statist project that imagines its authority completed by means of civil engagement, and yet, as we know all too well, this authority must be supplemented by very uncivil means. But setting violent suppression aside, I would further argue that the notion of civility itself is sustained through the exercise of what I call "euphemized violence," the dark underside of power that underlies any performance of the state's own civilizing imaginary.

If these issues of civility and population quality echo discourses from earlier in the century, it is important to recognize why late-twentieth-century scholars invoke this past in a conscious way. I am thinking specifically of the discursive opposition between the technological advancement of "material civilization" (*wuzhi wenming*) and the reinvigoration of an essentialized national identity in the sphere of "spiritual civilization" (*jingshen wenming*). These terms were first articulated by Chinese intellectuals living in Japan at the turn of the century. And it is clear that Japan, then and now, in many ways more so than the "West," provides the model for having successfully negotiated the tension between the two. Partha Chatterjee has suggested that the anticolonial nationalisms of Asia and Africa cannot be subsumed within a modular adoption of national models propagated by the West but are predicated on a *difference*, marked out by dual domains of the material and the spiritual, in which the latter bears the essential markers of national identity.[15] These spiritual resources reassure that the nation is the selfsame subject emerging out of an immemorial past, that it can, indeed, claim a past and a future. However, I would like to suggest that this split between the material and the spiritual does not derive entirely from the confrontation of "East" and "West" but circulates among the newly emerging nationalisms and the anticolonial struggles of Asia and Africa. Japan is exemplary here as a successful model of how to modernize the nation without sacrificing its cultural identity, an identity, moreover, that becomes created and solidified out of the process of defining national spirit.

These issues are implicit in the modern genealogy of the word *wenming* in Chinese discourse. This word exemplifies that "innovative classicism" discussed earlier in the case of *shehui* (society). Like shehui, wenming was part of a complex of social science concepts that came to China by way of Meiji Japan.

Most present-day accounts of the origin of wenming as a discursive entity trace it back to the ancient Chinese classics, thereby establishing an East Asian past for this word that is deeply historical. Two passages are frequently cited as the *loci classici* where the ideograph for *wen* (writing, culture, refinement) happens to combine with *ming* (brightness, understanding), anticipating in the classical language the arrival of the later binomial form of a vernacular speech promoted by the early-twentieth-century cultural reformers.

A passage from the *Shijing* (The book of songs), therefore, gives us, "When a dragon is seen in the fields, then all of heaven will be wenming." In his post-Mao commentary, Weng Qiyin interpreted this phrase to mean, "The people's prosperity depends on a good ruler." The author critiques this notion as smacking of idealist historicism that privileges a ruling elite, yet the association of wenming with good governance seems too useful to leave out. Although wenming here appears to refer somewhat generally to social stability, prosperity, and political unity, the author concludes that this passage "proves that our ancestors had the idea of civilization from a very early time."[16]

Most accounts then jump a couple of millennia to cite a passage by Li Yu, a minor literary figure of the early Qing dynasty, who wrote, "Avoiding the smell of grass will lead to wenming."[17] Here, wenming clearly refers to the cultivation and refinement of the literati, and this motto reflects the aspirations of a minor literatus of uncertain social origins seeking higher status in the widened opportunities for social mobility of the early Qing.

From this citation, the historical narrative then suddenly jumps into a discussion of "civilization" in the context of the nineteenth-century European narrative of progress.[18] Unsurprisingly, references to Morgan, Marx, and Engels then follow as part of the legacy of the Maoist period when the stage theory of cultural evolution was enshrined as the truth of historical materialism. But gradually, in the 1980s, references appear to the early figures of British and American social anthropology, E. B. Tylor and Clyde Kluckhohn, in which the notions of "culture" and "civilization" become collapsed in the definition of wenming, reflecting their complex relationship in Western theoretical discourse. The presence of these authors would have formerly been considered too contaminated by their identification of anthropology as a tool of imperialism during the Maoist era, but suddenly they carry the charisma of "modern social science."

Clearly the notion of "civilization" entered China with the introduction of Marxist thought, but Chinese intellectuals were also very aware of the notion as more than merely a theoretical category but also as a process, as a national strategy for radical social transformation. The notion of "civilization and enlightenment" (*bunmei kaika*) was a central element in the reform program of Meiji Japan in which the object of reform was not merely the formal institutional apparatus of government but the culture itself as well, in the urgent refashioning of the Japanese people into national subjects. "Civilization" provided the standard to measure relative backwardness, the distance that had to be traveled to "overtake the West" through the reform of the customs and even the "feelings" of the people in preparation for national sovereignty.[19]

Indeed, it was this expression of a national will or "spirit" that remade the notion of wenming into one that could be refashioned to fit its national context. Wenming can refer to Western civilization specifically. The *Xiandai hanyu cidian* (Dictionary of contemporary Chinese) suggests that an old usage of wenming applies directly to customs, habits, and objects imbued with the "flavor of Western modernity" (*xifang xiandai secai*).[20] However, very early in the twentieth century we see a split in the notion of civilization between material and spiritual development, which grants to the language of "national essence" the aura of science. This split between "material civilization" and "spiritual civilization" has returned with a vengeance in the 1980s, and much scholarly energy has been devoted to tracing its history as an indigenous theoretical resource for talking about modernization.

In his discussion from 1985, Tang Daiwang contests the apparent consensus that the May Fourth writer Guo Morou was the first to use these terms in the essay "In Praise of Wang Yangming," written in 1925. In fact, Tang cites a much earlier essay that appeared in 1902 in a Chinese progressive journal, *Yishu huibian*, published in Japan, which he goes on to cite at length to display its contemporary relevance.

In this 1902 essay, an author, writing under the name of Gong Fazi, notes the distinction made by Euramerican civilization between material and spiritual civilization:

> Aspects such as national feeling and "military spirit" [*wushidao*] belong to spiritual civilization. Other than this, all visible aspects belong to material civilization: clothing, food, living conditions, housing, and manufacture. Spiritual civilization is the vitality [*shengqi*] of the nation. As long as it is present, [the nation] will flourish; without it [the nation] will perish. Its necessity goes without saying.

However, he goes on to say:

> Material civilization helps to realize spiritual civilization. Those who today do not regard material civilization as worthy of attention are wrong. Mate-

rial civilization must come first, and spiritual civilization follows. Without materiality, where will spirit find its sustenance? If material civilization is corrupt, then there is no hope of recovery of the spirit, hence not only can spiritual civilization not be independent from material civilization, but those who wish to build spiritual civilization must first take material civilization as the base. This is absolute.

The author of this text invokes the Hegelian dialectic in demonstrating how spiritual civilization can push forward the level of material development. For instance, in the context of educational reform, the old-style academies must be replaced with modern schools. But to accomplish this, it is important to have a "vision with which to inspire the people." The Gong Fazi then goes on to suggest that Japan's successful political reform was due to its proper resolution of the relationship between material and spiritual civilizations. Having made a detailed study of Western civilization, the Japanese promoted the development of material civilization even when it came into conflict with indigenous custom and habits. This was necessary to change the people's old ways, but one should also be aware that material development does not ensure spiritual development: "If you act on this premise then you will lose everything." He concludes that the two must be raised together, not one to the neglect of the other, and ends with a plea that those engaged in reforming the national language pay close attention to both. Reading this commentary in the 1980s, Tang concludes by saying, "Eighty years ago, this author had already attained an advanced and original perspective on the long pursuit of the powerful aspiration of our nation for material and spiritual civilizations."[21]

In this essay we see reference made to "military spirit" (*wushidao*), which, along with "national feeling" (*aiguo xin*), exemplifies for the author what falls into the domain of spiritual civilization. This clearly is a reference to Japanese *bushidō*, or "way of the Samurai," which to some extent underlies what becomes recognized as the "difference" between Japanese and Chinese responses to Western imperialism. Japanese national strength, presumably based on its "military spirit," was in marked contrast to the deeply felt lack of such in the disintegration of Chinese sovereignty at the end of Qing. Clearly, what constitutes an advanced level of spiritual development is a strong sense of national will, a self-awareness. Japan is admired for its successful merging of its "tradition" of samurai loyalty and fighting spirit into the notion of the modern nation-state. And yet this notion of "tradition" does not appear to be questioned as something that is constructed as the "other" of modernity. Moreover, for the China of the 1980s to take Japan as a model, it must come to terms with the tragic consequences of the Japanese success in constructing an expansive nationalism which had high costs for China but which was also a major factor in the development of Chinese nationalism. But no longer is Japan by any means the sole example of a successful Asian national model, given the emergence of other polities that are identifiably "Chinese" or "Confucian" in Taiwan, Hong Kong, Korea, and Singapore.

What, then, does this split between material and spiritual civilizations mean for reform-era discussions about modernity and national identity? We might well question how this construction displaces an earlier Maoist rhetoric about the relationship between base and superstructure that asserts the power of the superstructure, the power of conscious will, to determine the course of history. In repudiation of Maoism, the splitting of wenming into "material civilization" and "spiritual civilization" reprivileged the power of the material base to determine the progress of cultural development in the last instance. This reprivileging of the material forces allowed the implementation of Deng's economic reforms without abandoning the ideological field entirely. "Spiritual civilization" was acknowledged to have a certain countereffect (fan zuoyong) or degree of influence over the material sphere, so that the party's ideological leadership could be reaffirmed. The pursuit of material development independent of ethico-moral development would lead to the brutalization of life and social disorder. Here, again, wenming discourse repudiates Maoist practice because it overprivileged the superstructure as a determining force in human development. This "superstructural determinism" is what led to the rabid policing of culture during the Cultural Revolution, which now is one of the critical signifiers of chaos (luan) and social disorder—indeed the very antithesis of civility itself. This is the privileged explanation for the spiritual "regression" of the Chinese people into a more uncivilized state.

In the early 1980s, the use of wenming was fundamental in formulating the reformers' position on the controlled use of the market to stimulate rapid economic development. It allowed more latitude to market forces without relinquishing political and ideological control. In this early period, the use of wenming effectively repudiated Mao's emphasis on ideology and culture (wenhua) as the primary arena for struggle and change. However, wenhua refused to go away, returning in the cultural debates of the mid-1980s as a hotly contested discursive field.

Here is where the considerable overlap between the English terms for "culture" and "civilization" also obscures the relationship between wenhua and wenming. And yet the semantic relationship between these two terms has to be firmly placed in the context of the heated political struggles that surround them. We see an important shift in the relative position of these two terms in political discourse. During the Cultural Revolution, wenhua defined the domain of struggle, in which a transformation of the superstructure could have a concrete material effect on human progress. Wenhua was the domain of cultural praxis. Wenming, on the contrary, appears to have been pretty much contained within a more specialized usage in the context of the stage theory of cultural evolutionism; its deployment was largely historiographical rather than central to debates about the pressing political struggles of the day.[22] Wenhua, as it was used in the Cultural Revolution, clearly had a class character, whereas the wenming discourse of the 1980s carefully skirts the issue of class by referring to the overall development of society rather than the different kinds of consciousness possessed by different class positions. In the post-Mao period, wenming is closely associated with the idea of modernization. But it is used officially to convey an idea of modernity that distinctly differs from that of the liberal capitalist democracies of the West. The goal is to establish a "socialist spiritual civilization" that offers not just an "alternative modernity" but also one that will supersede the dubious claims of the Western liberal democracies to be "the end of history." Increasingly, we are becoming aware of how much the models for a "Chinese" modernity are no longer, necessarily, "the West" but the illiberal capitalisms of Japan and Singapore.[23] And yet "the West," and the United States in particular, constitutes the object of desire in dreams of escape, in the rage to study abroad (*chuguo re*), in the fantasies about America as the liberation of one's body and mind and as offering the opportunity for unbelievable wealth.[24]

In many of these discourses that would seem to mimic a characteristically colonial articulation of power, the nation-state has taken on the role of father/oppressor as the civilizing agency. Moreover, we might consider that the greatest challenge to the "end of history" scenario is the rapid development of the "illiberal" market economies of the East.[25] This should give us pause in regarding the civilizing rituals of the Chinese socialist state as irreducibly "other" when the state's moral force is deployed to fashion a disciplined labor force for the global reorganization of capital. It begs the question of any absolute conceptual division between socialism and the liberal democracies and suggests an entirely new articulation of power, the full lineaments of which we have barely begun to discern. The discourses of population quality, downsizing, and neo-Malthusian projections are very much a global phenomenon in which American workers are increasingly subject to the evaluative gaze of capital and exhortations to greater discipline and productivity, simultaneously with the erosion of job security and its related benefits.[27]

What, then, does wenming mean as a contemporary *practice* of the state? In post-Mao China, it takes the form largely in the bestowal of status honors. Local party committees are instructed to evaluate the communities under their jurisdiction according to national models and defined criteria in terms of sanitation and social order. This evaluation in turn designates certain units as having "civilized" status and as able to provide local models for others to emulate. According to those functionaries who do "civilization work" in Kunshan, a county (now designated as a *shi*) just northwest of Shanghai, "civilized household" (*wenming hu*) status has become the baseline of social respectability, the "mass leading the few." The "five-good family" (*wuhao jiating*) is far more selective, giving a much smaller number of households a superlative model status, the "few leading the mass."[28]

Both statuses presumably work by means of an economy of face (mianzi), in which households gain or lose social respectability by their being selected or rejected for this honor. As an example of how these statuses come to constitute mianzi, I was told of a peasant family whose recently built house exceeded local regulations regarding house size. They tore down and rebuilt the house rather than lose their civilized status. Another family, ashamed at their lack of "civilized" status, stole the "civilized household" plaque (*wenming pai*) from their neighbors in anticipation of the visit of a potential daughter-in-law. Hence, through the accumulation of a vast number of these *petits récits*, the party tries to build a surface that gives the illusion of substance, that the moral force of the party alone has motivated these subjects to act as they do. The resort to financial penalties and other more coercive means is a normal functioning of power that is continually reinscribed as "abuse" (the other within), subject to the regulatory disciplines of the party itself. These plaques and status honors become ubiquitous in everyday life as the visible markers of the party's disciplinary power. The disciplinary aspect comes into view most clearly when the party seizes on the surplus value of a recalcitrant subject as a measure of its civilizing power. The discussion below examines in somewhat more detail how the party deploys its civilizing practices to awaken the Chinese masses to a consciousness of their own productive power.

Producing Productive Bodies

The Chinese peasantry, it would seem from post-Maoist representations, is an "object," that must be awakened from a state of torpor. The present discourse that speaks of peasant bodies articulates anew a long-standing concern over China's "failure" to attain the modernity that has proved so elusive. This discourse focuses on the productive powers of the peasant body, its incitements to labor, its disciplinization and enhancements to its "quality." Equally present are images of consuming bodies, but consumption itself can also be forced to produce as the stimulant to a growing commodity economy and culture. Undisciplined bodies, however, consume to the detriment of the nation, draining away its vitality. Their inaction in the domain of entrepreneurial endeavor signifies the immobility of the nation, its failure to transcend the material and spiritual barriers that obstruct its development as a world power. These images of producing and consuming bodies are embedded in state-sponsored constructions of modernity as "civility" (wenming) itself.

In tracking the present discursive construction of the laboring bodies of Chinese peasants and peasants-becoming-workers, we must invariably come to terms with how peasant bodies have been made to signify in history. The unremitting toil of peasant life represents, in some contexts, the "stagnation" of the Chinese economy (the endogenous factor theory of Chinese underdevelopment), in which the rapid population increases of the eighteenth century are understood to have overwhelmed the ability of the peasant economy to sustain a forward evolutionary motion. But this same peasant toil represents, in other contexts, the inexorable world-historical forces of imperialism that threatened to consume the nation (the exogenous factor theory) through the exportation of its surplus value elsewhere, including the export of laboring Chinese bodies. The world-shaking event of the socialist revolution unleashed a seemingly boundless productive energy not only within the discourse of socialist realism, in which the sum productivity of collective organization was greater than its parts, but also in Western projections of the numbing, antlike effect of an apparently boundless population mindlessly subordinated to a totalitarian authority.

This awesome potential is now almost universally understood to have been cavalierly wasted and broken on the overambitious mobilization tactics of socialist construction starting with the Great Leap Forward. The political upheavals that followed and the entrenchment of an egalitarian ideology put this massive laboring productive body into a state of quiescent stupor until the economic reforms once again unleashed its latent energies. "Eating from one big pot" (*chi daguofan*), the quintessential image of Maoist egalitarian policies, is above all a consuming image, but even more regrettably it is a consumption that "produces" surplus bodies that drain away the wealth of the nation. This history of representing Chinese peasant bodies and their labor reflects a recurring tension between images of the body as producing and consuming and of population size as wealth or liability.[29] What is effaced within the present deployment of these images is any consideration of class. What replaces class is a

new vocabulary of social analysis that locates peasant households on a supposedly common trajectory from poverty to wealth as well as from backwardness to civility.[30] I want to explore the post-Maoist discourse of the Chinese
peasant body in terms of the regeneration and enhancement of its productive
energies and the energies that are consumed in this production of producing
bodies.

Let us consider, then, the following story that appeared in the *Nongmin ribao*
(Peasant gazette) in 1987:[31]

> "A Gambler becomes a Double Civilization Household"
> In Zandong Village (Hebei Province), Yao Shengzhi, who once spent his
> time at home gambling, has become a "law-abiding, civilized, prospering
> household" [*zunji shoufa wenming zhifu hu*]. Yao Shengzhi now uses his
> dissolute past as an example to incite several dozen of his former gambling
> buddies to cast aside their old habits for a new life and walk the path to
> prosperity through hard work. Yao Shengzhi is sixty-three years old. Until
> 1983, his household was popularly known far and wide as a "gambling
> family" [*dubo zhijia*] and a "poverty-ridden household" [*pinkunhu*].
>
> Early in 1983, the county party committee selected Zandong Village as a
> pilot point for the construction of spiritual civilization. When a mutual
> reform group [*bangjiao xiaozu*] began to seek out Yao Shengzhi, he was
> lying on his *kang* and wouldn't rise. After being urged time and again by
> their good intentions and their offer of help, he was finally [caused to be]
> moved to cooperate with them.
>
> His change in attitude brought new changes to his household. In addi-
> tion to successful pig raising and farming fifteen hectares of contract land,
> he also carried out sideline enterprises of making grass twine and tailor-
> ing. The village also sold him cheaply ten *jian* of what was publicly owned
> old housing to run a guest house. He also runs a rubber-stamping shop
> that is now flourishing. From 1984 to 1986, his household income was
> more than eighty thousand yuan. He built a new house of thirty-eight *jian*
> and bought a color television and new furniture. All thirteen members of
> the household live in harmony and have attained the status of "civilized
> prosperous household" [*wenming fuyu hu*].
>
> After Yao Shengzhi's household had prospered through hard work, he
> devoted himself to making a contribution to the nation and to his fellow
> villagers. Last year, when he saw on television that his brother villages had
> suffered from hailstorms, he immediately gave five hundred yuan to the
> county government in aid for them. When he heard that the district was

going to establish a "foundation for science, education, and culture" [*ke-jiaowen jijinhui*], he immediately contributed two hundred yuan.

Yao Shengzhi has also enthusiastically aided the work of political and legal organs, persuading several dozen former gamblers in Xincheng, Rongcheng, Baxian, Renqiu, and other counties to give up their evil practice for good [*gaixie guizheng*] and stride on the path of rectitude. Chen Shangjun of Chenzhuang Village came to him to study gambling techniques in order to recoup his losses after losing all his money. Yao Shengzhi used his past experience to educate Chen into changing his ways for the better. Moreover, he lent him two thousand yuan to purchase a small tractor to get started in a transport business. Chen Shangjun not only abstained from gambling but also attained the status of "prospering household" [*zhifu hu*] through hard work. These last few years, Yao Shengzhi has subsidized the household sidelines of old gambling buddies to the tune of more than seven thousand yuan and has helped them onto the road to prosperity. Under his guidance, Zangang Township has put an end to gambling. Last year, the judiciary office established a propaganda station for legal knowledge at Yao Shengzhi's house. The County Public Security Bureau also not long ago issued to his household a "mirror plaque" inscribed "Abide the law! Labor to prosperity!" [*zunji shoufa, laodong zhifu*].

This story portrays very clearly the top-down nature of "thought work" (*sixiang gongzuo*): The county government decides to initiate a civilized village program and arbitrarily selects one village as a pilot project. A major objective of this initiative is the eradication of gambling. Along with ritual expenditure, gambling perhaps ranks highest as the very essence of "excess" and "waste" outside a productive rationality. But the two are linked in other ways in the context of Chinese culture. There has long been a close connection between ritual communication with the gods, divination, and gambling as a form of divination that informs one as to one's standing with cosmic forces. Although gambling is not productive of material wealth itself, it is a ritualized redistribution of wealth according to the vagaries of "luck." Businessmen in Taiwan and Hong Kong gamble daily as a prognostication of their business success. We know that Yao Shengzhi is "lucky," otherwise less successful gamblers would not seek him out to improve their gambling skills.

Can it be that Yao's gambling luck is to be transferred to business luck under the beneficent spiritual power of the party? Marked as a lucky man, he becomes the ideal raw material to be worked on by the party's activism. He will be made to produce more than just material wealth. What his astonishing transformation produces is a circulation of meaning that makes visible the power of the party's ideological practice to create a new social reality. Yao Shengzhi therefore becomes instrumental in the marking off of a geographically bounded area that has been cleansed of a potent marker of backwardness and social disorder. Within this bounded area is a further displacement in which the gambler's house itself becomes an energized node disseminating the therapeutic effects of "legal knowledge." Here, "legal knowledge" signifies the party's civilizing influence.[32] Yao's house is all the more effective a sign in this circulation of meaning because it bears the traces of its uncivil past that attest to the persuasive power of the party's authority.

How is this circulation of meaning accomplished in the text? At the beginning of the narrative we find Yao Shengzhi lying on his *kang*, the heated brick platform that is the physical as well as symbolic center of the northern Chinese home. His inability or unwillingness to rise from his inert position when the mutual reform group arrives makes him the very image of inaction, nonproductivity, even paralysis. His prostrate form suggests an almost drugged-like lethargy, the result perhaps of all-night gambling parties that threaten to consume him and drain him of his energies. He is therefore not just a consuming body (as opposed to a producing body) but also consumed himself by an activity that is the negation of productive labor.

The mutual reform group that comes to exhort him is a group of minor offenders that have been organized under party leadership to offer its members mutual support so that they desist from undesirable practices, such as gambling. Usually led by a party member or activist, these groups are a form of horizontal policing that supplements the supervision of the local party organization.[33] Yao finally accepts the offer of the group members to help him, but not until after being subjected to repeated assaults on his resistance to being reformed. Indeed, his very embodiment as an obdurate subject intensifies the "surplus value" that can be extracted from him in the project of making his capitulation signify all the more strikingly.

We know from parallel texts that the emotional exchange that occurs here is highly ritualized. The recalcitrant subject is engulfed by an overwhelming display of "human feeling" (*renqing*) expressed on his behalf. This often takes the form of "speaking from the heart" (*tanxin*), which must wrest an appropriate response from the subject at an emotional level, even to tears. Yao is therefore appropriately "caused to have his emotions be moved" (*shi ta shoudao gandong*). For him to ignore this offering of concern would shift the moral balance against him. Failure to respond to entreaties ritualized in this way affects one's "face," not just at the level of social prestige (*mianzi*) but the very fiber of one's moral being (*lian*), as one who is not responsive to the claims inherent in human relations, as one who will simply not see reason (*bu jiang daoli*). This pressure is intensified when the one who is doing the entreating is superior in rank. For instance, were the party secretary to exhort an especially obdurate subject, almost invariably, in these narratives at least, this reduces the subject, especially women, to a state of tearful submission. The representation of tears in these narratives conveys the inexorable persuasive power (*shuifuli*) of the exhortation. The horizontal relationship between Yao and the mutual help group perhaps accounts for the sustained resistance of the "target," yet this resistance makes the victory all the more extraordinary.[34]

Once Yao has allowed himself to be moved by this exhortation, however, it is as though his passive body were merely awaiting the invigorating stimulus of the party's notice to spur him to action in a startling array of entrepreneurial activities. Even when we learn that his household is composed of thirteen family members, we can't help but see the list of his new enterprises as impressively diversified across almost all the economic niches now open to the peasant household under the economic reforms: he farms, raises livestock, and simultaneously engages in handicraft, industry, and service enterprises, as well as becoming involved, at least indirectly, with the highly lucrative transport industry. Yao's household prospers, acquiring the significant markers of new prosperity—a large new house and a color television set. This sudden about-face in Yao's response to the efforts of the mutual reform group signals a possible ellipsis in the narrative, an ellipsis that holds at a remove other motivating factors at work in excess of the party's explicit reliance on "persuasion" to influence people's behavior. These extralegal methods may draw on economic sanctions and even physical detention or punishment, often under the guise of "persuasion," that operates as a kind of "euphemized violence" because its results are attributed to the power of purely moral appeals. Perhaps the erosion of Yao's resistance was merely a measure to gain respite from the constant barrage of exhortations to reform.

But Yao's transformation does not end with his entrepreneurial successes. He then begins to seek out ways to share his newfound prosperity with others. When Yao learns from his recently acquired television that disaster has hit neighboring villages, he immediately donates five hundred yuan in disaster relief to the county government. (He clearly consumes appropriately; the television becomes the means to solicit the support of a modern and responsive citizenry.) When he hears that the district government wants to set up a cultural foundation, again his response is immediate. As one "native" reader of the text has suggested, it is as though Yao were desperately seeking opportunities to exhibit his generosity as publicly as possible.[35] His choice of beneficiaries is also highly significant. The cultural foundation that the district government wishes to establish is an organ, usually established in urban areas or at the county level, to oversee projects for improving science, education, and culture in a local area. It issues permission for various projects and has a small budget from the state. It is not something typically found at the district level (*diqu*), except perhaps in those where the leadership is anxious to demonstrate a high level of cultural development. By means of such donations, the productiveness of Yao's business success is not confined to the production of material wealth but also spills over into the local establishment of "spiritual civilization."

But Yao's productivity as successful entrepreneur and public benefactor continues to produce at yet another level. He becomes an activist in the local campaign to eradicate gambling, and as an activist, he is all the more formidable because his own past carries the signs of the message. Perhaps, as the leader of a small group similar to the one that had exhorted him to rectitude, he in turn convinces all the members of his old circle to give up gambling. And he succeeds in this, not only through moral example and exhortation, but also through material support in lending them the working capital to establish enterprises of their own! In so doing, he may merely be repaying a debt owed to the local party organization, which undoubtedly provided the financial resources for him to "take off" in his entrepreneurial endeavors. The party has unleashed in him the energy not only to "produce" material wealth but to "produce" producing bodies as well. The entire township is rid of the evil of chronic gambling, but more important, it has gained a good number of productive and industrious citizens who have learned the value and benefits of their own labor. In return, Yao receives official recognition for his services in his designation as "law-abiding, civilized, prosperous household," a composite title that combines three established status honors in one designation. And this status is made public by the ritual bestowal of a mirror plaque (*jingbian*), a material marker usually presented with a ritual fanfare of gongs and drums.[36]

In this tale of transformation, we see demonstrated for us not only the party's agency made visible but also the inextricable links between material and spiritual development. These links are established early in the narrative, in the denominating strategies of the text that build a relation of cause and effect by means of a double chain of signifiers that label status honors and their antithesis. To be law-abiding (*zunji shoufa*) leads to propriety (*wenming*) and wealth (*fu*), whereas to be a gambling household (*dubo zhijia*) leads only to a state of impoverishment (*pinkunhu*) and diminished physical vitality.

But is persuasion alone, with or without the accompaniment of the various forms of "euphemized violence," sufficient to account for this startling transformation? The transition from a state of inertness to one of explosive energy appears to cover over yet another ellipsis, a gap in the text. What is hidden here is the tremendous expenditure of energies required to stage it. The production of productive bodies in this way is a production that also consumes the time and energy and even, as we shall see, the bodies of those who engage in this production. This consuming labor is hidden here because the specific effect intended by the story is the disvaluing of gambling. The focus is on the displacement of a negative practice. However, what is hidden here gets represented elsewhere when the "what" of the story is focused more specifically on the "work" itself—that is, the labor that goes into "thought work" (*sixiang gongzuo*). In another story from a journal directed at rural cadres, we find this intensive labor represented in a county-level outreach effort, the "party liaison households" (*dangyuan lianxihu*) in which individual party members are assigned to do intensive ideological work with one or a number of peasant households. In Suixi County (Guangdong), 8,764 party members (83.1 percent) were assigned to 26,895 peasant households (23.5 percent). In one specific case a woman member was assigned to a man nicknamed "manure pit stone" (*shikengshi*), who was notorious for gambling and fighting. In 1984 he had lost his family's water buffalo and bicycle by gambling. The party member assigned to his case spent her evenings with him studying legal knowledge and her days helping him to resolve his economic difficulties. By 1986 he had not only been reformed but his economic position had improved to the point where his annual income reached six thousand yuan and he had built a new house for his family. Still, the labor necessary for this transformation is only partially revealed, and in any case such an intensive approach is limited by the relatively small number of party personnel working with a much larger population. What remains obscured is the process of the careful selection of specific "work targets" (*gongzuo duixiang*) who richly embody the negative signifiers that become grist in the mill of meaning production. Parallel to this investment of labor is the invisible channeling of material resources by the local government into setting up the enterprises necessary to propel their targets into prosperity.

The demands of thought work are limitless in that they can never be met literally but only in the form of representative models that must be forced to produce beyond the bounds of a single case as signs in the larger order of meaning. And yet the drain of this limitless consumption of energies becomes in itself productive in similar fashion. In 1991, the film *Jiao Yulu* revived the cult of a model county-level party secretary from the 1960s to redeploy the image of the selfless party member. In the film, the hero unstintingly labors for the people as his body literally wastes away from stomach cancer. The intensity of this labor is emphasized in commentary that criticizes the desultory effects of local party organizations driven by the intermittent winds of political expediency in the post-Mao period. A campaign approach can not replace the thorough and careful work of a party organization that has thoroughly internalized ideological work as part of its basic program, one that has fully integrated the construction of both material and spiritual civilizations as two essential parts of a unified approach. Likewise, the trend to quantify (*lianghua*) concrete goals for ideological work is criticized because it leads to the production of empty statistics in pursuit of "form without substance" (*xingshi zhuyi*). One newspaper commentary bewailed the distribution of "civilized household" status honors to households that ill-deserved such designations in the pursuit of quantifiably impressive results. If the quantification of results leads to the desultory effects of pro forma attainment, then the expenditure of labor time on the part of ideological workers becomes even less visible. Jiao Yulu "hides" the drain on his body of his selfless labor for the people until this sacrifice can no longer be hidden in his collapse and death. It is a labor that must be hidden and visible at the same time, in that its "secret" is always revealed through the visible diminishing of the physical vitality of the hero. This process of revelation is an important one in the party's representation of itself as a secret benefactor. As something both hidden and revealed, this labor perhaps balances the other aspects of the party that share this contradictory character: corruption and moral lassitude. The danger, of course, is that the representation of the model makes reality look even more rotten by comparison. This aspect of Jiao Yulu was played up in political cartoons that portrayed party cadres emerging from movie theaters with faces red from embarrassment. In one, a peasant asks his leader, "Party Secretary, have you been drinking?" Here the red face is directly connected to the "big belly of power," "eating big and drinking big" (*dachi dahe*) at public expense, a different image altogether of "consuming labor." The faces of cadres supposedly reddened in their confrontation with the model suggest that perhaps the most productive effect of this consuming labor is not the literal completion of its goals, which can never be completely realized, but its production of meaning as a signifying practice: the inscribing of ideology on the party members themselves, a greater consciousness of the social gaze that constitutes "face" for the party as a collective body, but also the production of symbolic capital that claims the nation-space through self-sacrifice.

Productive bodies can be produced only by the labor of the party itself, not by the natural increase through sexual reproduction, which only produces consuming bodies and which therefore must be controlled. The body in its natural state, unsubordinated to a managing rationality, is incapable of producing accumulation. In this concern over the people's productivity, we see the party constituting itself as the historically necessary agent to lift the nation from a state of dependency and backwardness to autonomy and even world dominance. Peasant bodies therefore become the raw material to be worked on, to be disciplined in the name of "improving the quality of the people" (*tigao renminde suzhi*). This idea of improving the population is complexly related to the whole range of activities that constitute the objectives of ideological work in the reform period. A better-quality population will deliver to the state an educated and disciplined labor force, cleansed of the irrational tendencies of the body in its "natural" or uneducated state. The quality of the population and not its quantity is what assures the accumulation of wealth that will deliver the promise of a socialism "with Chinese characteristics." But for whom is this body mobilizing as a laboring body, a disciplined body, cleansed of its irrational appetites? Is it mobilized solely at the imaginary level to fulfill the demands of a rationality that defines the modern nation? In this disciplinization of the agrarian economy, we see the confrontation of a massive agrarian population with the new labor demands of an ambitious social program of modernization and economic development. Those who are being remolded to this new discipline are not proletarianized workers but a peasantry newly restored to some individual control over the means of agricultural production. The agricultural reform is clearly designed to appeal to the self-interest of the peasant household. Implicit in this design is the unleashing of a latent energy that had been paralyzed by the institutions of collective agriculture. Yet one might well remark on the apparent necessity for the party to engage in these hortatory exercises to zap that latent energy into life. This suggests that the scope of peasant initiative is still perceived to be uncertain and risky and still under the purview of the party-state. What is apparent in this account is that the unleashing of this productive energy cannot be allowed to fall outside the construction of a certain social vision. It cannot be allowed to signify the economy as a zone of autonomous action but must be harnessed by the party for its self-representation. One is tempted to suggest that the producing of productive bodies is primarily for the incarnation of a social vision in which even a decadent gambler can be mobilized for his own benefit and the larger social good. And yet the establishment of a spiritual civilization may also signify a readiness to entice foreign investment for local enterprises by holding out a population of docile productive workers who can be flexibly shunted between agriculture and the small-scale township and village industries that have supplied an important motor for

China's astounding economic takeoff in the last decade. Perhaps the two go together in an unholy alliance, a new configuration of power in which a "socialism with Chinese characteristics" joins forces with global capitalism.

Certainly, the gambler's story works to construct hegemony for the party. Gambling is one of those unambiguous markers of the forces of chaos that have been unleashed in the period of reform. It is a social phenomenon that feeds on the new wealth and mobility of the people, along with prostitution, pornography, drugs, corruption, and so forth. It is almost invariably included in the usual "laundry list of the "six evils" (*liuhai*) that have marked the goals of ideological work in the period immediately following the spring of 1989. In my interview with both peasants and urban people in Nanjing in 1991, almost all agreed that gambling is a social evil that had mushroomed over the previous three years. It is visible everywhere in the casual card games and games of chance on the street, jostling cheek by jowl with diviners also selling their services. Gambling is harmful because of its addictive quality, leading to the neglect of production, to the depletion of household resources, to intrafamilial conflict, and even to theft and violent crime. It is almost invariably a male activity and one that often leads to violence against long-suffering spouses. Hence, it is a concern of the women's association (*fulian*), which organizes gambling "widows" into shock troops to battle this evil.

Gambling also provides an ironic commentary on the excitement of sudden wealth that pervades China's postreform economy. A favorite topic of conversation is the scandalized appreciation of how much money some households have managed to garner for themselves under the new policies, especially the "independent households" (*getihu*) that are also perceived as the major consumers of luan activities. The rise in prostitution even in rural towns is seen as serving the needs of this economically and geographically mobile population. The lure of sudden wealth may tempt some to attain it through the vagaries of chance rather than through honest production of a socially valued commodity.

The gambler's story is therefore not just about disciplining the laboring body but also about the party's ability to address the sources of chaos unleashed by its own policies. And yet the display of these forces of luan as barely controlled threats to the social order also builds hegemony for the party as the only alternative to chaos. I am convinced that the lurid accounts of crime (including gambling-related crime) in the various "legal pictorials" (*fazhi huabao*) that have flourished in China for the last several years serve this hegemony-building effort. These are eagerly read by educated urban residents who absorb this powerful lesson in a state of shocked titillation that borders on the pornographic without ever quite going over the edge.

The gambler's story follows a predictable development within the conventions of socialist realist representation—the coming into consciousness of the subject under the party's direction—although the idiom of how this transformation is attained is specific to the post-Mao period (economic opportunity, rather than moral incentive, being the primary animating factor). The relation between Yao's performance and his subjectivity is not completely unproblematic; indeed, his repeated demonstrations of public spirit mark him as a desperate man. But the story is disrupted by the possibility of a subversive reading that suggests the gap between performance and subjectivity, in which uncoerced compliance is suspect and where the limits to power are acknowledged, if only implicitly. In other words, in representing Yao's desperate acts, the story suggests a posttotalitarian subjectivity, as described by Václav Havel, in which "one need not believe all these mystifications, but one must behave as if one did, or at least put up with them tacitly, or get along with those who use them."[37] One in effect suffers oneself to merge with the panoramic display of the party's social vision as a strategy of survival.

Achille Mbembe suggests that for the African postcolony there is a "vast space created for equivocation, simulacrum, bargaining and 'improvisation'" by both agents of power and common folk.[38] This is no less true for China, in which domination and resistance are complexly intertwined, occupying the same space and the same time. But this simultaneity does not preclude the possibility of a third sight/site in which subaltern rumor offers "revisionary sights" of the disjunctures and displacements of power. Such is the ultimate fate of the crackdown in Tiananmen in the whispered undertone that people adopt when talking of that time. Seated in the breakfast nook of our Seattle home, my son's nanny widens her eyes and lowers her voice, if only for dramatic effect, to evade the eye and ear of the invisible censor—an absent presence—as she speaks of the "crude methods" of the "uncivil" state (*zhei tu banfa queshi bu wenming*).

4 THE POLITICIZED BODY

Zhang Yimou's film *Hong gaoliang* (*Red Sorghum*) is striking for its imagery of the body.[1] Through its exaltation of the primitive aspects of peasant culture and its festive excess, the film aims to recoup the image of a prepoliticized, spontaneous body, still "intact" after the onslaught from the political rituals of the socialist party-state. At first glance, these images of the body might be too easily dismissed as a mythification of presocialist Chinese peasant society, a dream of lost plenitude when the body was not yet alienated from the "spontaneous" pleasures of the lower bodily stratum. However, the film constructs this grotesque body as a deliberate displacement of the politicized body inscribed within the rituals of the party-state.[2]

In this chapter I explore the discourse of the body against which the film's imagery is working. Therefore, my starting point is the question of how individual subjects become positioned in the state's own ritual forms and the extent to which these political rituals continue to structure people's lived reality. However, I push my argument further to explore how the production of docile political subjects in these ritualized ways undergirds a projection of the party-state as a subject written large, as the unified voice of the "people as one"—a projection that conceals the internal fragmentation and diversity not only of "the people" but also within the organization of the party.

I thus deal with the issue of subjectivity at two levels: at the level of individual bodies and at that of the body politic. My intent is to demonstrate that politicizing the body is not merely a manipulative project of the state to ensure social control and ideological domination but also essential to the party-state's self-identity, its creation of a self-referential reality that is in itself an ideological effect.[3] Finally, I explore how these processes of subject making, while they may resemble in certain respects the mechanisms of Foucault's disciplinary state, are also quite different from Western disciplinary technologies, both in terms of the degree of individuation of the political subject and in terms of Foucault's distinction between the visible and invisible modalities of power. In other words, I wish to consider the ways in which the operations of power may be specific to the contemporary Chinese socialist state.

The Power to Name and the Power of Naming

I begin my discussion by reading a newspaper account that will provide the ground for the discussion that follows.[4]

Exchanging His Huqin for a Plaque

In Xingfu Village, Maoping Township, Lianyuan City, Hunan Province, everyone is talking with great approval of how Zhou Yixiang won his plaque.

This year, Xingfu Village had a competition to designate "law-abiding households" [zunji shoufa hu]. Zhou Yixiang was the first to be affected. He resolutely put down the huqin [the horse-headed fiddle used by diviners] that had accompanied him from village to village as he defrauded people of their money by telling horoscopes [bazi]. He had resolved to change his heterodox ways for rectitude. He worked from dawn to dusk, competing to become a "law-abiding household." At the end of June, the village party secretary and the village committee appraised the entire village to select the "law-abiding households." Zhou Yixiang was passed over without mention. He saw the brightly painted red and gold plaques on the door frames of others and felt cut to the heart. The next day, the more he thought about it, the more agitated he became. He ran over to the party secretary and asked him flat out, "Why didn't I get a plaque?"

Liang Lunyu, the party secretary, recalled Zhou's past feudal superstition activity and the money he had fraudulently obtained in this way and felt that this was not up to the standard of a "law-abiding household." Old Zhou saw immediately what was in the party secretary's mind and argued his case: "If it was because I used to read horoscopes, I have washed my hands of it ever since you announced the 'law-abiding household' competition, and I promise to do it no longer." One of his neighbors tugged at a corner of Zhou's clothes: "Brother Yixiang, don't argue until you are red in the face and your ears scarlet. Anyway, there is no monetary reward. It doesn't matter whether you have a plaque or not." When old Zhou heard this, he became even angrier. He rushed at this fellow villager, saying, "You only know how to fart [ni xiaode gepi]. If there had been an award of ten or so yuan, then I wouldn't have said anything. It would have reflected badly on the issue of my reputation. But if it is simply a matter of qualifying for this status, then I must contend for it!"

Secretary Liang was very moved by what Old Zhou had said. That same night he called a meeting of the village cadres where Zhou Yixiang's request was earnestly discussed. In response to Zhou's application and based on his promise to engage no longer in feudal superstition, the party secretary and the village committee decided that they would designate his family as a "law-abiding household."

At dawn the next day, just as Zhou Yixiang rose from his bed, he heard a great clamor of gongs and drums at his door. It was Secretary Liang leading the village committee to deliver his "law-abiding household" plaque.

This story is very like others I have collected from newspapers of this period. And yet, despite its typicality, it is also arresting in certain of its narrative features that allow it to capture a very revealing moment in the everyday negotiation of power relations in the post-Maoist state. However, the nature of this story as a *petit récit* deployed by the propaganda apparatus of the party demands that it be examined from two perspectives—first, from the perspective of its representation of the real, that is, the operations it describes as actually taking place on the ground; and second, from the perspective of the text as a text and the ideological effects it produces as an artifact to be read. From this latter perspective it is clear that the very strategies on which the state must now depend to make the narrative work as intended also point to where the limits of power may be drawn.

We may begin, then, with a discussion of the story as a representation of a contemporary political ritual. The competition for model household status described above is one of a number of similar "ceremonies of objectification" that distribute subjects onto a bureaucratic grid for the purpose of specification and judgment. But even more important than the ability of these ceremonies to subject all to the panoptic gaze of power is their ability to position subjects in a ritual display of a transcendent reality. The bestowal of status honors, through the issuing of ritual markers and public processions, demonstrates the power of the state to define discursive positions in political culture through its classificatory strategies, its power to name, to sort persons into the hierarchically arranged categories of a moral order. I would assert that while this power to name does not go unchallenged (for example, by competing discourses of family, kinship, social relations, or ritual hierarchies), it does exert a powerful force in defining the subject in contemporary Chinese political culture. But this power of state ritual to determine the subject confronts an even more potent challenge in the post-Mao period—a popular distrust of the ideological, a legacy of the excessive use of political ritual during the Cultural Revolution. Yet despite the party's present emphasis on liberalizing the economy (and perhaps even because of this), its ideological project remains critically important to its self-definition.

The question then arises of what it means, in the post-Mao period, to be inscribed within the symbolic order of the state through rituals such as the one just described. The neighbor who reminds Zhou Yixiang about the monetary worthlessness of the award may in fact be indicating an even more general disregard for what it signifies at the symbolic level.[5] However, before dismissing such ritual markers as meaningless, we should perhaps consider what the implications might be of not receiving one. What does it mean for the party to create a category that is inscribed within a totalizing symbolic system and to sort people into it or into its negatively defined other? This categorical exclusion of individuals from the social body isolates them in a state of extreme moral, as well as political, ambiguity.[6] The "law-abiding household" plaque, as a material item of display, is a binary code that encompasses all through its very presence or absence. At one level, these designations are signs that connote a subliminal message about submission to the power of the state. To aspire to inclusion within the connotations of this sign is to announce, in Václav Havel's words, that "I know what I must do. I behave in the manner expected of me. I can be depended upon and am beyond reproach. I am obedient and therefore I have the right to be left in peace."[7] Conformity with the model appears to originate from a "disinterested conviction" in the moral values it represents. Zhou Yixiang presents his claim for this status as if his only concern were a regard for official propriety and not a fear of the various forms of political harassment to which a negative classification might make him subject. In this sense, his seeking to be reinscribed within the model is, as Havel suggests, a dignified cover for his own subjection. But this subjection is one that is shared by all those who suffer themselves to be evaluated and who subsequently display the markers that identify them with the party's moral leadership. Individuals thereby actively comply with the forces that make them subject to the symbolic order of the state. They allow themselves to be absorbed into the "panorama of everyday life," which is composed of signs, such as "law-abiding household" plaques, which maintain the play of appearances and which give substance to the claims by the party-state to be a highly visible arbiter of everyday practice.

Yet what becomes inscribed through these designations is a propriety not solely defined by the state but one that is also heavily imbricated with popular notions of respectability. The quality of law-abidingness defines a value not entirely alien to a sense of local propriety, although the behaviors that constitute this value in terms of local sensibilities may differ significantly and even contest those of a centralized authority.[8] At the same time, we cannot assume that the state's definition of propriety has failed completely to influence popular notions of correct practice. Zhou's failure to receive a plaque thus marks him with a lack of propriety that spills over into a position not just of political ambiguity but of social and moral ambiguity as well. This lack is therefore something that may not be easily deflected from one's inner sense of worth but must be construed as a very real attack on one's social respectability, one's face (mianzi).

In this instance the power to name is the power to discriminate between those who fulfill the requirements of the model and those who do not; and it is a power that the party reserves for itself, as a "universal" and "transcendent" authority.[9] As shown by our story, this authority is exercised in practice by the local party secretary, albeit supported by committees of local worthies. What I would like to suggest is that, with the diminution of party control over economic practice in the post-Mao period, the reform of everyday practice has become a heightened locus for concern by a party anxious to exert its ideological authority and leadership at the local level. In making such a suggestion, I contest the accepted wisdom that the post-Mao period has seen an end to ideology and a return to a more "rational" pragmatism in the political and economic spheres. Those everyday activities in which local party officials continue to exercise their powers of discrimination are precisely where we see a restoration of the arbitrary power of local officials to determine the distinction between what is and is not—a power that, in some important respects, has not diminished in the post-Mao reform period. Moreover, although much about this exercise of power is specific to its socialist context, it would appear to be continuous with certain practices of the imperial state. Indeed, one is tempted to invoke the notion of the "rectification of names" as something eternal to any construction of power that is essentially "Chinese":

> Classical Chinese philosophers focus on names (distinction making) and desires rather than beliefs and desires. To be able to acquire a shared naming convention a human must have or acquire the ability to make a distinction—a *shih* (this), *fei* (not this). Along with this ability comes a socially appropriate attitude toward the things distinguished in this way and a set of dispositions (desires) involving them. Chinese philosophers fasten on these acquired discrimination abilities and the attitudes (desires) which accompany them rather than on the creation and modification of

beliefs. Our "raw impulses" are tuned when we internalize ways of classifying and categorizing things. Thus, language shapes behavior.[10]

However, this process of naming has a distinctly ideological function: certain people get to name, others are relegated to acting accordingly. In the classic distinction that we make between orthopraxy versus orthodoxy as somehow capturing the difference between East and West, this dimension that is specific to a particular modality of power gets displaced onto something called "Chineseness."[11]

Confucianists conceptualized government as guiding this process of discrimination and setting up models for the moral edification of the masses. In the late imperial period, these models were promulgated by the local gentry who were deeply inculcated in Confucian values. In the socialist period, the local party organizations have replaced the gentry as the responsible agents for guiding the design of models for local emulation. Throughout the socialist period, the local party secretary has been the critical link between the universal discourse of the state and the particulars of local practice. His motivations and willingness for playing this role reveal the complexity of his political subjectivity, which is composed of a complex mix of both conviction and will to power and not always easily reduced to one or the other.[12] But, however complex his motivations might be, his power to judge between what is and is not is a powerful mechanism for control, and we would be mistaken if we were to attribute this process of rectifying names to its deep cultural roots. Oppositional pairs have a deeply ideological function in all systems of meaning, and this is especially true in totalizing systems of meaning in which alternative coding is repressed or the intent is to obliterate prior coding through a revolutionary transformation of values.[13]

In Chinese political culture the opposition between *shi* and *fei* often takes on more than discursive form—it is inscribed onto bodily dispositions, one's carriage and positioning in the rituals of power. This was more overtly observable in the struggle session of the past, with all its attendant techniques of the body: the submissive stance with bowed head, the wearing of dunce caps and placards—all the means through which one's face, the measure of one's social respectability, is destroyed. Post-Mao literary re-creations of that earlier period have powerfully detailed the violence of an ascriptive system that reduced one's moral status to one's class background and thereby determined one's inclusion either among "the people" or the ranks of class enemies. However, in the successive political campaigns of the 1960s, as more and more categories of persons were named as class enemies and excluded from the social body, the arbitrary nature of the class-status system was also made more visible.[14] This was particularly true as the authority to draw the line defining class enemies became disseminated and contested among rival political factions during the Cultural Revolution.

Despite this erosion of the power of class background to ascribe one's position in the status hierarchies of Chinese socialist political culture, I am suggesting that the distinction between shi and fei remains a potent oppositional coding of the post-Maoist period, although the terms in which it is configured and the degree to which the authority to name may be concentrated in a unified party identity may be changing. At the same time, despite their reduced salience in political culture, the categories of class remain a subterranean code in the post-Mao period, one that can be applied to mask other, more real contradictions in Chinese society in periods when political conflict sharpens, as it did in the spring of 1989. For instance, attempts by the central leadership to redefine the massive popular demonstrations for democratic reform as a "counter-revolutionary activity" incited by a "small minority of people" (*jishaoshu ren*) were intended to displace popular characterizations of this movement as a "patriotic democratic movement."[15]

Although the distinction between shi and fei remains and continues to be coded in terms reminiscent of the Maoist period, it takes on the less confrontational mode used to deal with "contradictions among the people."[16] The aim of these distinctions is therefore no longer to exclude a pariah group but to absorb as many subjects as possible into the embrace of a state-defined standard through the reformation of behavior. Shi and fei now mark the distinction between "backward" (*houjin fenzi*) and "advanced" (*xianjin fenzi*) in radically new ways that reflect the modernization ideology of the Dengist state. It is the transformation of these elements from backward to advanced status that now becomes the primary means through which these activities produce their results. Thus, although the overt rituals of humiliation and the use of physical violence have been abandoned, the objectification of targets is still no less important, as they are now the vehicles for the circulation of signs in a play of representations that makes power visible.

In returning to the story of Zhou Yixiang, we see an opposition based not on antagonistic class positions between individuals but defined by contrasting states of being in a single individual—from a state of benightedness to enlightenment, from feudal superstition to socialist propriety. In his transformation, we see reinvented a classic structuring figure of socialist realism that marks the difference between spontaneity and consciousness.[17] Once again, we see the antithetic positioning of the politicized body, whose bodily dispositions are guided by consciousness—"party mindedness"—against a prepoliticized past, in which the inchoate pleasures of the spontaneous body disrupt the social and political order, but for quite different political effects. It is perhaps no accident that many of the pleasures of the lower bodily stratum, celebrated by Mikhail Bakhtin, define those domains of practice that are the targets of the party's civilizing zeal. And they are targets precisely because, as figures of excess—large-scale banqueting, gambling, ritualized reciprocity, and sexual reproduction—they offend the technological rationality through which the party seeks to reform society.[18]

However, the assignment of these categories is not merely a discursive act. It is a call to action. Households and individuals that are marked as "backward" are subjected to an unremitting pressure from the entire spread of party organizations—the local party branch, the youth league, and the women's association. Throughout the 1980s, new organizations were also called into being expressly for this purpose, variously titled: social ethics appraisal committees (*shehui daode pingyi hui*); village people's educational activities group (*cunmin jiaoyu huodongzu*); councils on weddings and funerals (*hongbai xishi lishihui*, to discourage ostentatious family rituals); or civilization committees (*wenming zu*). These groups are generally composed of a mix of party personnel and persons of communally recognized high moral standing, selected under the direction of the local party organizations.[19] "Backward elements" become the target of all these diverse groups in a great mobilization of concerted attention. They are cajoled, publicly shamed, and generally pestered into conformity with model behavior. This attention leads to tearful renunciations of former behavior that are offered not as a literal submission to the powerful pressures exerted on them but in a public recognition of the tremendous concern and trouble that the party has expressed for them through these very activities. To fail to respond to these efforts would be, in effect, a refusal to reciprocate this lavish demonstration of human feeling (*renqing*), a violation of propriety itself.

The tearful denouements of these humble dramas are essential to their operation as signs of the party's own efficacy, its successful operations on the social body.[20] Backward elements thereby provide the raw materials to be worked on by the machinery of the party organization; they become the stimulus to reanimate a deadened party apparatus during a period of increasing alienation from and deteriorating prestige among the people. And, indeed, images of the body cluster thickly in communicating this possibility. These organizational innovations to mobilize the sleeping potential of the local party apparatus are described as "resensitizing the deadened nerve tissue" in, may I suggest, the extremities of the body politic.[21]

We would therefore be in error if we attempted to understand these rituals of objectification solely in terms of their specified ends—the reformation of behavior. They are also rituals of subjection, of subject making; they produce docile bodies that transform these bodies into signifiers that figure in a master narrative of progress toward a socialist modernity. These rituals objectify subjects in a way that does not individuate them but causes them to be subsumed within a mass identity, the "people as one," for whom the party becomes the solely authorized voice. If, as Michel de Certeau has suggested, "every power is toponymical and initiates its order of places by naming them," then the power to name, in this sense, is a negation of otherness that appropriates what is other into the self.[22] To be named is to be heteronomous; it means to be absorbed into another's reality, to be subject to the rule of the other.

As I have noted above, the power to make these distinctions is essentially a discursive one; it is a speech act, an act of naming. But just as the power to name, in a sense, illustrates how things can be done with words, the power of that doing, as Pierre Bourdieu has suggested, does not issue from the speech act itself but from its empowering institutional structure.[23] The local cadre has the power to name because he or she is inscribed within a larger social vision that organizes the subjectivity of the state—as a subject written large, as it imagines itself as a palpable force in society. But a great part of that imaginary subjectivity of the state is its presumption to speak as the voice of the people. This presumption is one that results from a confusion of identities that must be constantly reproduced. The party clearly has the power to delineate the models, but it is continually rediscovering them anew as creations of the people. It appears in a state of perpetual surprise at this creative energy. The masses lead and the party propagates and promotes the best effects of these popular impulses. And yet the model is always part of a larger, more universal signifying system. Therefore, the delineation of the model is by no means a purely local phenomenon, despite the fiction of press accounts reporting on local areas that specific models are the novel creations of the people that must, in the best tradition of the mass line, be gathered up by central authorities for the purposes of propagating their good effects more widely.[24]

This is a subtle point but one that can help us focus on the mysterious process of how the party as a subject written large constitutes itself as a self-referential reality. If the process of "suture" is when the subject recognizes himself or herself in the discourse of the other so that an identification is formed, then the process I am describing here is a curious inversion of this.[25] The party continually sees its own reflection mirrored in these models, and it misrecognizes itself as the other, in that the models are identified with the creativity of the people. This misrecognition allows the party to take up these models as representing the will of the masses; it underpins the party's assumption of the delegation to it of the popular will. The party authorizes itself to "represent," in the sense of "speaking for," the people as a unitary social body. Any dissent with the party's will must therefore come from "outside the people."[26] In this circular progression of the subject, we have what Michel Pêcheux calls the "Münchhausen effect" in honor of the legendary baron "who lifted himself into the air by pulling on his own hair," in which the subject is caught within a network of signifiers so that he or she—in this case, the state—results as a "cause of itself."[27] This circular relationship in the sphere of politics has been sketched by Bourdieu: "It is because the representative exists, because he *represents* (symbolic action), that the represented or symbolised group exists and then in return brings into existence its representative as representative of a group. We see in this circular relation the roots of the illusion which makes the representative appear even to himself as the *causa sui* since he is the cause of that which produces his power and also because he thinks that the group would not exist—or not fully exist—if he were not there to embody it."[28]

If we substitute the party for Bourdieu's representative, we can then begin to address the process of what he calls "political fetishism" in which the act of delegation authorizes the party's voice to speak for the masses. But once that authority is made self-evident, it becomes the principle of political alienation in which the party is now the sole source of social agency, thereby rendering the masses as an "inanimate object."[29] Again returning to Bourdieu:

> Someone speaks in the name of something which is made to exist through this very discourse. A whole series of symbolic effects in everyday politics rests on this sort of usurping ventriloquism, they consist in speaking and yet making it appear that it is someone else who speaks, speaking for those who give one the right to speak, who in fact authorise one to speak. Usually when a politician says "the people, the masses" he invokes the oracle-effect. This is the act which consists in producing the message and deciphering it at the same time, in making others believe that "I am the other" that the spokesperson is a simple substitute for the people, is truly the people in the sense that what he says is the truth and life of the people. The usurpation which resides in the fact of affirming oneself as capable of speaking *in the name of* is what authorises the movement from indicative to the *imperative*.[30]

This self-referentiality of the party as a subject written large is an ideological effect; it is what gives the system its inner coherence, without which, as Václav Havel suggests, it would "collapse in upon itself . . . in a kind of material implosion." And because ideology is ultimately subordinated "to the interests of the structure . . . it has a natural tendency to disengage from reality, to create a world of appearances, to become ritual. . . . It becomes reality itself, albeit a reality altogether self-contained, one that on certain levels (chiefly inside the power structure) may have even greater weight than reality as such."[31]

Who Is Spoken Here?

Although this subheading may at first glance appear ungrammatical, what I ask is what subject position this story is reinscribing. At first glance, the story would appear to register the transformation of Zhou Yixiang himself, whose subject position traverses a fundamental antithesis in the discourse of the party—from backward to advanced element. However, this text works doubly as a tale of transformation, and the subject that is reinscribed is not really Zhou Yixiang, whose transformation is described but not truly effected by the text, but the party secretary himself. To demonstrate how the story does this, it is possible to show how it works in a readerly way, in which the reader is assumed to be a passive consumer of meanings fixed in the text, so that the reader is stitched into a position that works to constitute the larger subjectivity of the state. In other words, this reading of the socialist realist text can make visible the mechanisms within it that contribute to its ideological effect, its construction of a self-referential reality.[32]

We can start by noting the proper names that define character and place, as well as the attributes that cluster around these proper names. The story centers on three protagonists, only two of whom have proper names: the diviner, Zhou Yixiang; the party secretary, Liang Lunyu; and an unnamed bystander. Connecting the three is a dual axis of power. The relationship between Zhou and the party secretary is clearly on a vertical axis, while Zhou's relationship with the bystander is horizontally inscribed. The implications of this triangulation of relationships will be made evident later in a discussion of how the narrative unfolds.

The attributes that define character cluster most thickly about Zhou himself; and these are incorporated into a larger conceptual scheme of what it means to be "backward," that is, feudal, self-interested, untrustworthy, uncivilized, and so forth, as opposed to what it means to be "advanced," or "law-abiding"—the antithesis of all that is backward. What is intriguing about this story in particular is that all the attributes that inscribe both backward and advanced statuses cluster about the diviner from the very beginning. He has undergone the transformation from one status to the other, but this transformation has as yet gone unrecognized in the eyes of power. The dramatic tension of his being caught between demonstrates all the more clearly that these semic markers are not neutral but are "ideologically symptomatic"; they inscribe the text with power relations.[33] They make possible "strategies for understanding persons and places which are really ways of signifying and controlling those persons and places."[34]

In contrast, the coding of the party secretary is somewhat less defined—we know his proper name and we know that he is powerful—but the values attributed to him are not clear from the start of the narrative; and indeed, they become clearer only in the unfolding of the text. The attributes of the bystander are the least well-defined. We do not even know for sure if he was successful in attaining model status, which might have determined some status distinction in his relationship with the diviner, a relationship that is otherwise horizontally inscribed between two relatively powerless people. At the same time, Zhou is given the opportunity to demonstrate his moral superiority over the bystander by rejecting his insinuation that money is the universal standard of value. The bystander performs the narratological function of a "helper" who allows Zhou to achieve his goal and the narrative to function as it is intended. He also provides Zhou with the pretext to switch codes from the infantilizing discourse of the slave, in which he begs for recognition, to the uncensored speech of the spontaneous body, which releases his anger in a direction away from a direct confrontation with power.

Next we may chart the sequence of events that seem to unfold in a predictable order. This is most apparent in "fixed generic forms," such as the socialist realist tale of transformation, in which there is a high degree of "previsibility."[35] This predictability confers a sense on the reader of having been there before— the textual equivalent of déjà vu. Indeed, the formulaic nature of socialist realist literature is invariably pointed out in attempts to define its essential character. But this story is particularly arresting in the way it does not follow the typical chain of events. More typically, competition for model status locates and identifies backward elements on which the party apparatus can work. The tale of transformation details the coming to consciousness of the backward individual and charts her or his progress toward model status. This transformation frequently takes the form of moving from a state of passivity or even paralysis to one of activism and vigor. In Zhou Yixiang's case, however, this transformation was already accomplished at the beginning of the story, and instead, we have an account of his struggle for recognition.

The narrative unfolds in the following order. An omniscient and invisible narrator specifies time and place and the history of the events that precede the moment when the narrative shifts into direct speech. In the exchange between

Zhou and the party secretary, only the direct speech of the diviner is represented, whereas the narrator summarizes what is going through the party secretary's mind. The party secretary is silent, yet we are allowed to follow his inner thoughts. Zhou responds to this silence by an apparently clairvoyant understanding of the party secretary's internal thought. He is, after all, a diviner who knows how to read the signs correctly! He counters the party secretary's silence with a sincere disavowal of his former practice. This vertical exchange is then displaced by the interference of a third party who enables Zhou to authenticate his sincerity through an unleashing of emotion. This displacement is highly significant. Throughout this second exchange, the party secretary silently listens, at a slight remove, like a voyeur, to an exchange not ostensibly intended for his ears. Zhou's uncensored speech is authenticated by its horizontal trajectory, by the exhibition of his anger, and by its discursive marking by vulgar speech—the reference to farting is certainly not "civilized" (wenming), but it imbues the atmosphere of Zhou's speech with the spontaneity of the lower bodily stratum. It installs a verisimilitude of peasant earthiness that *knows no pretense*. It disrupts the text with an officially disvalued discourse for calculated effect. Again the party secretary remains silent while the omniscient narrator, who we must recognize as the monological voice of the party itself, informs us that he has been moved by Zhou's speech.

In this sequence of events, we see power being reinscribed in the elliptical moment. The party secretary is apparently convinced more by Zhou's second exchange with the bystander than he is with Zhou's more direct submission to power. If it is now generally assumed that all exchanges on the vertical axis must give rise to the lie, then the second exchange becomes necessary to install a stronger effect of the "true." If the first exchange must be understood as a performance on Zhou's part, then the implication is that when he speaks to his neighbor, he is no longer "performing" but is speaking the uncensored language of truth. Both exchanges are, most likely, performances, the second of which exemplifies the Bakhtinian idea of the dialogical angle, in which speech operates at multiple levels of meaning and is directed to more than just its ostensible interlocutor. In his "spontaneous" and "uncensored" speech to his neighbor, Zhou may still be performing an "inauthentic" self, but one that has the stronger effect of the "true." And yet, in the story, Zhou's uncensored speech cannot be allowed this power, despite its presence in the discursive structure of the narrative. The party secretary refuses to reveal himself as swayed by the power of Zhou's uncensored speech in such a public way. Instead, he silently withdraws; he submits Zhou's application for model status for reevaluation by the bureaucracy of power and then "surprises" him the next morning, with a clamorous procession that reaffirms the power not of Zhou's performance but of the party's paternal authority. In the narrative structure of the story, the panopticism of the party is preserved; it hears what is not intended for its ears. But, even more important, it controls the conditions under which it offers itself to view.

In the realist text, the hermeneutic development of the narrative moves the reader toward the disclosure of something hidden. However, this disclosure is not just the revelation of the "truth" but also a closure—a fixing down of meaning, the closing off of other interpretations. The hermeneutic code projects "a stable subject about whom things can be ultimately discovered." But in the structure of the socialist realist text, this process of discovery is not strictly parallel, for reasons that will be explored in the concluding section of this chapter. Briefly, the process of discovery here does not probe under the surface into the psyche of the subject; it is not a process of understanding the subject more deeply, revealing something hidden that is peculiar to the individual. What it reveals is the hidden agency of the party's appeal to a universal ethical standard. In this sense, the hermeneutic code in the socialist realist text does parallel its operation in the realist text to the extent that it reinscribes "a culturally determined position or group of positions to which the reader is expected to conform."[36]

In the brief confines of our story, there is not much room for a sustained suspension of the central enigma. The question of whether Zhou Yixiang has indeed been "misclassified" as backward is equivocated briefly in the attribution to him by his neighbor of a desire for financial gain. But his sincerity apparently convinces the party secretary, who is taken by surprise by Zhou's vehemence. This is the moment of revelation when the ideological practices of the party show themselves to be working effectively. This element of surprise is perhaps the central clue to understanding the text as being "about" the party secretary himself and not about Zhou Yixiang at all. After all, the probable readers of this article are rural cadres and not ordinary peasants. The reader will therefore recognize the party secretary's surprise as his own surprise in "discovering" that these sorts of emulation campaigns do in fact have the power to effect the dramatic transformation of marginal characters such as Zhou Yixiang.

The symbolic structure of this narrative is closely tied to the figure of antithesis, what Barthes refers to as the most ideological of oppositions. It sets two categories or states of being "ritually face to face like two fully armed warriors."[37] Antithesis "admits of no mediation between its terms. They are represented as eternal and 'inexpiable.' Any attempt to reconcile them is seen as 'transgressive.' "[38] These binary oppositions are, therefore, "central to the organization of the cultural order." They define the normal, the moral, the orthodox, and the good by a principle of exclusion that denies or denigrates alternative modes of being. They fix the subject into a stable meaning that even in the process of transformation from one term to the other is no more than a movement between fixed positions that does not challenge the symbolic economy of the opposition itself. To be defined as a backward element allows for "the power of legal substitution" in which "backwardness" quite automatically and "naturally" signifies a wealth of other values. This "order of just equivalence" is the anchor of the readerly text in which meaning is stable and signs do not circulate beyond a fixed universe of connotations.[39] The power of this order is demonstrated in the story when Zhou Yixiang's neighbors attribute to him a material self-interest in his wish to change his status. Practitioners of feudal superstition are characterized in the discourse of the state as the purveyors of a "false commodity" for the purposes of personal gain. This attribution to him of a hope for material gain threatens to force Zhou Yixiang back into the negative category from which he aspires to free himself. For Zhou to traverse the distance between opposed terms, he must rearticulate his being from a love of material gain to a regard for his moral character—what in the Chinese idiom translates as "face."

Zhou Yixiang's vehemence and the party secretary's surprise, however, point toward yet another transformation that the text itself is working to effect—a restoration of faith in the party and in the efficacy of its technologies of social engineering. This transformation, which is less visibly articulated than the other, regulates the distinction between negative and positive visions of the party bureaucracy—between party functionaries which are apathetic, unimaginative, and pro forma in the exercise of their duties and those which are activist social agents who judge on the basis of "facts" and not on the routine application of set categories. The rural cadre who reads this text undergoes an experience of anagnorisis, a re-cognition of his or her own truer self, a coming to know himself or herself anew as a committed party member endowed with a sense of his or her own political agency. The party secretary's reaction is recognized as the reader's own surprise, and the reader finds herself or himself "hailed" by the text and thereby reinscribed with a renewal of faith in the efficacy of the party to effect real social change. At least this is the way the text is supposed to work. Its weak point lies in one's reading of Zhou's vehemence—whether the reader is convinced by the "effect" of Zhou's spontaneous outburst as being outside the rationality of control. This vehemence, if it is read as "true," presents itself as a lesson to be learned by the party and its agents that comes from "the people"—here represented in the lowly person of Zhou Yixiang. It attests to the power of the party's categories in defining social respectability and thereby becomes the means through which the party renews its self-image as a spiritual vanguard. The motivation of the retired diviner to jump into his new role as an advanced element does not go entirely unquestioned, hence the equivocation about his possible interest in a material reward, but it is not problematized in any way that would challenge the moral coloration of any alternatives to the party's definition of "the good," of what it means to be "civilized."

The symbolic antitheses that are set up in this short narrative are fundamental to the maintenance of the cultural code, which is here that of socialist realism. As a cultural code, socialist realism transcends its usual characterization as a mere protocol for art and literature, becoming a part of lived reality itself. The representation of society as it is desired to be, rather than as it really is, becomes a means to effect one's sense of reality magically. It invites one to participate in the play of appearances that for the moment becomes the reality. But the transience of this effect demands that this reality be constantly re-inscribed. Therefore, the revelatory transformation of the party secretary is one that has been experienced before in endless textual repetition. Each return offers an opportunity to realize the model, to redeem oneself and in the process to redeem the authority of the party, an authority that rests on this demonstrated efficacy of its social technologies.

If the "reading effect" of this text is to reaffirm the party's leadership in a period when that role has been increasingly challenged and brought into question, then the "who" that is spoken here is not Zhou Yixiang or even the party secretary but the party itself, asserting once again its illusory inner coherence and unified will. The important question now becomes: To what extent is this effect limited to those who are already caught within the embrace of this ideological system as its representatives? In this text, are we seeing the party merely gesturing to itself? And to what extent does the urgency of this self-affirmation betray a lack of decision or conflict within the party about its role? Even before the events of 1989 it was quite evident that the party was going through a period of intense self-reflection in response to its deteriorating relationship to the masses. In the aftermath of the crackdown the problem of *dangqun quanxi* (the relationship between party and masses) became a more critical issue for many party members who were scandalized by the slaughter and who had genuinely hoped that the possibility for dialogue might have opened new avenues of communication between the party and the masses it claimed to represent. The repression of the democracy movement was an all too effective reminder of the illusory quality of those pseudo-democratic reforms of the 1980s.[40] And, finally, we must also ask to what extent this self-referential reality retains the power to pull the participation of others from outside the party into its ritual performances, because these performances should never be underestimated as displays of empty formalism. They are the very enactment of subject making and political subjection within an ideological system that aims to structure people's lived reality by making the people themselves become the signs that construct a socialist reality.

In determining the reading "effect" of our story, however, we must also regard the question of whether such texts can be read only as a readerly text, where meaning is fixed and alternative interpretations are foreclosed. But even the most readerly text opens onto a world that exceeds it and that lends to the text the possibility of a plurality of scandalous readings that threaten to disrupt all the mechanisms that work internally to fix its meaning. A more cynical interpretation of Zhou Yixiang's transformation would read it as a tale of imposture, the specific genre of which could here be called "the apparently reformed individual." Such a reading would acknowledge all those forces of political intimidation that compel Zhou to jump into the play of appearances, while recognizing that his participation must be accompanied by the consciousness of playing a role in a larger fiction, a consciousness of an inauthenticity of being. This awareness of one's own duplicitous participation in the play of appearances is in itself a passive recognition of the truth. Zhou is offered no dignified alternative but to participate in the party's socialist realist fictions about its role as the true representative of the popular will.

But must we assume, as Havel suggests, that Zhou Yixiang's supposed consciousness of his complicity in the construction of this dual reality can be construed only as a measure of his degradation? Is this not granting the state too much power? The text lends itself perhaps to yet another interpretation of the play of power relations represented there. Zhou Yixiang's very insistence that he be reclassified might also be read as a subtle form of resistance to the powerful discourses of the state. Zhou Yixiang's metaphorical tapping on the shoulder of the official may also be read as a moment of active resistance. The diviner is setting for himself the limits to which he is willing to allow the discourses of the state the power to redefine his person. Zhou Yixiang is essentially saying to the party secretary, "I have played your game up to this point, recognize me now—or forever lose this opportunity to use me to make visible your power." For, if the party were to ignore this subtle reminder of the limits to its power, it would risk a negation of its very basis. The alienation of the players from the game may result in their quiet refusal to play. Their willingness to subject themselves to the symbolic order of the party is the necessary precondition for any sustained production of a socialist reality. Nor does this refusal necessarily take the form of a direct political opposition. Rather, it may take its form in the arena of what Havel has termed the "prepolitical" that encompasses the sometimes infinitesimal resistances of everyday life. In Zhou Yixiang's case, perhaps his only alternative would be his refusal to allow his exclusion from a state-defined morality to redefine his inner sense of moral worth, to exercise his freedom to choose to be excluded.[41]

Power and Visibility

This brings me to a concluding point. My analysis of the text based on methods of reading the realist text assumes that one can apply the same methodology of reading to the socialist realist text. This is a big assumption unless one takes into account the significant differences between these two very different cultural productions. Barthes's semiotic codes, for instance, were aimed primarily at reading the realist text, which is the specific product of a sociohistoric moment—the nineteenth-century realist novel.[42] The difference that must be accounted for is perhaps in the ways they create specific kinds of reality. The realist novel installs an effect of the real within a fictional space, and it does so through the individuation of its characters based on the kinds of knowledge of the human psyche that are produced by the disciplinary technologies of Western capitalist society—the silent and invisible modes of knowledge that are coextensive with a particular economy of power—what Foucault calls "biopower."[43] The socialist realist text, it would seem to me, operates according to quite a different principle. It projects a utopic fiction onto the space of lived reality not through the individuation of its characters but through the classification of its characters into coded positions, representations that are moral exemplars, clusters of signs that must be made visible in order to circulate throughout the social body and thereby to produce the effects of power, making the party, in its turn, also supremely visible in a veritable and dazzling display of presence.

In China we see many technologies of power that appear at first glance to be fully "disciplinary" in Foucault's sense of this term—the placing of persons onto a grid which makes even intimate areas of practice visible to a panoptic gaze and which exposes to that gaze the gaps between actual practice and the model; the meticulous rituals of criticism and self-criticism, which on the surface appear so analogous to the individuating rituals of the confessional mode; and the dossiers, which record each person's political history, that resemble, at least superficially, the scriptural economy of the disciplinary state.

What I would suggest is that the knowledge produced by these technologies is a knowledge that is quite differently constructed. Subjects are not constituted as objects of knowledge in a science of the individual so much as they are classified into a system of signs that locates them as factors in a historical drama, a master narrative about the consciously directed progression toward socialism. The location of actors in this narrative becomes a mode of inquiry into a discourse that represents itself as more truly "scientific" than any claim to knowledge of the bourgeois social sciences—in the discourse of historical materialism, as it is spoken by the post-Maoist state, history itself becomes the fetishized object—a teleological project that authorizes the repression of human freedom and masks the entrenchment of a system of state power.

What we are observing here is perhaps not altogether a disciplinary technology in Foucault's sense but something that resembles more what he called a "semiotechnique" that to work must make its subjects visible to the panoptic gaze of an invisible and anonymous power as well as create a visibility that is produced at large via the circulation of signs throughout the social body.[44] Signs play on the surface of subjects, reordering their outward practice rather than their inner psyches. It is not that these techniques fail to affect one's sense of self, but they do so more in terms of a submersion of the self into a moral category, a state of selflessness that merges into the collectivity, rather than through an elaboration of the self in all its particularity. The goal is not so much the orthopedic refashioning of the individual so that deviance is made to conform to a norm presumed to be already present in the social body as a whole but the radical re-formation of that very social body, in which old practices are displaced by new, in the utopic projection of a new social reality.

Finally, although the spatial metaphor of the panopticon may still apply as an adequate figure of the operation of power in the Chinese socialist state, it must be amended to suggest that its working is contingent on the hypervisibility of the apparatus of power and its operations on the social body. The tower at the center is not entirely a darkened space inhabited by an invisible gaze but an illumined stage from which the party calls, "Look at me! I make myself visible to you. Your return gaze completes me and realizes my power." To repeat the opening line of our story, "Everyone is talking with great approval of how Zhou Yixiang won his plaque."

5 NEO-MALTHUSIAN
FANTASY AND NATIONAL
TRANSCENDENCE

In March 1991 I arrived in China with my husband and two young children. From the moment we stepped off the plane in Shanghai, we sensed a reaction to the plurality of our children that was almost palpable. As we walked the crowded streets, the vendors, mostly elderly women, would tap out a tattoo with their wooden clappers to the accompaniment, "You liangge yo-o-o" (There are two of them). One asked why we had been allowed to have more than one child. My husband replied that it was because we were foreigners. This answer seemed to satisfy by putting us into a special category, not unlike China's national minorities, who are generally known to be subject to different policy restrictions regarding birth limitation. Although I was well aware that reproduction was a matter of intense public scrutiny in China, I was nonetheless unprepared for the extension of this scrutiny to my family, despite our being so obviously marked as outsiders. We never experienced this attentiveness as hostile; rather, it registered as astonishment, not unmixed with approval. But this focused attention from strangers made our having two children into an anomaly that had to be explained again and again. The surprise that our condition aroused began to make me wonder whether the idea had become established in China that people from "advanced industrial nations" voluntarily did not have more than one child. I began to ask myself, To what extent had the meaning of the one-child family policy expanded from a mere remedy for underdevelopment to become a sign of the modern itself?

In this chapter I focus on the discursive construction of China as a nation that is "excessively populous" (*renkou guoduo*). In suggesting that this notion is one that is actively constructed, I am not trying to argue whether China is indeed "overpopulated" but rather that we should look more closely at what the issue of population is made to mean in post-Mao political discourse. This issue yields a certain "surplus value" that has made population a very productive discourse throughout the reform era, dramatically reshaping people's sense of national purpose. Therefore, I direct my discussion toward the ways in which the phenomenon of overpopulation is experienced in everyday life. In this context we see at play complex images of the body as a consuming or producing body that articulate the pedagogical imperatives and disciplinary practices of the Chinese socialist state. Given the tremendous power of population discourse to shape people's concerns about the national destiny, we must also consider how it figures in oppositional discourse, as well as in popular expressions of hope or despair.

The issue of population penetrates so deeply into the national psyche—it circulates so widely among different social interests—that it begs the question of what gives it such hegemonic power. No policy is more resisted at the level of popular practices than the one-child policy, and yet no other policy has greater power to reinvigorate the imperative for strong, centralized control. At the height of the student movement in 1989, when students and intellectuals all over China were demonstrating in support of expanded political rights, the issue of reproductive rights was never once mentioned. Indeed, population was raised by the demonstrators as one of the crucially important problems faced by China today, one that must be handled at the level of national government. How can we understand the popular acceptance of such a painfully austere policy that has so much power to restore the statist ambitions of party leadership?

Raising the Quality of the People

Following an animated discussion of Chinese cuisine, our host turned to one of the Chinese guests and said, "China should, by rights, be a great and prosperous nation." The implication was that China had somehow fallen far short of this expectation. This produced a lull in the conversation, as we all contemplated the implications of such a failure.[1]

The railway compartment contained two women. One was middle-aged, dressed in a white polyester pantsuit. Her sunglasses made it difficult to read her face. She seemed almost asleep at times; at others, she stared out of the window with a sour expression that seemed to register extreme distaste bordering on despair. This was her first trip to the mainland after her flight to Taiwan as a young girl. The other woman was in her twenties, returning home from Shanghai after escorting a friend on her way to study in Japan. The older woman explained she was visiting relatives left behind so many years before. "My uncle told me Shanghai was a beautiful city." Her tone clearly registered disbelief. Indeed, the *bund* and other famous sites of the prerevolutionary colonial city looked shabby and worn. Eventually, the filth of the train and the surly unwillingness of the train personnel brought forth the agonized question, "What is wrong with the Chinese people, why can't we do anything right?" The younger woman calmly replied, "The quality of the people is too low, and the reason that the quality of the people is too low is because there are too many people."[2]

The fieldwork excerpts above illustrate the degree to which a sense of despair about the national destiny pervaded China's urbanized citizenry in the early 1990s and how closely this sentiment was tied to the issue of population. In particular, the second passage is exemplary in that the woman from Taiwan, as an outsider, was casually instructed by a young woman with words that might have come right out of party circulars addressing the issue of population quality for the benefit of basic-level functionaries. What is striking about these examples is the degree to which they suggest the everyday contexts in which these concerns circulate in social discourse. What has made the problem of population so ubiquitous to social life?[3]

With the announcement of the one-child family policy in 1978, population has insistently been raised not just as a problem but as a principal causal factor in China's failure to achieve its national destiny. However, the 1980s witnessed a subtle but profound shift in China's discourse on population from an emphasis on quantity to quality. The significance of this shift has spread far beyond the domain of reproduction as an object of state control and scientific study into the very heart of the Chinese national imaginary. Population quality has become central to an emerging Chinese cultural critique that, as the Chinese economy has opened out to the world, has turned in on itself, reassigning the onus of underdevelopment from Western imperialism to factors endogenous to Chinese society. The impact of this notion is marked by its apparent ease in traversing the boundaries between party rhetoric and everyday speech, between establishment intellectuals and dissident critics. In its wide circulation throughout Chinese society, the issue of population quality orchestrates popular sentiment with the aims of a Communist Party intent on reconstituting its hegemony in the post-Mao era. And yet this issue also provides the means to launch a powerful oppositional politics as a sign of the failure of socialism in China. To understand fully its complex dimensions in Chinese political discourse, we must track its circulation among its many discursive locations. Moreover, we must also track the issue historically, noting its resonance with

Chinese constructions of modernity early in this century as well as its connections to the global reorganization of capital in the late twentieth century.

The notion of population quality covers a wide range of discourses and practices: birth control, childrearing, sanitation, education, technology, law, eugenics, and so forth. It is difficult to convey how pervasive the project of raising population quality has become in party rhetoric in the last half-decade.[4] The party focuses on the presumed low physical and educational quality of the population, its ignorance, its excessive size, its lack of discipline, and the genetic impoverishment of minority or isolated populations. But official rhetoric, even when it is most vague, becomes tremendously elaborated within the language of everyday life. The comments that people make about population quality often express popular concerns about China's ambiguous position as a socialist nation in a world where it must confront the rapid industrialization of the "four little dragons" (Taiwan, Korea, Hong Kong, and Singapore) and Japan, as well as the collapse of socialism in the Eastern bloc. At times, this language conveys a widespread despair over China's ability to attain a modernity that continually eludes it. At the same time, by invoking concerns about stability and social control—the fear of *luan* (chaos)—the problem of population produces willed consent for a strong, centralized state. Implicit in this fear is the fear over China's inability to transform its massive population into a disciplined citizenry that can be harnessed for a unified national purpose. Hence, we have an important linkage here between the issues of quantity and quality and their prioritization in the national agenda.

These fears about social disorder must account, at least in part, for the apparent hegemonic status of the one-child family policy, perhaps the most stringent population policy in world history. In its dramatic demographic distortion of the Chinese population and in the pain it produces for individual families and women, this policy suggests a monumental form of national self-mutilation. And yet, while it is easy to get people to talk about their thwarted wishes concerning reproduction, it is almost impossible to elicit direct criticism of the policy (at least to a foreign researcher). Must we assume that this reluctance to criticize the population policy openly is a measure of how much the power of the state is internalized within the speaking subject? To suggest so would obscure the complex ways in which population provides the means to articulate concerns about the nation that circulate well beyond state discourse.

To understand how pervasive this issue has become, we can begin by tracing its trajectory in the last decade. The notion of quality may have achieved its first post-Mao prominence in Bo Yang's controversial essay "The Ugly Chinaman." This essay by a Taiwanese author, first published in 1985, was quickly introduced to a mainland audience, where it had a profound impact on Chinese intellectuals.[5] The compelling issues it raised about cultural impediments to the development of civilization and democracy in China set off a period of intense "cultural self-examination" (*wenhua fansi*). Not long afterward, a major report on rural poverty sponsored by the State Council firmly laid the blame of China's backwardness onto a deficiency in the "quality" of the population. This report was used as reference material in the writing of the television series *Heshang*, which pointed toward the massive size of the rural poor as a primary factor in China's economic backwardness.[6] Yet despite this association with oppositional voices pressing for political reform, the issue of population quality has far from disappeared from state planning in the years since the crackdown. Rather, it seemed to achieve renewed impetus, occupying a privileged position in the eighth five-year plan launched in 1991.[7]

Even more impressive to the ethnographer is the degree to which the notion of population quality suffuses everyday speech to articulate concerns about China's present and future. But it is a multivocal concept, meaning different things in different contexts: in party rhetoric, in eugenics discourse and law, and in discriminating or articulating specific subgroupings or social interests (intellectuals versus workers, Han versus non-Han ethnic minorities, core versus periphery) within the larger mass. This is most apparent when people (including party officials) in the 1990s "joke" that the best development policy for China would be to kill off half its population or when intellectuals suggest that more play should be given to competition and "survival of the fittest" or bemoan the fact that those killed in the crackdown were students and not peasants. The latter examples, especially, draw attention to deep rifts in the imagined community of the nation in which the mass of rural poor is seen by some members of an intellectual elite not just as an expendable surplus but also as a serious obstacle blocking China's drive to attain wealth and power. Clearly, this idea of the low quality of the population plays well among urban people and intellectuals, especially when the referent is the unwashed masses of China's economic periphery. Indeed, the construction of *pianpi* (isolated) areas in the political rhetoric of the last half-decade points to a widespread consciousness of a dramatic reterritorialization of China in which rapid development has become concentrated in the wealthy coastal provinces better integrated into the global market.

But how does this notion play in the places that are labeled as "backward" and "peripheral"? A *getihu* (entrepreneurial householder) from the interior of Fujian Province traveling home from the city of Xiamen in late May 1989 told me that the economic reforms are only "on the surface" and will spread to villages such as his own only when there is political reform. The inhabitants of the hinterland do not necessarily place the causal factors of their poverty and backwardness within themselves but point instead toward their distance from a government that disvalues and excludes them from the selective and highly circumscribed locations of special economic processing zones.[8]

Yet there can be no question that this premise of improving the population lies at the very heart of the party's efforts to restore its hegemonic position in the post-Mao period. The unwashed masses are the raison d'être of the state—they are what constructs a pedagogical project that is anterior to any discussion of political reform. Following Foucault, we see "sexuality" (in its broadest sense as the sexual reproduction of the population as a whole) as the entity that becomes "the theme of political operations, economic interventions (through incitements to or curbs on procreation), and ideological campaigns for raising standards of morality and responsibility: it was put forward as the index of a society's strength, revealing of both its political energy and its biological vigor."[9]

In the population discourse of the reform period, the massive size of the Chinese population is blamed for dissipating the effect of all modernizing efforts. However, the project is not limited to reducing the growth rate but is extended to "raising the quality of the people" (*tigao renminde suzhi*). This idea suffuses party policy from the imposition of birth quotas to its ideological practice of "building socialist spiritual civilization." To some extent, the project of population is directed at defining socialism against its capitalist "other." Reproduction becomes the locus for the imposition of a planning rationality that will demonstrate the superiority of socialism. In this sense, China's population policy exemplifies or even raises to a new level what Foucault defines as the rationality of the modern state: the management of the population, for its own sake, rather than for the enrichment of the monarch, is a rationality of the state that is "proper to itself."[10] The long-term commitment to the birth policy is to bring production and reproduction "into a proper balance."[11] Society is viewed as a vast machine subject to the fine-tuned regulation of a strong central governing authority. In official speeches in 1991 celebrating the seventieth anniversary of the party's founding, Mao himself was credited with saying in 1957 that lacking a birth policy is a form of "anarchism."[12] Western practices of voluntary "family planning" are dismissed as characteristic of a capitalist liberal autonomy unsuited to China's stage of development. If China's many millions of peasant households were to make their own reproductive decisions, the population would rebound at an unimaginable rate.

This rationality takes on elaborate form in the pedagogical functions of the state. The project of raising the quality of the people is at base an educational project, and many of the activities deployed toward this end are educational in character—the issuing of books of general knowledge (health, childrearing, law, technology, and so on), the disseminating of this knowledge through adult education programs, the holding of local and national competitions to test this knowledge, and the bestowal of status honors to households and local party organizations for achievements demonstrated in these areas. Here we see that the issue of population becomes the means to express the persistent problem of how to produce a modern citizenry out of undisciplined masses, a problem that acquires new urgency with the dissolution of collective agriculture and with the new freedoms accorded to the household economy. Implicit in this project is the discourse on the quality of Chinese labor that must be contextualized beyond national borders to acknowledge the evaluative gaze of global capital. Given the opening of China's borders to transnational capital flows, the success of the economic reforms becomes contingent on the selling of Chinese labor on a global market, with its more rigorous norms of discipline and skill.

However, the population policy is also seen as a "play on time" in its stringent application for rapid results. For the national leadership, the last ten years of the twentieth century are seen as a critically important turning point invested with tremendous urgency. Production must be developed to insure the stability of the socialist system. This urgency has only intensified with the collapse of socialism in what was the USSR. Yet the policy does not address primarily fears of a demographic crisis (the threat of famine) but fears of a cultural and political crisis. It is explicitly conceived as a strategy to speed the pace of development so that China might attain its rightful place in the world before the rate of population growth renders such a transition impossible. China's population policy is a test of national will, a race against time and history.

The issue of population quality is not limited to the projects of the state but is tremendously elaborated at the level of everyday practices. Perhaps I was exposed daily to this set of concerns because I had very young children with me during my field research in 1991. My infant son, especially, became the medium through which people would discuss at length the differing qualities of children's bodies East and West. I found myself caught up in a complex mirroring process, one in which China's internalized sense of lack was becoming expressed, sometimes in explicitly concrete ways, through the material body of my infant son. People would squeeze his arm or leg and comment appreciatively about the hardness of his flesh, the pallor of his skin, his size, the depth of his cranium. The appearance of my children in public places would invite the occasional person to deliver impromptu lectures to anyone willing to listen. The conclusion would be that "the quality of body" (*shenti suzhi*) of Western children was higher. They were larger, more supple, and had a glow of health presumably lacking in Chinese children.[13] This focused attention to my child's body reflects a deep and abiding concern that relates bodily quality to national strength. Early in this century, a modernizing national elite rejected Confucian ideals of scholarly cultivation that associated physical frailty with cultural refinement. Mao, who had been an avid physical culturalist in his youth, also clearly linked physical strength to the revitalization of the nation. This pervasive articulation between bodily vitality and national transcendence continues in present Chinese cultural practice.

This attention was not limited to my son's physical condition but was closely related to his intellectual development. People would comment on his responsiveness to others, his eagerness to explore things, his strong will. These traits were praised as indicators of superior intelligence and creativity, but the subtext here is clearly that they also produce a less controllable child. This ambivalence is heavily inscribed in the word *pi*, used to describe naughtiness in children. When parents complain that their children are *pi*, one detects a secret satisfaction mixed into their irritation. One senses the dilemma of being caught between fears of social disorder and cultural stasis. This shows itself both in the subtle critique of the Chinese tradition of paternal authority as constraining creativity and intellectual freedom and in the concern often expressed that the next generation of single children will be overindulged, self-centered, and difficult to control. Yet on the afternoon of June 4, 1989, as I talked with a male university professor about the bloody crackdown in Beijing, he said, pointing to his daughter: "Her generation will not stand for this. And that, too, will be a kind of progress."

This concern with children's physical and intellectual development translates directly into the accelerated development of a commodity culture beginning in the mid-1980s. The child becomes an intensified site of commodification, as well as providing a site of remolding the cultural and physical resources of the nation. One's child becomes the focus of a lavish expenditure of newly commodified, highly processed nutritional supplements and gimmicks that promise to increase the intellectual development of the child. The commodity becomes the supplement for what is lacking in the national culture, an expenditure that is made to fill in what is missing. The child's body becomes the repository of expended value, presumably justified by its heightened "quality," which compensates for the loss of more reproduction. The figure of the child, by means of the very practices intended to enhance its development, comes to express not only concerns for the national future but fears about the loss of class position on the part of urban parents who experience an intense anxiety about their ability to maintain a foothold in the middle class. In the highly volatile atmosphere of reform-era economics, which has witnessed the mercurial rise and fall of fortunes and the possibility of almost undreamed-of wealth, none of the old strategies for status enhancement remain secure. One's single child must therefore be prepared for the greater competition of the marketplace not just in China but on a global stage as well.[14] Indeed, this heightened concern among urban parents for the quality of children's bodies is closely linked to their fears of falling into the mass. The incredible elaboration of "modern childrearing" practices among this class is an urgent project of maintaining a critical distance between themselves and these "others."

This popular concern with physical and intellectual quality has to be understood within the context of a national narrative, structured on the premise of Enlightenment history, in which China's developmental progress has been arrested in the realization of its early promise. Intrinsic to the idea of the nation is an identity that is deeply historical; the "people" must also retain an identity that is primordial in character. And yet it is precisely this primordial character of the people that marks them with the negative characteristics of an unenlightened mass, irrational in its belief in the supernatural and not responsive to the claims of national purpose. Once again, we return to the problem of the fear of the crowd. How can its unruly nature be made over into a disciplined citizenry? To constitute a popular sovereignty fundamental to the notion of the "modern state," the "people" have to be remade into national subjects by means of a national pedagogy that reveals to the people their image as national subjects. The people cannot be invested with political sovereignty until they have been subject to an extensive and prolonged remodeling, a "qualitative" transformation of the population. This construction of the people as unready for the political process has a history. Indeed, some of the eugenics discourse of the post-Mao period eerily echoes that of Chinese eugenics proponents of the 1920s.[15]

Early in this century, among Chinese intellectual circles, the discourse of race improvement became closely tied to concerns for national renewal. Eugenic theories, originating in Europe not long before, provided Chinese nationalists with a powerful explanatory framework to understand China's weakness. Some of these early eugenics proponents saw the "degeneracy" of the Chinese people not as an outcome of "natural selection" but as a direct result of the destabilization caused by the intrusion of Western imperialism. Fears of national subjugation and racial extinction became inextricably tied in the national discourse of that time.[16] Eugenics offered the promise of "cultural selection" (*wenhua xuanze*), the scientifically managed propagation of the people to supplement the natural processes of selection destabilized by foreign imperialism. While eugenics thinking was important among elites, it was never programmatically pursued, although the Guomindang government was sympathetic to many of its aims.

Eugenics was rejected outright by Mao, who saw it as a tool of imperialism. Indeed, the discourse of class elevated the rural masses as a progressive force in history. Mao's pronatalism was consistent with his trust in the masses to provide the motor force for China's development, at least until the devastating famine of 1959–62 signaled the limits to his politics of mass mobilization. The return to the concern with population quality in the post-Mao period mirrors earlier eugenics thinking in suggesting that the low quality of the Chinese people is due once more to the destabilization of natural selection, with the causal factor this time being Maoist economic policies, which placed insufficient controls on reproduction. The issue of population quality now goes much further than the debates among a small elite to become the very ground for constructing political authority in the post-Mao period.

In China the project of modernization suffuses everyday life with its language, its reform of practices, people's consciousness of commodities, their access to them or their lack thereof, and the symbolic value of these things that far exceeds their practical uses. Commodities become the markers of a stage of development, the tangible indicators of a society's wealth and vigor. There is a certain pride of achievement in this. A constantly recurring conversational topic is the recital of the material ways in which one's daily life has been enriched by the ownership of washing machines, color televisions, refrigerators, and so forth. Indeed, the various projections of different birth rates and their consequences for the future are not uncommonly charted in terms of the availability of just these sorts of commodities. This illustrates all too clearly Václav Havel's suggestion that the "really existing socialisms" fall prey to a commodity fetishism more extreme than in any capitalist society because it leads to the surrender of human dignity in exchange for these symbolic markers of modern life.[17]

At play here are images of the body as consuming bodies or producing bodies. In the discussion of China's population as an overlarge, ignorant, and backward mass, the Chinese body is seen as primarily a consuming body, its productive capacities made quiescent by the egalitarian policies of the Maoist era. The consuming demands of this body are out of balance with its productivity. The birth policy is intended to coordinate population and economic development, to bring them into an ideal alignment that will speed progress to the attainment of *xiaokang shenghuo* (the state of being "comfortably well off"), as frequently defined in terms of the purchase of commodities as well as in living conditions more generally—housing, care for old age—and with visions of a lifestyle that is actively purveyed in television programming and advertising.[18]

To turn unproductive consuming bodies into producing bodies disciplined to consume appropriately requires a concentration of resources by limiting population growth. This issue is the crux of the issue of quality versus quantity. For there is apparently not a universal consensus among Chinese population experts on the necessity of such a rigorous policy of population limitation. One recent account of China's current population crisis reports that there has been some debate within academic circles over whether the principal contradiction is quantity or quality (the need for education). But the author uses the quality argument to stress the supremacy of the quantity issue. The population exceeds the ability of a modern nation to meet its increased educational needs.[19] Only with increased quality in education can Chinese labor become sufficiently productive for modernization. At work here are the complex forces of the global restructuring of capitalism that has moved apace with China's reform years. The global market for labor mirrors back an image of Chinese labor as cheap but undisciplined. The attainment of civilized status by rural townships signals not only the successful production of new national subjects but also the readiness of a disciplined workforce to be absorbed into the global economy.

The "eugenic" aspects of China's population discourse are therefore primarily focused on improving education and nurture. While the eugenics discourse does entail what Foucault refers to as the power of "disallowing life itself," it purports to do this in a decidedly egalitarian fashion.[20] "Eugenics" is used in the Western-language literature as the translation of the Chinese *yousheng youyu*, which means more literally "good birth, good nurturing." In its broadest sense, the meaning of "yousheng youyu" refers precisely to the concentration of resources in childbearing and -rearing that will produce a higher-quality population through improved medical care, nutrition, and education.[21] The idea is to reproduce less in order to reproduce better. In this sense, the project of yousheng youyu is intended to redress the perceived inferiorities within the Chinese people themselves. Even when the project is phrased in terms of "improving the race," it is still aimed at improving the conditions of nurture, rather than reflecting a concern for racial purity. According to Foucault, the "eugenic ordering" of Western society "was accompanied by the oneiric exaltation of a superior blood."[22] In China the "stuff" to be eugenically ordered is not blood and the extirpation of all threats to its "purity." What is important is downsizing the population to allow for the disciplined ordering of bodies subject to a central educating authority.[23]

Having suggested that Chinese eugenics discourse is focused primarily on the supposed deficiencies within the dominant ethnic group of Han Chinese, it would be mistaken to suggest that it ignores China's ethnic minorities. But its application here must be understood in the complete context of how China's internal "others" are constituted as a total object of knowledge against which the national narrative of progress and modernity is constructed. Ironically, the national minorities have been subject to more relaxed birth policy restrictions than has the Han majority. Many of these groups are quite small in terms of total population size. Yet the current eugenics discourse, when it does focus on statistics of congenital defects both physical and mental, often takes its examples from cases where a large number of these appear in isolated minority populations or in places that are defined as backward and remote, which leads to inbreeding.[24]

Here it would appear that population size takes on an inverse meaning—the supposed inferiority of the minorities is due to the smaller size of their population providing a smaller marriage pool. One wonders whether we see here a scientific rationale for the construction of national minority populations or those from the "remote" countryside as congenitally backward to a degree that goes beyond mere ignorance or what can be redressed through improved education.[25] The obvious danger of this is in the possibility of forcible restriction of reproductive rights among isolated populations deemed to be inferior. This possibility looms larger with the passing of a eugenics law in 1991 that may bring the force of law against transgressors.[26]

Consuming Labor

There can be no question that the birth policy has been the very center of party activism at the local level throughout the 1980s and early 1990s. This alone suggests a critical repositioning of the locus of party control from production to reproduction. As one township-level official remarked to me in 1991, "We used to manage production; now we just manage babies."[27] In the Jiangsu countryside, local party leaders, when talking about "ideological work," brag of achieving 100 percent compliance with both the birth policy and cremation. The land is too littered with bodies both living and dead, dissipating resources that must be concentrated. Results are not only expressed in percentage points of compliance with the birth policy but also in terms of phantom population statistics of the unborn.[28]

The central government's resolve to continue its stringent birth policy is clearly stated in the eighth five-year plan released in the spring of 1991. The rhetoric insistently reasserts the importance of birth limitation as equal to that of economic development. But it also acknowledges that at the local level the two have been, in the past, "grasped hold" of with differing degrees of activism—"one hand hard, one hand soft," economic development being given greater priority.[29] And yet in southern Jiangsu, where I did field research in 1991, the policy is pursued rigorously in many rural areas. An article on the "Sunan model" also appearing that year claimed that in some areas of this region, demographic changes that took one hundred years to achieve in the West had been accomplished in only ten years.[30] The birth policy is frequently stated to be a massive effort unprecedented in history, and China's achievement in birth planning, to be a contribution to the world. Clearly, there are large stakes at play in demonstrating the superiority of the socialist system.

The birth policy is at some level a form of signifying practice that defines a sense of purpose and reconstructs the will of the party from the central government down to the basic-level organizations. Especially during the demoralized years since Tiananmen, the party has been obsessed with the idea of reactivating its "paralytic body," commonly expressed as *fahui zuoyong* (to play a role, to deploy energies) in the renewal of its leadership role. Nowhere is this clearer than in press accounts of model birth policy workers. These accounts follow the conventions of those which represent model party members more generally. One of the most ubiquitous themes is the notion of party work as consuming labor, a labor that expends completely the energies and even the physical bodies of party members. This theme of consuming labor is exemplified by the film *Jiao Yulu*, which was required viewing for all party members in 1991. As mentioned earlier, this film dwelt with particular emphasis on the theme of selfless labor as embodied by this model party secretary who carries on his ceaseless endeavors for the people while attempting to cover up the ravages of stomach cancer that visibly consume him and eventually result in his death.

Birth control work lends itself splendidly to this theme of consuming labor. It is acknowledged as the most difficult task of local government and is referred to as "the number one difficulty" (*diyinan*). It is therefore a perfect medium through which the party can represent to the "masses" its spirit of self-sacrifice and commitment to the national good. But this theme of consuming labor takes on specific images in the case of birth policy workers, who are often women. Not only do they lose their health, youth, and even their personal safety to the demands of this labor, but the cost to them may also include the sacrifice of their children and the welfare of their households. Birth policy work is so demanding that it virtually requires the dereliction of women's roles as mothers and household managers.

In one profile of a model birth policy mother that appeared in the national press, the most detailed aspect of the narrative is the "unnatural" refusal of this woman to fulfill the obligations of her social roles.[31] Ties of kinship and friendship are given no consideration in her impartial treatment of all out-of-plan births.[32] This public rectitude is the implied standard for all party cadres. What seems extraordinary, however, is the degree to which this woman is praised for abandoning her roles within the family. She "risks everything" for the "work of the party" and therefore "fails to fill with credit" her role as mother. Foremost in her failure is her apparent neglect of her three children, who are abandoned during the day like "orphaned swallows." Her son falls off a bridge and lies unconscious for hours. A neighbor scolds her, "How can you neglect your children?" Weeping, the woman strokes her son's head and answers, "My duties are so heavy, I can't divide myself, but can only do an injustice to my children." She is therefore not an unfeeling mother but one who sacrifices her children to a higher responsibility.

This sacrifice, however, points to a contradiction in the text that goes unexplored. How is it possible for a woman who so resolutely pursues the termination of out-of-plan births to have three children herself? Did she have them before the one-child family became the desired norm? And what does her overabundance of children imply for the legitimacy of her work? Must she sacrifice her children in this way so that she can convince others to give up their reproductive hopes? Does her maternal neglect signify a denial of the value of children implicit in the lost pregnancies of other women?

But her children are not the only ones to suffer; her household economy also languishes from neglect. She absents herself for days, doing intensive work on recalcitrant cases. Her pigs die, and finally she decides not to raise any animals because she can not look after them properly. With the economic reforms, other households, engaging in household sidelines, prosper one by one. But her household remains poor. Her elder brother asks her, "Why do you expend your energies uselessly on this task?" She answers: "I am a party member. I must not think of the cost to myself."

At the end of the account, this birth worker is described as aging and worn from fifteen years of "cultivating a wasteland full of thistles and thorns." And what are her rewards? She has gained the love and esteem of the women in her community. To demonstrate this point, some of them are quoted as saying that they often think of having more children. But they don't dare to come up against "Old Yu." This statement attests less to the affection between Yu and other women and more to the divisions between women, between those state functionaries whose subjectivities are clearly inscribed within state-inflected goals, whose rewards appear in the form of status honors from the party hierarchy that certify their contribution to the future of the nation, and those "unenlightened" women who still have their subjectivities more narrowly circumscribed by their duties to kin and family. These women functionaries are the very image of *funu*, which Tani Barlow glosses as "national woman," whose liberation launched her as a political subject harnessed to the interests of the state.[33]

In a second account, picking up many of the same themes, a woman birth worker is physically attacked and beaten into unconsciousness.[34] Nevertheless, after the incident she insists that her attackers not be arrested or forced to pay penalties, as long as they truly understand and support birth policy work. The guilty parties are put into a difficult position. Even if popular sentiment initially supported their action as a righteous blow against oppressive government, the birth worker's refusal to bring down the full fury of the law turns the moral balance against them. They have no choice but to comply, apparently moved to tears by her selfless response. We see here how such birth work becomes a kind of "euphemized violence." Persuasion through "thought work" and social pressure, the approved methods of obtaining compliance with what is still policy rather than law, becomes supplemented through direct appeal to coercive possibilities. One local cadre reported to me that in recalcitrant cases the local government would stop all electricity and water services to the household, in short, "not allow one to live" (*bu rang ni shenghuo*).[35]

Moreover, coercive measures are made to look like not only "persuasion" in these representations but even "nurturance." The social isolation of the birth policy worker, produced by a loyalty that transcends kin and community, is redressed by her role as a caring party member. Her dedication and offers of help in her official capacity induce tears and emotion in her "work targets." This emotive component is critical in the claiming of moral ground while covering over the exercise of coercive means. Party work induces tears—of gratitude and of shame. Weeping almost always marks the capitulation of the "recalcitrant case." Intrinsic to the party's project to restore its relationship to the masses is its self-representation as a closely tied friend and benefactor, a *tiexinren* (a person stuck to one's heart). Ideal birth policy workers must therefore be willing to lavish care and attention on their targets. In these accounts, women who consent to abortion are shown to be moved to tears by the flood of thoughtful attention during and after the procedure that must stand in marked contrast to the perfunctory character of most health care in China. This cultivation of obligation and sentiment is obviously much more labor intensive than the more brutal expediency of coercive measures, although as suggested above, the two go hand in hand.

This woman's dedication to her work leads her to an even more thorough dereliction of her nurturing role within the family. She goes off to deal with a difficult case, leaving her feverish son at home. He dies and is buried under the yellow earth. The same earth that covers her son also covers centuries of the history of the Chinese people. Their need is greater than her own need to assume the role of mother. This theme of historical continuity is important; it underscores the timeless cycle of blind reproduction uncontrolled by a central planning intelligence. Despite the accumulation of centuries of Chinese history, the place is defined as the quintessence of *luohou* (backwardness) for which the only remedy is the disciplinizing intervention of the birth policy. This relationship between luohou and overpopulation is not demonstrated; it simply goes without saying.

What, then, is this consuming labor producing? In her work on the bioeconomics of nineteenth-century European discourse, Catherine Gallagher looks at the symbolic circulation of value between images of productive and nonproductive labor. The bodies of working-class men and women were seen to have been diminished by the displacement onto others of the value they created in the extraction of surplus value from their labor.[36] In post-Tiananmen China, the bodies of party members engaged in the laborious activity of party work are shown to be expended in the massive effort to modernize a vast agrarian state. Others become wealthy, but the dedicated party member neglects her own welfare and that of her family in the extravagant expenditure of time and energy demanded by the expectations of her role. Whether or not we believe that party members are selfless, dedicated people or ambitious political opportunists or something in between, what cannot be denied is the tremendous amount of energy deployed to project this image of the party and its members as a laboring body producing productive (if not reproductive) bodies and not a parasitic growth on the social body. Despite all the cynicism of a posttotalitarian age, the trope of self-sacrifice remains as a potent sign of the nation-space, a marker that claims for its bearer a heroic role in China's struggle to "come to its own."[37]

The Indicators of Social Disorder

In the discussion above, China's vast population is currently constructed unproblematically as "illth" and not "wealth."[38] The word "illth" is the word John Ruskin used to critique Malthus's suggestion that a growing and healthy population ultimately leads to catastrophic ends, famine and plague, as the outer limits imposed on population growth. Nineteenth-century bioeconomics reversed the wisdom of an earlier political economy that saw populousness as a sign of a nation's health and vitality. The definition of population as "illth" is also linked to twentieth-century discourses which emanate from Euramerican places and which point to the underdevelopment of "third world" countries as rooted primarily in their population problem, rather than in unequal exchanges of wealth and power, capital and labor, on a global scale.[39] Hence the attribution of overpopulation in the late twentieth century carries with it tremendous disciplinary power in the significant sanctions that work both materially and symbolically to put the nation in its place in the global community. Yet despite the tremendous disciplinizing power of population discourse on a global and national level that disvalues bodies in their sheer numerousness, popular practices continue to assert the value of bodies in their singularity. What should not be ignored is the tremendous pain caused by lost or terminated pregnancies because of the stringent application of the one-child family policy imposed on China's population. The party-state openly represents the modes of resistance to this policy as a problem of incomplete pedagogical work. Less explicit is any discussion of the "hunger" for bodies that the policy produces. One exception is the issue of care for the aged. Homes for the elderly are supposed to take up this responsibility, a promise generally regarded as overly ambitious given the burden that the aging population will place on single children in the next generation. Another exception might be the recognition that the demographic imbalance between the sexes attributed to the birth policy will lead to a large population of unmarried men, who will turn to alcoholism, prostitution, and hooliganism because of their exclusion from a "normal" family life.

Less explicit are other ways in which the "hunger" for bodies might link with the discourse of social disorder. The liberalizing atmosphere of the post-Mao period has given rise to a new kind of journalism dedicated to the investigation of the underside of society. One of the recurring themes in this new genre are stories about the traffic of bodies, mostly the sale of women and children. This traffic has become an important sign of the forces of social disorder that have been unleashed by the economic reforms.

The traffic in bodies is made possible by the new mobilities of the reform period. Organized rings of human peddlers abduct, transport, and sell human beings across vast geographical spaces. Most ubiquitous are women from the poorer interior provinces (Sichuan, Anhui) who are transported to the more prosperous coastal areas and sold as brides. Stories of this kind abound in the new legal pictorials that can be bought on almost any urban street. They are consumed by an educated, urban elite, and yet the sensationalism of the reportage verges at times on the pornographic. This is especially true of stories about the traffic in women that linger on the depiction of rape.

The true scandal of these stories is the frightening way in which they represent the reduction of women and their reproductive power to the status of mere commodities, a scandal that is reflected in the escalation of bride-price exchanges, what the state refers to as "buying and selling marriages" (*maimai hunyin*). The stories of rape or "first night" rights taken by these brokers in human beings highlight the theme of women as commodities that can be possessed (used), exchanged, and even returned for resale if they fail to satisfy the buyer. The theme of woman as commodity is exemplified by the photographic display of women being bought and sold in the marketplace that accompanied the sale of a highly celebrated book of reportage devoted to this social issue.[40] The "market" that moves women's bodies across the length and breadth of China in a series of complex, hidden exchanges becomes quite literally concretized in the depiction of these women as caged in an unnamed location, presumably a marketplace in fact, scantily clad with price placards hanging from their necks. That these photos are "staged" is almost indisputable. The photographs themselves bear the record of when the images were shot, dated only a few weeks prior to publication; the "models" are clearly the same in each shot, but with their clothing exchanged.[41]

When urban people talk about the phenomenon of the abduction and sale of women, it is as if they were speaking about a foreign country. Perhaps this explains the heightened shock delivered by a famous piece of reportage about a Shanghai graduate student who was abducted while en route to Beijing to do research and sold to a peasant household in Shandong. The scandal of this story is the movement of embodied value out of its "proper" circuit of exchange. The educated, refined bodies of urban elite women are found to be infinitely substitutable with poor peasant women from Sichuan and Anhui in the commodification of women's bodies, presenting a confusion of bodily values that violates the sanctity of an imaginary divide. The urban identity of the victim intensifies the vicarious horror of the reader, a horror that derives from the distance the narrative is compelled to construct between city and country.[42]

And yet, with the suburbanization of the peasantry in the wealthy coastal regions, the divide is constructed more along the axis between coastal areas and places of the interior—the very divide that these women traverse as commodities. This imaginary distance, therefore, is constantly crossed by the exchange of women that tends to flow toward economically more prosperous regions. Forced abduction by human peddlers (*renfanzi*) is only the extreme end of a continuum. The flow of women from poorer villages seeking to marry into wealthier areas includes many who go voluntarily; some may fall into the hands of unscrupulous "marriage brokers" who then sell them to the highest bidder, depriving them of any choice in selecting a mate. How widespread this new social ill has become in the last ten years is difficult to fathom, but the social commentary on it has virtually exploded. One indication of how common this traffic is perceived to be is indicated by the short fictional piece "Baoying" (Retribution) about a man who abducts and sells a young girl, only to return home to find his daughter has been stolen by another trafficker.[43] These stories about the commodification of women raise an important corrective to those apologists for China's reproductive policies who suggest that an indirect benefit lies in an enhanced status for women as desirable commodities in short supply in a highly competitive "marriage market."

This flagrant display of the forces of social disorder in the semiofficial press not only titillates; it has a much more serious role in constructing hegemony for the party. In making disorder so shockingly visible, these stories reinforce fears of the return of "chaos" and enflame the public concern for social control (not to mention the way they construct the low quality of the population). However, another, more subversive reading of this literature makes visible the suppressed popular concern for what can only be understood as a dearth of bodies. The abduction and sale of women and children point toward an unfulfilled hunger for bodies that are seen not as consuming but producing bodies, essential to the reproduction of the household unit newly empowered by the economic reforms.

But this traffic in bodies is not limited to this illicit trade by human peddlers. It also appears in the sanctions used to discourage out-of-plan births. In many areas, fines are used to penalize excess births, although the amount may vary in relation to the known wealth of the household. Wealthy, independent, entrepreneurial households may pay fines in the tens of thousands of yuan. In some cases, the fines appear not to act as a deterrent but as a de facto tax on out-of-plan births. The unabashed readiness of more prosperous households to pay the price leads one to suspect that having extra children may be a new form of conspicuous consumption in the countryside. This suggests new dimensions of resistance to the allocative power of the state in which its penalties become the basis for status enhancement.[44] Moreover, the fines are not always applied equally but often only in those cases in which the offending household is known to have financial assets, operating, in effect, as an indirect tax on wealth.

The modes of resistance to the policy are too numerous to catalogue; a fascinating project might be to attempt to categorize them according to the *Sanshiliu ji* (Thirty-six stratagems), the classic Chinese text of cunning intelligence, of wile and warcraft. The first stratagem, "cross the sea under cover" (*mantian guohai*), more freely translated as "hiding in plain sight," is amply illustrated by a woman of my acquaintance from an entrepreneurial peasant family who hid in a friend's apartment in the walled compound of the Provincial Party Headquarters throughout her pregnancy so that she wouldn't be forced into an abortion she did not want. Once this woman gave birth she was fined fifteen thousand yuan (roughly three thousand U.S. dollars). She subsequently named the boy "Wanwu" (literally, fifteen thousand) but was persuaded by her university-educated brother to change the baby's name to the more literary "Tao," which has a homophonic association with "to run away." Indeed, the last of the thirty-six stratagems is, "When all else fails, run away" (*zou wei shang ji*).

This leads to another theme in the reportage of social disorder: the appearance of a growing "floating population" (*liudong renkou*) that has been loosened from its bureaucratic moorings in the household registration system. Some of these itinerant people consciously use their newfound mobility to gain reproductive freedom.[45] Many take up trades that connect them with the marketplace and the petty commodity economy grown increasingly vibrant in the period of the reform. Although this gypsylike population is able to slip through the bureaucratic structures of control, it has increasingly become targeted by the state as requiring stiffer regulation, particularly with regard to the birth policy. However, the floating population as a discursive category includes more than just itinerant entrepreneurs: it also refers to the flow of peasant laborers who traverse the distance from the impoverished periphery to the more prosperous coastal provinces. The presence of large numbers of homeless laborers, living on the streets or housed on the ground floor of the high-rise construction sites they are hired to build, generates a good deal of discussion about social disorder and the comparative value of bodies. Although their cheap labor fuels the explosive expansion of the reform economy, their very presence raises the specter of social disorder and political instability. They are the uncivilized crowd that has not yet been made into a modern citizenry, the unsightly but indispensable presence in the heart of China's civility.

This affiliation of the floating population with the marketplace as commodified labor allows yet a further subversive reading of the state's own discourse on the value of bodies. The official disvaluation of too many bodies as excess, as dissipating and debilitating the wealth and vitality of the nation, is confronted with the revaluation of the body in the marketplace where its productive and reproductive powers become commodities to be bought and sold. The marketplace provides an autonomous zone in which bodily value can be reconstituted in opposition to the regulated values of the state not just as commodity but as household labor power in a growing entrepreneurial economy. I do not mean to valorize the market uncritically as a zone of freedom when here it so clearly represents unfreedom for women. My intention is merely to locate a social space for the active revaluation of bodies that counters its disvaluation in the population policies of the state.

Central to my argument is the suggestion that "population" is not a self-evident problematic of political economy but is first and foremost a discursive category that must be understood in its broader context of signification. Population discourse in post-Mao China, as it has elsewhere, expresses concerns about the circulation of value and the potential of the nation to transcend its position of weakness and poverty to become a major actor in the international community of nations. Moreover, any attempt to identify the concern with "population quality" as belonging exclusively to the state would misunderstand its broad articulation with a wide array of interests and concerns in post-Mao China, all of which produce different meanings and different political registrations for what appears discursively as the same language. Mapping the complex ways in which notions about population circulate throughout Chinese society helps us to account for the hegemonic power of China's population policy, as well as to locate the agency of ordinary people in defining what population means in the context of their immediate concerns and future hopes. The notion of population quality can be seen as perhaps the most pervasive currency of exchange in "the politics of perception and experience" throughout the period of China's economic reform.[46]

6 CHILI PEPPER POLITICS

> The language of the law, which is supposed to be universal, is, in this respect,
> inadequate; it must, if it is to be effective, be the discourse of one class to another,
> which has neither the same ideas as it nor even the same words.
> —Michel Foucault, *Discipline and Punish*

Zhang Yimou's film "*The Story of Qiu Ju*" (*Qiu Ju da guansi*) is the story of a
young peasant woman's unrelenting search for legal redress for what she re-
gards as an abusive exercise of power.[1] The village head (*cunzhang*) has kicked
Qiu Ju's husband in the groin, temporarily incapacitating him and arousing
concerns about his future fertility (given the ever hopeful prospect of a change
in the birth policy). The injury seems, at first, to be inconsequential, but the
question of what should constitute adequate compensation looms large for
most of the film as Qiu Ju pursues her grievance at ascending levels of political
authority. The case is settled at each level apparently *in her favor*, and yet she
fails to feel satisfaction. The reasons for this are clear enough to Qiu Ju, although not necessarily to those around her. She does not seek financial compensation for her injury but instead wants a public avowal of where the limits to
power lie. In Zhang Yimou's own words, "What Qiu Ju wants is *shuafa* [*sic*]—a
word used in the film that does not mean an 'apology' but an answer, an
explanation, a clarification."[2] The political stakes in this apparently minor
matter gradually come into view as Qiu Ju realizes the impossibility of obtaining her desire. Were the village head to recognize her demand for a clear
accounting of where the limits lie, he would lose his ability to govern effectively.
"I have to lead this place," he retorts to the official who urges him to take a more
conciliatory approach.

The efforts of mediators to resolve the conflict quickly with a monetary
compensation are derailed by the village head's intransigence. He throws the
carefully counted and folded bills at Qiu Ju's feet and tells her that she must bow

her head to him as she bends over to retrieve each one, a movement that would force her to ape the ritualized subordination of the *ketou* (kowtow). This humiliation she refuses. Only when the village head redeems himself at a moment of need does Qiu Ju feel satisfied, but not before the ponderous gears of the legal system have been set in motion, leading to his arrest and detention. The legal means of redress, therefore, are never appropriate to the situation; they are either insufficient or violently in excess of what is desired.

Zhang Yimou's depiction of Qiu Ju's struggles to make power accountable to its limits suggests a new articulatory politics in which one class *speaks* to another. Indeed, here I want to explore the notion of narrative address that captures the multiple meanings of "address" as not only a "speaking to" but also a "hailing" in the Althusserian sense of constituting a subject in the very act of addressing it.[3] Zhang Yimou is quite consciously hailing the mass of China's peasantry as a subject capable of claiming political agency. However, the film addresses its subject in such a way as to produce a rhetorical effect quite different from that of the conventions of socialist realist representation, even when on the surface it appears to be faithful to those very conventions. Read as an ironic commentary on socialist realism, the film offers a strategic site from which to explore how peasant subjects are constituted in the political rhetoric and practices of reform-era China. The film begs the question of how the party's civilizing rhetoric "speaks" to the people and the kinds of subjects that are made possible or impossible by such an address.

These questions are central to the larger concern of how a nation's people can be mobilized as a modern citizenry, disciplined to the goals of governance. How the undisciplined mass is to be made into "the people-nation" is a central problematic in many postcolonial contexts because of its very indeterminacy—"the people," called into being by the pedagogical operations of the state, may begin to challenge the established structures of governance. In the reform period, these dual objectives of democratic reform and civic discipline—of constituting the rural masses as a citizenry that is both self-governing *and* orderly—are embodied in the institution of village compacts (*xianggui minyue*).[4] Drafted by township and village governments in the post-Mao period, these compacts are intended to reinstitute normative rule by means of an economy of "face" in communities whose social order has become threatened by the disintegration of collective organization and the new mobilities in rural areas.

However, the Chinese state's promotion of these compacts as an institution of "self-government" raises critical issues about the politics of representation. The compacts imaginatively position the rural masses as their author *and* object.[5] The "masses" are thereby made subject to a pedagogical practice that they, as active subjects, are said to be the authors of—a neatly recursive maneuver that covers over the fact that the compacts frequently work to reaffirm the power of the local party apparatus. The compacts are therefore akin to the power of constitutional reforms as a mode of what Prasenjit Duara has called "writing the people into being," the creation of a "people-nation" in the very act of "representing" one. One could suggest that this recursivity in the construction of "the people" is inherent to the process of political representation in the modern state.[6] However, the compacts carry this confusion between subject and object, pedagogical and performative, to a heightened degree, perhaps reflecting the pressures, generated both domestically and internationally, for political reforms. Indeed, I argue that this lack of clarity is "functionally induced."[7] The compacts are primarily pedagogical, conveying an officially approved model from above, but they do so under the guise of the performative, as a spontaneous "eruption" from below. This maneuver gives the "appearance" of popular political participation without seriously challenging the concentration of power in the party apparatus.[8] And yet the compacts, as a pedagogical practice, always carry with them a potential performativity that may prove difficult to reign in. For, once called into being, "the people," increasingly subject to burgeoning forces outside the force field of party control, begin to realize an agency of their own that then confronts their fetishized representation in the rhetoric of the state.[9]

The Story of Qiu Ju insistently draws attention to the gaps that are smoothed over and hidden in power's self-representation. It turns a critical gaze on the concentration of power in the hands of local officials that is exemplified by the ironic slippage in Chinese between "personal power" (*renquan*) and "human rights" (*renquan*). The film is all the more pregnant with this irony in its apparent depiction of the operations of the newly remodeled legal system as operating *exactly as it ought*, with officials fulfilling to a heightened degree the Communist Party ideals of earnest and self-sacrificing service—so much so that no less a personage than Li Ruihuan (head of the Ministry of Culture) praised the film as one worth advocating through the government propaganda apparatus![10] Despite this official approval, the film explicitly invites the Chinese "masses" to question the everyday exertion of power. It anticipates, through the figure of prolepsis—the representation of a thing as actually existing before the fact—the coming to awareness of the masses own agency in the political process. And it does this by closely examining the system of dispute mediation as instituted within the post-Mao political reforms. It is in this context that we see Qiu Ju resisting the subtle forces that insistently attempt to pull her back into the scripted position of a passive acquiescence to power. Her struggle with these forces is a struggle to assert a new kind of subjectivity within the protocols of state bureaucratic power. In her direct use of the institutions of the political reform, we see revealed the inability of power to reform itself. Reform must come from elsewhere, and it comes here from a semiliterate peasant woman in the deep hinterland of the Shaanxi countryside. She exemplifies how a single person can trouble the existing relations of power by taking literally the state's claim to be a government accountable to the people.

The Facts of the Case

Let us review the facts of the case to explore more carefully how the film envisions this political possibility. Qiu Ju and her husband, Wan Qinglai, had begun building a chili pepper drying shed on agricultural land without having first received official permission. They had submitted an application for the construction, but as Qiu Ju later explains to public security officials, the village head was slow to respond, and the family decided to build without a proper permit. Qiu Ju's family are peasant entrepreneurs, in bureaucratic parlance, a "specialized household" (*zhuanye hu*) engaged in the production of a single commodity for sale in the market. Their house had already been filled to capacity with garlands of drying chili peppers. Indeed, these cascading strings of red frame the domestic scenes of Qiu Ju's household, just as similar garlands of maize provide background color to the village chief's home. They are the scenic equivalent to the long hallucinatory banners of dyed cloth that frame the action of Zhang's earlier film *Judou*. Chilies are an important accompaniment to a bland diet composed mostly of grain products, and in the film they may signify a refusal of blandness in realms other than merely gustatory ones. Draped to excess with these chilies, the Wan family home presents an aspect of repleteness, being filled to capacity with the products of their labor. To expand production and increase the scale of their enterprise, they clearly need additional space to store and dry their chilies. With their failure to procure the proper permit, the family runs headlong into the local exercise of power, which, even with the retreat of direct state power over production, continues to constrain and limit the economic initiative of peasant enterprises. Despite the past ten years of economic reform, a certain anxiety persists regarding the recurrence of widening economic differences, so that sudden wealth is often inscribed as "going over the top" (*fu guotou*), sometimes resulting in the efforts of a certain type of local official to limit the size of household enterprises.[11] The Wan family's decision to build their shed constitutes a fundamental challenge to the village head's power to constrain the scope of their enterprise. He claims the authority of regulations governing land use but fails to produce them in writing. In fact, as the public security officers later inform Qiu Ju, there are stipulations, often included in the village compacts, that enforce compliance with national policies regulating the use of agricultural land.[12] However, the primary concern in these regulations is usually with the misappropriation of land for use as housing sites. The Wan family's stated intent had been to build a structure that was closely related to agricultural production, an area where the regulations may, in fact, be less clearly stated.

But this initial challenge to the village head's authority becomes quickly overshadowed by another. When the village head intervenes to halt construction, Wan Qinglai angrily retorts that the chief is good only for raising hens, a pointed reference to the village head's repeated failure to produce a son. The insult reflects not only on his failure but also on his infringement of the birth policy—his large number of daughters standing as incontrovertible evidence of the inequities of power. Therefore, the insult operates at a number of levels. It brings to the surface an interesting circulation of the violence of the birth policy working here in this confrontation between local leader and villager. The pain that the policy produces in thwarted reproductive desire is one that is generally shared. However, the pain that the policy produces for the village head, insofar as even he may not try again with impunity, is transferred by the kick to Wan Qinglai's crotch. The circulation of this violence moves more typically toward the woman who fails to bear a son, a movement that reasserts itself later in the film when the village head holds Qiu Ju's baby and taunts his wife with "her" failure.[13] As the village head is himself a victim of the policy, one can almost sympathize with his impulse to kick his taunter as a pointed rejoinder to this reminder of his emotional pain as profound as Wan Qinglai's more physical one. The psychological blow to the village head's fertility is balanced by a physical one in which male fertility is brought into question on both sides, a leveling in reproductive potential.

And yet there are clearly inequities of power operating here. Just as the village head carries the authority to limit the scope of the Wan family's production, he also carries the power to limit their reproduction, while allowing his own to remain, relatively speaking, unregulated.[14] Indeed, had the blow been aimed elsewhere, we might well wonder whether it would have led to such a deep sense of injury, given the heightened tension about reproduction produced by the policy. It appears to be the specificity of the blow that compels Qiu Ju to question more generally the right of the village head to assault a villager with impunity. Therefore, the spontaneous response of the village head to a deeply felt insult becomes transformed into a searching inquiry to the limits of power. The irony, of course, is that the blow that causes the grievance is not the one for which the village head is eventually punished. The legal machinery is interested only in the x-ray of Wan Qinglai's broken rib as the physical evidence to determine whether the attack can be classified as a criminal assault. As I will elaborate below, this shift in legal interest from one blow to another replicates the general disavowal of power of the means it must use to achieve its ends, a means that must, for the system to operate smoothly, be a violence that leaves no marks.

Let us look at how this disavowal operates in the procedural apparatus of dispute resolution. Rather than appealing to the formal legal system, Qiu Ju initiates her grievance by applying to local authorities, who employ the procedures of mediation to effect a harmonious conciliation. At the outset we have a difference established between the language of mediation, in which both parties in the conflict accept partial responsibility for wrongdoing, and the language of the law, which takes on a more directly adversarial relationship in the attribution of wrongdoing. When Qiu Ju fails to find satisfaction through the mediation process, she is instructed to appeal to higher authorities until the mediation process is exhausted, and only then to seek out more formal legal means. Doubtful, she asks, "If I bring suit, then will the right thing be done?" She is asking, in a sense, how a certain balance in her relationship to the village head can be restored, a balance that had been disrupted by the "negative reciprocity" of the blow. As we are soon made to see when it comes time for Qiu Ju to give birth, village life is still highly interdependent and based on relationships built through ties of reciprocity and obligation. This was portrayed earlier in the film when a parcel of purchased snacks misrepresented by Officer Li to Qiu Ju as a gift from the village head potentially carries the power to restore that balance—that is, until Qiu Ju discovers that it is really Li who made the purchase and not the head. A gift from the head would have put him in the inferior position of acknowledging that he had been in the wrong and needed to make amends.

When Qiu Ju asks whether a lawsuit will make things right, she is seeking some sort of acknowledgment on his part of his transgression. Officer Li understands this and urges the head to say "a few nice words." As we soon discover, the legal system cannot produce this result, and yet the head's inability to respond to Qiu Ju's demand has everything to do with the specific economy of power in reform-era China. This paradox results in the series of misfirings as Qiu Ju pursues her desire to higher and higher levels of the legal bureaucracy. In a particularly comic moment, she discovers at the last moment that the suit she had initiated with the help of a lawyer has been lodged against the director of the Provincial Public Security Office. He in a sense becomes a proxy who stands in for legal bureaucracy, placing her in the difficult position of injuring some-one who has shown her kindness. She balks until the director himself tells her that he does not take it personally, the proper procedure ensures that "the right thing be done."

The judgment of the court only reaffirms the outcome of informal media-tion. The suit fails to produce the desired result, forcing us to recognize that the director knew all along that Qiu Ju would lose. The court scene is only one more means of "instructing" this ignorant peasant woman in the transcendent wisdom of the mediation process. The responsibility for the wrong keeps get-ting displaced upward in the process of appeal as a repetitive object lesson for the masses that the justice to be obtained there is the same as that already available locally.[15] No wonder Qiu Ju begins to suspect collusion as she is placed further and further into the position of one who is inherently unable to be satisfied, a pregnant hysteric whose whims must be indulged.

In her isolation, her only option is to seek satisfaction at the next higher level of legal formality. Only when she presses criminal charges against the village head for physical assault does the legal apparatus act, but in a form that wildly exceeds Qiu Ju's desire. And it does this because *it speaks another language*—the abstracted language of the law which can address only the positivity of docu-mented evidence of physical injury but which cannot ever adequately address the legality of the assault itself in its complex social determination. The state's culpable reliance on the personalized power of its local officials cannot be exposed. The village head must be sacrificed to leave the larger question of power and its limits unaddressed. The final moment of the film, which focuses on Qiu Ju's stunned face in a prolonged stop-action shot, registers her shocked realization that "the right thing" *cannot* be done—that the system is incapable of delivering it to her. We are then left poised between different readings of where this understanding might lead her—either to despair over the futility of any sort of political action or a realization that justice will never be won by passive acceptance of the institutions in place but only with an insistent and unrelenting demand for power to recognize its "proper" limits.

The Law of the Supplement

The post-Mao political reforms appear in the film in its depiction of the process of dispute mediation and its relation to the legal system. The institution of dispute mediation is not an innovation of the reform era but has been retained alongside the newly reconstructed legal system as a supplementary means to handle disputes. A comprehensive village compact includes stipulations for the appointment of a cadre in charge of mediation (*tiaojie ganbu*) and the process of dispute resolution.[16] It is this supplementary aspect of the mediation process and its encompassment within the village compact that is of interest here. For the supplement, as that which "substitutes for" or "fills in" what is missing, is a sign of power's own effacement.[17]

This "supplementary" aspect of the compact is clearly represented in the rhetoric that attempts to define its relationship to the formal legal system. The compact is promoted as a model for "self-government." It therefore becomes a mechanism whereby the functions of horizontal policing are internalized into the local community. The contents of the compacts give a punishing specificity to areas of everyday life presumed to be too trivial or too pervasive to be dealt with adequately by the state legal apparatus.[18] It addresses issues of social order that are beyond the scope of the law or the present capacity of the legal system to handle. Therefore, the compacts are supplementary in both senses: as a substitute and as a filling-in for what is lacking in the law. They are supposed to operate entirely through the force of moral persuasion and public opinion. Yet the charters regularly exceed this limit in their stipulation of financial penalties and even physical punishment and detention to ensure compliance—abuses of power critiqued repeatedly through official organs as "crude methods" (*tu banfa*) but so ubiquitous that this fitful critique of localized instances is no less than a bland disavowal of where the responsibility for these abuses of power properly lies.

Indeed, the routinization of this disavowal suggests yet another example of the "euphemization" of the violence of the state, in which the local party officials operate as "loose cannons" to deliver results desired by the center in exchange for the local concentration of power in their hands.[19] In other words, the supplementarity of the compacts gives special license to local officials to abuse the proper limits of their authority, and this ability to exceed the limits is something that the center is absolutely dependent on in order to function at all. This is especially apparent in the context of birth policy implementation. The one-child family is policy and not law. However, it comes down on the heads of millions of peasant households with all the punitive force of the law, so that from a peasant perspective the difference between policy and law is often a moot one.

The blurring of this distinction is critical to the reproduction of power of local officials in the post-Mao period. Qiu Ju's request is impossible precisely because it falls between the clear divisions of the law and party policy, as the latter is supposed to be implemented according to a certain "work style" pre-scribed by party traditions of self-sacrificing service. Her asking for "clarifica-tion" insists that the gap that lies between the two, in which the moral authority to govern takes on the coercive force of the law, be made clear. Her demand undermines the very basis on which the party retains its power. In the post-Mao economic reforms, rural cadres may have lost much of their power to direct production, but that loss has been subtly restored through a repositioning of the loci of control. The reform era continues to witness a formidable concentra-tion of power in the hands of ten thousand "local emperors" (*tu huangdi*). Rather than appealing to some notion of a timeless "Chinese" culture that ineluctably predisposes the Chinese to a system of "arbitrary personal power" (*renzhi*), I would prefer to focus on the more recent historical factors in China's struggle for national sovereignty and its drive toward modernity to understand the functional determination of this particular distribution of power.[20] In other words, what forces converge to reproduce the uncannily persistent power of the local leader? I shall return shortly to this question.

The Collision of Languages

The language of the law claims to be comprehensive and universal, invested with an objectivity that transcends the particular. However, the law speaks in a language that cannot be readily understood by Qiu Ju but must be *translated*. This difficulty of communication between the language of the law and that of everyday life is suggested when she learns from other plaintiffs that one must not approach the law bearing merely one's own words but with a written document describing one's grievance. She procures this document, but it is nonetheless indelibly marked by the curious "back translations" of the quasi-literate marketplace scribe who writes letters for hire and for whom cost is determined by the level of gravity desired. The public security officials are amused by the awkward pretension of the letter in which a kick in the groin becomes transmuted into an "attempted homicide." These misapplications of language only serve to intensify the "alien-ness" of the legal system, its formal rituals and language, in the process securing Qiu Ju's positioning as an ignorant peasant woman who seizes on a commodified mode of access to the law rather than being able to inhabit its language and spaces confidently.[21]

This theme of the language of the law as something that must be translated is reprised throughout the film. Again, in the scene in the Public Security Office, we see a variation on the "good cop, bad cop" idea. The first officer reads out the appropriate legal passages, speaking the lofty, universal language of the law, and the second officer, turning in his seat to face Qiu Ju, immediately translates the legal language into one that *addresses* Qiu Ju *directly*. Another instance occurs when the legal decision for her suit is read in court: we do not see Qiu Ju's defeat reflected on her face until the lawyer turns to tell her, "We lost." Only then does she understand the full import of what she has just heard. Finally, at the very end of the film, Qiu Ju's stunned face shown close up registers the full horror of what the untranslatability of languages has wrought.

Indeed, I would argue that this problem of translation across languages reveals the significant gap between the formal and informal legal systems mentioned earlier. Qiu Ju's desire is impossible precisely because it falls between the two, dramatizing their inability to form together a seamless and unproblematic unity. Moreover, this problematic linkage is not just a defect in the system that merely needs to be pointed out and fixed; rather, its very ambiguity provides the necessary space for the party-state to reproduce its power.

The film helps us to see how this works by showing us the two systems as two separate legal cultures, each with its own language. The village compact itself may be seen as a vehicle of translation that conveys the law into the norms of the community. Indeed, the impetus to draft compacts was often encompassed by "the dissemination of legal knowledge" movement (*pufa jiaoyu*) of the late 1980s. But as a vehicle of translation it also magically transmutes national policy into something that operates locally as "the law." The ironic result of propagating legal knowledge among the masses, however, is their heightened ability to cite the law against the arbitrary use of power. Increasingly, peasant subjects, such as Wan Qinglai and others newly empowered by the economic reforms, may require written documentation that clearly states the legal basis for the decisions of local officials and may even take local officials to court in pursuit of their grievances. In other words, they have adopted the language of the law to counter the "illegalities of power" that operate unchecked in the countryside. In the language of local officials, these new peasant subjects who use the law to challenge their authority are called *diaomin*, a pejorative label that targets such households as "troublemakers."[22] Diaomin stand in contrast with another category of troublemakers called *dingzihu* (nail households) who act much more spontaneously and violently to the arbitrary exercise of power, resulting often in punitive responses from the state.[23] Both categories stand in opposition to *shunmin* (obedient subjects), a label that is perhaps condescending at best. Whereas dingzihu may be more generally marginalized as social deviants, diaomin are often respected as able and savvy agents deploying legal means to confront powerful officials.[24] The pufa jiaoyu campaigns of the 1980s may have been pedagogical in intent, redefining the terms by which "obedient subjects" could be recognized, but the letter of the law, once disseminated as "popular knowledge," becomes the very means by which power is confronted with its own self-image.[25] If diaomin are primarily agents acting locally in pursuit of specific goals, the political effects of their actions may indeed be scattered and uncoordinated with respect to pushing for more systemic reforms.[26] However, one wonders what new possibilities open up when diaomin are actively solicited by an oppositional elite to regard their confrontations with local officials as direct challenges to the system as a whole, the smooth operation of which is so heavily reliant on these localized sites of power. The film reflects back a different set of possibilities that disrupt representations of such peasants as an irritating problem with which local cadres have to deal. If the label diaomin typically carries a negative connotation, it is elevated by the film to become a heroic subject position actively soliciting emulation more broadly. If a million "Qiu Jus" were to pursue their grievances with such determination, then the state's dissemination of its own arbitrary violence downward to these myriad localized sites would stand exposed. Indeed, the title of the original story on which the film is based carries this message in coded form. The Chinese surname "Wan" can also be read as "ten thousand." Hence, "Wanjia sugong" can be translated either as "the Wan Family Lawsuit" or as "Ten Thousand Families Go to Court."[27] If ten thousand families all demand the same justice as Qiu Ju, the cumulative effect would be like that of water wearing away the hardest stone.

Therefore, the film captures both state strategies of fixing individuals into subject positions and the ways in which subjects might resist this positioning. Qiu Ju pursues her grievance by an appeal to the legal system, much as a diaomin would. Yet, the village head and other officials subtly position her as intractable and vindictive. Her failure to fall into her scripted position—her obdurate resistance to all the forces that insistently attempt to push her into a passive acceptance of the system as it is—places her outside the category of "obedient subject" and into the more socially transgressive category of "troublemaker." Even the solicitous attention of the officials that she encounters in her movement upward in the legal hierarchy is, in a sense, exerting a moral obligation on her to be satisfied, which she steadfastly refuses. As the film progresses, she becomes more and more isolated as socially deviant, carrying her grudge *beyond all reason*, precisely because she has ostensibly "already won." Why is it, then, that she can experience her "victory" only as a humiliation?

The answer to this question lies in the public nature of the confrontation between the village head and Qiu Ju in which the village head's ability to be a leader is pitted against Qiu Ju's social respectability, thus revealing the real stakes in the game. We are quickly made aware of the public stage on which this drama is being played out. When Qiu Ju visits the village head in company with the officer mediating her case, she is asked to step outside and immediately confronts the collective gaze of a group of villagers eagerly watching from a distance. The village head cannot be found to be in excess of his authority for having struck a villager; to find otherwise would result in an undermining of his ability to lead. It would court the kinds of insubordination exemplified by Wan Qinglai's taunt. If the regulations on land use are ambiguous, open to interpretation, then the confrontation between Wan Qinglai and the village chief is a struggle over how it is to be interpreted. "I am the law," the village head retorts to the Wan family's insistence on seeing the actual "letter" of the law as textual document. In the context of the economic reforms, where the rules that govern economic and political life tend to be murky and unpredictable, the authority of local leadership depends on the ability to foreclose the free interpretation of policy and the law. Once this authority is challenged, it collapses like a house of cards. The village head knows this, which explains his intransigence in the face of Qiu Ju's request for an explanation.

Instead, the system employs a method of damage control in which compensation is paid so that a *wrongful* exercise of force is transmuted into the lesser charge of *excessive* use, leaving the village head's leadership more or less intact. This move is accomplished by means of a money equivalent that measures the wrong according to a calculus of economic loss in doctor's fees and lost labor time. Two hundred yuan is not an insignificant sum, being equivalent in the mid-1980s to about one month's income in the Shaanxi countryside. The ability of the village head to hit a villager goes unquestioned, while the excessive exercise of this force becomes a measurable quantity that can then be balanced through an abstract, impersonal money equivalent. The fine levied against the village head is an inverse mirror of the widespread practice of using village compacts to levy fines on various infractions, rather than depending solely on the use of moral persuasion and social pressure to give the compacts their "binding force" (*shufu li*). This practice contravenes the official models for the compacts, but along with physical detention, corporal punishment, and confiscation of personal property, it is almost universally relied on to give the compacts their disciplinary power. The fines in particular come under heavy criticism for creating inequities under the law. One is free to break the rules if one has the means to pay the price. Moreover, the schedule of fines becomes a potential source of income for local governments, which makes them financially dependent on fining illegalities for their normal functioning.[28]

If the money equivalent was intended to restore a balance, how is it that this transfer misfires? The immediate answer is the village head's use of the moment as a ritual of subordination to restore Qiu Ju's proper position with respect to his authority—that is, on her knees. However, if Qiu Ju had stooped so low, she would have been viewed as willing to humble herself "only" for money. In other words, the real object of her quest would no longer be perceived as a demand for political accountability but as an opportunistic exploitation of the village head's momentary "loss of control" for financial gain. The abstract equivalent of money in a sense removes the language of mediation from the complex tissue of social relations and reduces it to a quid pro quo, as "blood money." One can almost anticipate the village head's relish in recounting the transfer: "Oh, yes, I gave her the money all right, but I made her crawl to pick it up." The language of market exchange intervenes to save face for the village head. It translates an exercise of power into the abstraction of an impersonal exchange of equivalence that magically does not touch on his face (mianzi).

Although Qiu Ju refuses to fall for this setup, she nonetheless becomes increasingly isolated in her quest for satisfaction, until even her husband abandons his support. Indeed, the solicitousness of the public officials helps to highlight the transgressive nature of Qiu Ju's refusal to be satisfied—her being unreasonable—that surpasses even the understanding of Gong Li, the actress playing Qiu Ju.[29] This solicitousness should move Qiu Ju to tears, in recognition of her share of the error whereby her insistent desire puts so many lofty personages to *such* inconvenience. A power that descends to address her directly with so much concern morally obligates Qiu Ju to listen and be moved by such attention. The gathering pressure, working on her and her family, fails to rein in her implacable desire for accountability. And yet, even as the sting registers on her face, the film refuses to allow Qiu Ju to respond in the expected, scripted fashion.

If the language of the law is universal and thus "abstracted" from the context of specific social relations, the compacts, in contrast, "particularize" the law, addressing local issues of social order and using a mode of address that is overwhelmingly personal. We see this in the contrast between the formally symmetrical, distant spaces of the law court tableau and the almost conspiratorial huddle of Li's visit as he bears gifts. We see it also in the arcane legal language of the court officials and the intimate appeal made by Li for Qiu Ju to act accordingly, to respond out of a deep sense of moral obligation to a power that addresses itself directly to her. Li, the officer in charge of mediation, rebukes Qiu Ju for carrying her complaint to a higher level. When she finds him leading home a stray ox, he tells her, "This is all I am good for," meaning, of course, "*You* have reduced me to this," and also, by implication, "You must feel shame for making me, a conscientious and caring official, lose face by not responding to my appeal." He apparently only humbles himself for his failure because he intends to make her feel shame.

Qiu Ju is thus repeatedly positioned as morally insufficient, unresponsive to the claims of social relationships. Her very personhood is at stake in claiming the legitimacy of her demand. And yet, despite her rejection of social pressure to constrain her behavior, it is also clear that she is not seeking an abstract impersonal justice but merely the right of "the people" to call power on its own illegalities. Qiu Ju has not abandoned the communitarian norms of face or the obligations of reciprocity (*bao*). She is willing to make her own peace with the village head when he responds to her need for assistance at the birth of her child. Indeed, her newborn infant's "full month" celebration (*manyue*), the ritual of successful reproduction, promises to become the site of reconciliation, a final misfiring that catastrophically concludes the film when the village chief is carried off for detention. In Zhang Yimou's own words:

> There is a gulf between the kind of family justice that she claims—the village is like a big family—and the justice dispensed by the Court. . . . [But] if you don't ask a question, nobody will ever give you an answer. You always have to fight in order for something to be done. In China, you have to try twenty times, and spend years in order to solve the most minor problems. Officials don't make any mistake really, but in the end, there's never any answer. To request that something be done is the beginning of democracy. With this film, I wanted to say that every Chinese—and not only the peasants—should do the same thing: to fight for their rights and discover themselves in the process.[30]

As suggested above, Qiu Ju's story reveals a gap between the law and its supplement that calls into question the total structure of power, not merely its localized abuse. The problem lies not with individuals. The village head is not an inherently evil character but one who is caught up in an economy of power that demands the consistent disavowal of its arbitrary exercise. I will now further consider how the film's narratorial tactics neatly invert the official petits récits which work to disavow the reliance of a centralized "superpower" on these "infralevel" excesses.

The Question of Gender

Wan Qinglai's incapacitation from his injury effects a gender reversal in the household's relationship to authority. At first he is angry and supports his wife's decision to fight back. Midway through the film, however, we see his increasing sensitivity to the circulation of gossip regarding his case and his willingness to be mollified by the cash payment, which he accepts indirectly from the hands of the village head's wife after the obligatory "three refusals." In Chinese society, to suggest that "people are talking about you" (*you ren jiang ni*) carries a tremendously potent force to constrain people's behavior. The situation escalates to the point where Wan Qinglai is taunted about not being able to control his wife, so that when Qiu Ju sets out once more, he yells angry words at her, telling her not to come back. Qiu Ju, in a sense, assumes the burden of confronting the power of the state, while her husband lies recumbent in the background, felled by an attack on the very center of his male potency, which must be nurtured and conserved back to health. One of the commodities Qiu Ju brings back from her adventures in the city is a tonic labeled "Man's Treasure," which reflects the way in which concerns about male potency becomes fetishized in the marketplace. Qiu Ju's activity, in contrast to Wan Qinglai's enforced passivity, effects something of a gender reversal, in which a woman sallies forth to do battle with forces much larger than herself.

Yet Qiu Ju is not just a woman but also a pregnant one, carrying before her at all times her increasingly evident moral claim on the officials of the state to respond to her with solicitous attention. The one-child family policy produces an environment that intensifies reproduction as a site of great anxiety and concern. Even before the current policy, the socialist state has availed itself of the reproductive domain as a primary means by which it can promulgate a normative family form and discipline the domestic sphere.[31] Qiu Ju is therefore able to turn the state's "solicitous attention" to women's reproductive health into a resource that ensures her reception wherever she goes. When she is sent back to her lodging via the personal limousine of the director of the Public Security Bureau, the guesthouse manager's wonder marks this as an unusual attention. One rather doubts that she would have been so treated had she not been pregnant. Yet one is made painfully aware of the condescension hidden in the attention; its very excessiveness is a signal to Qiu Ju that she has stepped outside the bounds. Her relentless pursuit of such a petty matter puts everyone to rather great inconvenience, while endangering her unborn child with her perilous travel by foot over the icy Shaanxi countryside. Her unnatural lack of concern puts a burden on everyone else. The attentiveness of officials insistently points out her lack, a subtle form of social control intended to limit the scope of her activities.

How are we to understand the gendered positions of Qiu Ju and her husband? Is gender really central to the kind of subjectivity Zhang Yimou is attempting to solicit? Or is Qiu Ju merely a post-Mao continuation of an older literary tradition of strong women characters? Meng Yue has suggested that the "strong woman" character in Maoist literature is not really a "flesh and blood" person but a certain idealized political subject construction through which the male narrator strips himself of sexual difference in the projection of his own desire onto a female counterpart. Meng points out that Li Shuangshuang, the heroine of the 1950s film that bears her name, is the perfect example of the female image that stands in for the political authority of the party. Li Shuangshuang exemplified the dynamism of the party's moral authority by pushing her backward husband toward collectivization. In this earlier film, a new model of marital "equality" results in the "disciplining" of male actors that goes beyond sexual politics in the domestic sphere to encompass the profound structural transformation of agricultural collectivization.[32] In many respects, Qiu Ju recalls Li Shuangshuang to mind as an idealized representation of political agency. But here she is not intended as a stand-in for the party's moral authority but serves as the agent who exposes the gaps in the party's own claims to that authority. If Qiu Ju is a "quotation" of the "strong woman" characterization of Li Shuangshuang in terms of her function in the film, she has neatly turned the party's deployment of gender back on itself.

Moreover, far from the "disembodied" heroines of revolutionary narrative that Meng Yue critiques, the physical claims of Qiu Ju's reproducing body fairly scream for attention, most forcibly in the course of her difficult labor. The difference here is that the Qiu Ju's pregnant body reasserts claims that stand outside the party's self-legitimating economy of representation. Moreover, the claims of the body intrude not just through the register of reproduction but also through that of sexuality. Qiu Ju's concern for her husband's sexual potency is expressed in, among other things, her purchase of medicinal tonics that promise its hastened restoration not just to him but to her as well.[33] It was, after all, this particular blow that galvanizes her desire for political accountability. The claims of the body are made here to occupy insistently a space that resists incorporation into the state's representational apparatus that otherwise attempts to appropriate the body for itself. One could argue (in a more general way than Meng Yue's analysis would allow) that the heroic figures of revolutionary narrative *are* embodied, if only in the murderous assaults of class enemies on their physical integrity. Similarly, the embodiment of self-sacrificing party officials takes the form of consuming labor that diminishes their physical integrity for the greater good.[34] Qiu Ju's grievance inverts the state's self-representation by superimposing the physical violence of a "class enemy" on the figure of the local party official, one who is supposed to be sacrificing his own bodily integrity rather than assaulting the bodies of others. If Qiu Ju's em-bodied aspect marks a departure from the heroines of revolutionary narrative (as desexualized women who lack flesh and blood), Meng Yue's analysis can nonetheless lead us to the conclusion that Qiu Ju does continue the tradition of elite male narrators' using female characters as a displacement of their own desire rather than exploring gendered subjectivities for their own sake. Gender is used here as a commentary on the effects of power more generally and not just on gendered relations of power.

From the Country to the City

The location of the film in the arid loess uplands of Shaanxi carries with it complex layerings of signification. In the 1980s, the northwest figured as a popular background setting for epic films about peasant life, amounting to a cultural trend referred to as the "northwest wind" (*xibei feng*), which lent itself to multiple modes of nostalgia circulating in Chinese cultural discourse at that time.[35] The northwest has long been considered the site of the early origins of Chinese culture and therefore figured prominently in the "searching for roots" (*xungen*) cultural movement of the 1980s.[36] Shaanxi Province also figures importantly in China's revolutionary history, being where the Chinese Communist Party's policies of land reform and class struggle were engineered and refined in practice. And, finally, this locale has the reputation, despite these associations of cultural and historical progress, of being a profoundly dour landscape of crushing poverty inhabited by a tenacious peasantry tempered by their struggles with nature. These associations came into play in the late 1980s with the nostalgic retrieval of a great Chinese civilization of the past, the golden age of the party's moral legitimacy, and a primordial peasant culture untouched by the contradictions of modernity. And yet the locale can also be made to present a critique of the socialist era. Almost a half-century has passed since the founding of the People's Republic, yet this "cradle of Chinese civilization" remains impoverished. The film manages to go beyond the powerful pull of nostalgia to assert the co-temporality of Qiu Ju's world with the national present tense. It does so by collapsing the apparent chasm between the developed core and the backward hinterland in suggesting that even a semiliterate woman from an isolated rural village is capable of a political agency that has the power to unsettle the system to its very core. In so doing, it attempts to undo the narrative of the state that declares unequivocally that the Chinese people are not yet ready for political reform and will not be ready until they are subjected to a prolonged and extensive process of remolding.

The film works against the turn in the political culture of the early 1990s toward a nostalgic yearning for the Yan'an period and the early years of the

People's Republic of China, what Lisa Rofel has referred to as "liberation nostalgia."[37] This nostalgia was actively cultivated in the officially generated celebration of the film *Jiao Yulu*, which resurrected the image of a model party secretary from the early 1960s. To insure large audiences, work units distributed numerous free tickets to this film, which was required viewing for political study in spring 1991. The visible consumption of the party secretary's body by cancer as he labors for the people's well-being recalls the "thematization of excess" of traditional moral tales of filial piety.[38] This nostalgia for the political commitment of the 1950s is combined, nonetheless, with an ironic recognition that history has incapacitated one for this sort of blind political certainty. The response to the film *Jiao Yulu* on the part of young intellectuals I knew was, "Zheiyang de ren tai shaole!" (That sort of person is all too rare!). One senses the desire to believe in the model of Jiao Yulu, but mixed with the awareness of the "impossibility" of such a model. It is important to note that this "liberation nostalgia" is not limited to party circles alone but is more generally distributed among the population at large, and how ironically this media blitz of nostalgic films and television drama plays in the present period. This irony comes from the increasingly blatant gap between the model and the reality, so that the model itself becomes a beacon pointing to what is so profoundly lacking. In his film, Zhang Yimou rewrites the subtext for the theme of consuming labor by juxtaposing the model of the self-sacrificing local official with its apparent costs: the unquestioned submission to authority and the overdependence of power on an economy of face that personalizes the "face" of power.[39]

As already suggested, the film, to make its point, does not shrink from representing the disjunctures of "development" in 1990s China but instead vividly dramatizes the distance between the city and the country—first and foremost, in the many departures and arrivals depicted in the film. We see Qiu Ju and Meizi, her younger sister-in-law and constant acolyte, moving upward through a nested series of central places of increasing size and sophistication that terminates in the urban splendor of Xi'an. The horizontal movement of travel through the Shaanxi countryside is also recoded as a progressive movement "upward" by the "ethnographic" depiction of the various modes of transport encountered on the journey: from foot travel to tractor-pulled carts to the long-distance bus. Qiu Ju finally arrives in the city, only to discover modes of transport such as the pedicab which may not be technologically as sophisticated as the city itself but which provide a service that must be paid for instead of being offered "for free" (as it often is in the countryside). Indeed, their fleecing by the urban pedicab driver is the first cultural trauma experienced by the two women in the city, women easily marked as ignorant peasants, "earth dumplings" (*tu baozi*) and ripe targets. The market towns and city places present a significant difference from the cultural landscape of the countryside. The camera loves to dwell on the surreal juxtapositions of commodified images for sale in the market town—traditional New Year's images jostle for attention with the seminude embraces of movie couples whose images travel internationally. Xi'an's city streets offer up a parade of commodified bodies and subjectivities—permed hair, hot pants, a young couple's tearful altercation—that stand in strong contrast to Qiu Ju's more "traditionally" inscribed body, whose padded clothing clearly marks her as alien to this more commodified world.

On Qiu Ju's arrival, the city of Xi'an, as the terminus of this movement upward, appears in the background as a smog-shrouded mirage of high-rises. The urban street scenes convey an almost palpable sense of anxiety and tension, heightened by the camerawork that uses a telescopic lens pushed to its limit, lending a jittery quality to the film and an extremely shallow depth of field that distorts the spatial relationship between objects so that they loom over each other in an almost hallucinatory way.[40] In one scene, Qiu Ju leaves Meizi waiting while she seeks out a public lavatory, only to find on her return that Meizi has wandered off. The soundtrack at that moment exhibits subtle changes as the camera closes in on Qiu Ju's anxious reaction, so that one experiences vicariously the thin whining aural sensation of a serious panic attack. Meizi returns, and Qiu Ju, in great relief, rebukes her, "You shouldn't wander off like that! Someone might grab you," giving voice to her fear of the city, in which young peasant women are vulnerable to being seized on as commodities.[41]

To a certain extent, the differently inscribed bodies of urban and rural women are juxtaposed on the body of Gong Li as the actress who plays Qiu Ju. As the principal actress in many of Zhang Yimou's earlier, more mythic, and sexually explicit films, Gong Li carries with her an aura of sophisticated glamour that is, presumably, alien to the figure of Qiu Ju. Despite her serious attempts to remodel her body through the liberal use of padded clothing and a swaybacked slouch simulating the physical carriage of pregnancy, the question arises as to whether she has been able to distance herself successfully from the already circulating images of her body that convey a significantly different "culture" of the body and the location of Gong Li's particular body in a metropolitan culture. The juxtaposition of Gong Li's body with that of Qiu Ju thus draws attention once more to the realization that the film is the projection of an elite desire to articulate a politics across an almost insurmountable divide. The question remains as to how this reinscription of Gong Li's body would be received by a rural audience. Would they be able to enter fully the fantasy space of the film, or would they view it as another condescension in the pedagogical interventions from "above"?[42]

The Transformative Magic of the Market

If we view *The Story of Qiu Ju* as an allegory about the emergence of individual agency in reform-era China, then surely we must recognize the presence of the marketplace as an enabling, but perhaps not sufficient, "cause." Qiu Ju paves her way up the hierarchy of the legal system through the sale of chili peppers, which she and her family have produced as a commodity for sale. Part of the comedy is the repeated motif of her setting off for yet a higher level of the legal system, accompanied by her young sister-in-law and a load of red chilies that underwrites each leg of her journey. Indeed, as suggested earlier, the chili peppers could be seen as a metaphor for Qiu Ju herself and her refusal to be backed into the "bland" and nonirritating position of the "obedient subject."

Her newfound economic mobility is also mirrored in her ability to buy "city clothes," which look odd especially when worn over her padded peasant clothing, an effect accentuated by the ungainliness of her pregnant body. Despite the comic effect of this masquerade, do we not also have a hint of a new ability being rapidly acquired to embody new subjectivities through the purchase of commodities obtained in the market economy? Although this act of "cross-dressing" may not be convincing at first, Qiu Ju appears to wear her disguise with increasing confidence every time she reaches for her new jacket to head off for town. In her transformation from ignorant peasant to savvy marketeer, we see the magic of the marketplace at work, a power that extends its magic by way of the new commodities that Qiu Ju brings back for her menfolk. In suggesting that the market is a place of magic and transformation, I do not mean to imply that this process is "liberatory" in all its dimensions but merely wish to point to a proliferation of possible subjectivities, some of which derive from a commodity economy but which may not be entirely divorced from the state and its exhortations for peasants to aspire to a "reasonable standard of living" (*xiao-kang shenghuo*). Do not these abilities to "refashion" oneself suggest new ways of being disciplined through consumer desire as well as having agency as an economic and political actor?

The role of the market is not limited to the frame of the film, however, but becomes an enabling factor in the film's being produced at all. Just as Qiu Ju had to go over the head of the village head and seek recognition of her grievance at a higher court of appeal, so did Zhang Yimou have to depend on foreign investors and his growing international acclaim first to make his film and then to ensure that it, along with his earlier films, could actually be shown to Chinese audiences.[43] If the market is an enabling factor not just in Zhang Yimou's overcoming political obstacles to make his film but also in his ability to "imagine" Qiu Ju's coming into a realization of her own agency, then what does this have to say about the current debates about China's political present and future? Do we just assume the liberal narrative of the power of the market to lead inevitably toward an increasing rationalization of political power, or do we concentrate instead on the multiple and uncertain discursive possibilities opened up by a coming together of forces, inherent in a moment when newly constituted subjects begin to flex their muscles?

If the market economy has unleashed forces that threaten the party's monopoly of political power, what might a new economy of power possibly look like? There is no clear answer in Zhang Yimou's film, yet the film goes beyond being merely an invitation to reflect passively on the arbitrary nature of power. It actively seeks to call into being a subjectivity that acts on those reflections. At the end of the film, Qiu Ju is faced with the realization that she has succeeded in her quest only too well. Having finally made her peace with the village head, she must now face once more the arbitrary working of power. One can only imagine her starting out on a new series of journeys, this time on behalf of her old enemy to seek his release from prison.

Lydia Liu's discussion of the discourse of individualism in May Fourth literary and philosophical debates shows the multiple articulations of what that category has been made to mean. Her purpose is not to decide which theoretical construction of the individual is most desirable for China or even which one is most "Chinese" but merely to examine carefully how the terms of the debate are set and the uses to which they are put. For, as she warns, such amnesia or forgetting of the discursive history of such powerful constructions threatens to enact a "return of the nightmare."[44] Her careful retrieval of this history actively deconstructs any attempt to identify the terms of the debate as belonging to the unproblematized abstractions of "China" and "the West." What then, does such scholarship enable? If scholarship is to constitute a truly political praxis, as Michael Taussig has suggested, must it not go beyond establishing the truism of the "constructed" nature of ideological categories? What if, instead of mere deconstruction, we were to direct our practice to nothing less than "more" construction? "What a sociology that would be!"[45] I am not sure that it is in my place to imagine some proleptic vision of a popular sovereignty "good for China." Nor do I wish to claim the possibilities opening out of the present transformations of Chinese society for any universalizing theoretical project. Rather, I would prefer to follow Liu's model of noting how the terms of debate are set and the uses to which they are put, while in sympathy with Taussig's argument for a politically engaged scholarship, I wish to note the possibilities opened up by new articulations of market forces that may not necessarily be unambiguously liberatory.[46]

In the analysis of the relations of power in the Chinese socialist state, the question should not be whether the present modality of power is somehow more "Chinese" but rather how the concentration of power in a myriad tiny centers somehow produces the effect of a single center. Who can dispute the unmistakable aura of power in the personage of a local party secretary? Multiply this "local emperor" (*tu huangdi*) or "red sun" (*hong taiyang*) several thousand times. Is this concentration of power in this personage not just as much a legacy of the campaign mentality of a party organization tempered under the conditions of guerrilla warfare? The party, having taken power, continued to face the guerrilla conditions of rapid economic development during the Maoist era and beyond, requiring a tactics heavily dependent on popular mobilizations and plays "against time."[47] The relative autonomy for a thousand tiny centers to deliver results up the hierarchy of command is just as much a legacy of how the modern Chinese state, under conditions of imperialism and cold war politics, took a form that was in some respects overdetermined for it rather than deriving entirely from some long-standing and immutable Chinese conception of the social order.

A refusal to link the appearance of village compacts to some essentialized model of Chinese culture and its overreliance on renzhi is in a sense to take a position within the culture debates of the 1980s. Jing Wang notes how the controversial television documentary series *Heshang* criticized the Chinese predisposition to look toward the past as a "repository . . . of society's ideal form" and argued for a wholesale rejection of many aspects of Chinese "tradition," its overcentralization of power, insularity, and submissiveness to authority.[48] *Heshang*'s critique is, in a sense, just as essentializing as the discourse of Confucian revival that, in the wake of the abrupt economic takeoff of the 1990s, may yet add strength to a post hoc argument for a "Confucian capitalism" that has a magical affinity with the capital logic of the late twentieth century—for instance, the often-noted characteristic of post-Fordist capital to seek out familist and mafia-type labor organizations.[49] As Jing Wang states, "The official project of the Confucian revival is thus potentially dangerous in that it operates in the mode of the 'metaphorical identification' of the subject with the state, of the private with the public spheres, of morality with loyalty, and of past with present."[50] This dangerous identification between subject and state raises the issue of how, in the rapidly overheating economy of the 1990s, a popular sovereignty should be constituted.

It remains to be seen whether the "villagers' committees" and other democratic reforms remain signs of an imaginary discourse or whether they provide the means to perform into being a new kind of political agency that exceeds the pedagogical intentions of the center by asking questions, by speaking back to power, and in so doing whether they step out of the recursive cycle of the state's inscription to engage in a genuine dialogue. As a new articulatory practice, Zhang Yimou's film is perhaps a start, but it is no guarantee, nor should we underestimate the ability of such practices to be reabsorbed by the very power they seek to question.

7 THE NATIONSCAPE

On a day trip to Shenzhen, the showplace of China's economic reforms, one need not forgo an encounter with five thousand years of Chinese history. On the contrary, in the midst of gleaming high-rises, broad boulevards, and industrial parks, one can gaze, almost with a single glance, at a comprehensive array of China's most famous tourist sites—all replicated in miniature. On over thirty hectares overlooking Shenzhen Bay, a magnificent theme park named Splendid China (Jinxiu Zhonghua) offers an expansive display of China's national landmarks representing its long cultural history, its natural landscape, its ethnic diversity—all within a highly compressed space.[1]

Susan Stewart suggests that in the social space of the miniature its diminutiveness does not correspond to a "reduction of significance" but is rather emblematic, a container well suited to "aphoristic and didactic thought."[2] She is writing of the exploration of miniature worlds in literature that rests on devices establishing a referential field, "a field where signs are displayed in relation to one another and in relation to concrete objects in the sensual world."[3] Indeed, we see these devices replicated in photo displays of these miniature landscapes, where we see the image being viewed by giants or, caught in the process of production, the artisan at work on the "finishing touches" that complete an object already phenomenal in its detail. In a magazine photograph of a mimic miniature display in Teng County, Shandong, the body of the artisan juxtaposed with the product of her handiwork creates a sense of wonder by causing the object to point outside itself, toward the scale of the human body (Figure 2).[4] The photo's extremely shallow depth of field in which the artisan's face is rendered out of focus intensifies the difference in scale. This reference to the human body works in tandem with other photographs that edit out any betrayal of the image as miniature. The object is displayed as if its diminished scale derived solely from the photographic frame itself and the object were

Figure 2.   Artisan at work. (*Liaowang zhoukan*, October 26, 1992, no. 43, color insert)

nothing less than the essential image of what it represents. In another photograph from the same source, this time of a miniature Potala Palace, the object appears to rise from the shadows against a neutral background, heightening its hallucinatory quality as the essence of the original, an effect, however, that depends on our knowing it is a miniature (Figure 3).

How should we be reading these miniature landscapes? At one level they speak the totality of the nation in time and space; they offer to the viewer a surreal simultaneity of the architectural monuments of Chinese civilization over five millennia—a compression of time that matches its reduction in physical size, redoubling the intensity of its ideological effect. The miniature offers a transcendental perspective akin to what Benedict Anderson calls the "bird's-eye view" of modern mapmaking. However, whereas he notes the importance of boundaries in modern maps as demarcations of an "exclusive sovereignty wedged between other sovereignties" that become fixed in the process of colonial expansion, Splendid China does not pretend to this cartographic convention.[5] Its boundary serves to demarcate the space of representation, within which the nation can be rendered as a total concept, a timeless essence, as something not determined by what it excludes or what it abuts up to and against. The boundary of the model becomes in this sense inwardly referential, detached from what lies outside itself,

Figure 3.   The Potala Palace. (*Liaowang zhoukan*, October 26, 1992, no. 43, color insert)

timeless because it assumes the eternal verity of the idea of "China" as a bounded entity. This boundedness offers the conditions of a "total surveyability," a "historical depth of field" imaginable only retrospectively, positioning the economic miracle of Shenzhen as the most recent element in a historical series emerging out of the mists of the past.[6] "At the centre, the nation narrates itself as *the* nation," uncomplicated by the difference instituted at its margins.[7] Note, therefore, the unproblematic inclusion of the characteristic housing styles and landscapes of a number of "national minority" peoples, not excluding the Potala, the "type site" of Tibetan Buddhism.[8] Indeed, the incorporation of tiny figurines of monks and other worshipers in front of Shenzhen's miniature Potala does not negate the secularized aspect of the nation-state but embellishes the representation of it as tolerant of religious expression, of its diversity within. A powerfully divisive force is hereby domesticated and rendered purely as display.[9]

Splendid China lies within a referential field larger than the one immediately within the boundaries of the park, for well within the orbit of the viewer's gaze, one observes the nearby profile of a modern city. Therefore, how do we place this park as a working site of signification within the total context of Shenzhen, which in many ways represents its antithesis or transcendence? Within this larger frame, we must note the tension between one space of representation and another. The miniature landscape compresses five thousand years of history into a tiny space, but it does so enclosed within the larger space of Shenzhen, a place whose history as an event spans only a decade. The whole of the nation in space and time is therefore contained within the part. But Shenzhen is no ordinary fragment of that larger whole; it is both interior and exterior to the nation-space. Its status as a "special economic zone" gives it this hybrid character both in terms of its integration with global capital and as a potent sign, as one of a heteroglossia of models in a sustained debate over China's proper road to modernization.[10] Indeed it was Deng Xiaoping's (also known as "the Whirl-wind") "southern progress" (*nanxun*) to Shenzhen in spring 1992 that set in motion a reaffirmation of enterprise capitalism that led to the startling 14 percent growth in China's national economy in 1993.[11] Shenzhen is itself no less a space of representation, so that the "shell," which sets apart this miniature landscape from what surrounds it, is not a point at which representation ends but points to where one representation becomes enclosed or embedded within another. Might this juxtaposition express a "split" in post-Mao constructions of the nation? Is the "contained" thereby represented as the "germ" or the imma-nent "spirit" of that which contains it? Might this layering of representations express the ambivalent temporality of the nation-state as being always caught "between" its simultaneous desire for being deeply historical and yet undeni-ably modern?[12]

As noted previously, both these desires are indelibly inscribed in the word *wenming*, meaning "civilization" or "civility," which is used to refer both to China's glorious past and to its dreamed-of future. *Zhongguo wenming* refers retrospectively to "Chinese civilization" and to its historical role as center to a wider cultural sphere, whereas *wenming* by itself can mean that which is subject to an assumed universal standard in the acquisition of modern regimes of order and industrial discipline. Wenming encapsulates what has been called the "Janus-facedness" of the national imaginary, looking toward the past to face the future; it marks simultaneously a place of plenitude and of lack.[13] But how do we situate the appearance of Splendid China at this particular moment, a moment that brings to completion a long-running debate about Chinese cul-ture and its relation to modernity, a debate which expressed considerable anx-iety about the adaptability of Chinese culture to modern modes of disciplinary power? Perhaps we can best read how Splendid China resolves this anxiety by noting carefully its absences, what it fails to include.

Splendid China reaches back into deep antiquity in its mapping of the nation-space, betraying a curious blindness in its exclusion of the sites of a revolution-ary tradition that once represented itself as a "rupture" in history. Nowhere in this model do we see Mao's birthplace, the mountains of Jingganshan, or the post-Liberation monuments of socialist construction. Indeed, with the one possible exception of Sun Yatsen's mausoleum, China's past is represented in the absence of any sites that speak of its modern history, which is in fact the history in China of the national idea itself![14] The absence of this history illustrates Geoffrey Bennington's aphoristic observation, "At the origin of the nation, we find a story of the nation's origin."[15] It is as if Shenzhen itself has become the new signifier of revolutionary rupture in the dramatic upheaval of enterprise capitalism. Shenzhen, hurtling toward the telos of modernity, *is* the present "time" of the nation, but one that all the more requires the calming certainty of a timeless identity residing within.[16] The embarrassment of Maoism, as an irrational derangement of China's "natural" course of development, is therefore secreted from view, only to return in manifestations that can best be described as "uncanny."

But it is perhaps emblematic that this reassuring image was constructed in Shenzhen, a place that contests the unquestioned totality of the nation. In the fitful starts and stops of the economic reforms, its booms and busts, its reterritorialization of the country along the contours of a radically uneven development, Shenzhen marks both the hope of a national future and a serious threat to the authority of the center and its ability to hold the nation together. Within the bounds of the model, we see the Forbidden City, and by extension, Zhongnanhai, still the seat of national political power, diminished in size and magically transported into the heart of the new order. My reading here is motivated by the often overt confrontation between Guangdong and Beijing, in which the former has been newly empowered by its economic linkages to the outside to assert its independence from central control.[17]

Splendid China reassures the viewer that the model, in its exquisite detail, is in fact an accurate copy of an original existing somewhere in a pure reality.[18] It holds time in suspension, essentializing the meaning of deep antiquity in its very stillness, a stillness that belies the economic upheaval going on "outside," affirming the nation as an eternal unity, made of an essence that does not change, that allows it to cohere together. Splendid China does not, in this sense, narrate the nation—it tells no story; it does not move in time so much as offer up the nation to the viewer as a self-evident object of contemplation. The miniature scale of the model is what gives it its object-nature, lending to it a sense of distance, as if viewed from a long way off, a distance essential to the "objective" gaze of the viewer, that curious "combination of detachment and close attentiveness."[19] In this sense, then, its diminutiveness installs a similar effect to the glass panes that separate viewers from commodities on display, "endowing goods with the distance that is the source of their objectness."[20] The

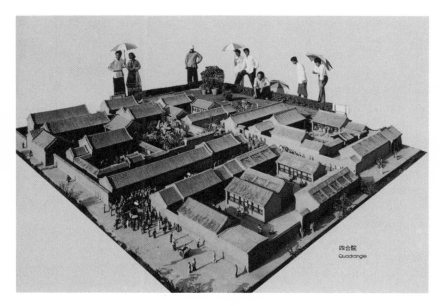

Figure 4.   From the guidebook to Splendid China. (*Jinxiu Zhonghua*, p. 53)

mode of display that reveals while it veils and withholds is one that manufactures desire.[21] This effect of distance is not dissipated, even when the boundary between viewer and object is violated in a photograph in which one of the onlookers has left the pedestrian path and is squatting within the space of the miniature (Figure 4). Indeed, the contrast in scale intensifies the effect of distance in its sheer proximity.

But Splendid China is only one of a number of material representations that suggest how the nationscape is imagined.[22] This chapter is conceptualized as successive readings of a series of material productions that, beginning in the late 1980s, convey how this desire and ambivalence for a national past are becoming displaced onto commodified forms along with the expansion of a market economy in China. China's "old towns," for instance, fulfill these conditions admirably, composing in their multiplicity a set of variations on a theme, reconstructing the antiquity of the nation in the very process of its commodification. They are at once a re-creation of the "color and flavor" (*guse guxiang*) of the past *and* a marketplace, enclosed within a modern urban space. As such, they represent a shift in focus from the totality of the nation to the deep continuity of a particular place. Old towns have proliferated with bewildering speed in the last half-dozen years. They are something of a marketing phenomenon, one that cannot be fully explained in terms of satisfying the demands of international tourism for an authentic China rendered up for consumption. They are produced, equally, if not more so, for domestic consumption and contemplation. I want to explore the tension between the inside and the outside of these spaces of representation while also noting carefully the tension between what lies inside and outside the circuit of commodity exchange with which these spaces of representation are so tightly bound. What sorts of nationscapes lie outside the commodity form, and how do practices of the nation inhabit hidden spaces in the interstices of everyday life recalling to memory a very different "time" of the nation?

The Old Town

What I am calling an "old town" (*fanggujie*) is the recent practice of reconstructing a street or an entire neighborhood to re-create the aspect of an earlier time.[23] The term in Chinese, unlike the English translation of "old town," is more explicit in its practice as representation. The Chinese *fanggu* means literally to "emulate" or "copy" the antique. Throughout the last decade this mode of tourist development has taken on the momentum of a major trend in local efforts to promote the expansion of a commodity economy. My focus here is on one rather extensive project of this kind, the Fuzimiao market area in the city of Nanjing. This site has a long history, especially in its associations with the literary and market cultures of the late imperial period.

The name "Fuzimiao" refers to a Confucian temple that was once located there. Nearby were the provincial examination halls where literati competed to attain imperial degrees. The area was also famous for its restaurants, brothels, and other leisure sites in a complex mix of literary culture with the demimonde. In the mid-1980s, Nanjing City embarked on a major project to restore the historical value of the area and rebuild it as a tourist site. While preserving the few structures that actually date from the late imperial period, builders razed large areas and replaced them with a vernacular architecture of white stucco walls and black-tiled roofs, in a style evoking the picturesque aspect of Jiangnan cities. This retrieval of a vernacular architecture parallels the popularity of a "rural" (*xiangtu*) painting genre that depicts a Jiangnan landscape undisturbed by the rapid transformation from agricultural to industrial production during the reform era. The reconstructed buildings of Fuzimiao primarily house shops and restaurants, whereas the streets of the quarter are filled with the semi-permanent booths of a bustling street market.

The "old town" and the miniature landscape described above enact very different practices of interiority. The miniature is doubly enclosed—not just by the defined boundaries that mark its limit but also by the contrast in scale that the miniature excites at its very horizon, trapping the observer "outside the possibility of a lived reality" that can be imagined only within its tiny spaces.[24] In contrast, the old town provides a context that must be inhabited, unfolding in time as one moves through it. Its horizon is discovered reluctantly, by a reverse form of trial and error, through sudden encounters with jarring reminders of the modern city which encloses it—a motorway, a line of unadorned apartment blocks—and which alert one to the imminent danger averted simply by turning back into the enveloping confines of a dream landscape. Yet, despite this sense of enclosure, the modern city does intrude in the unchecked flow of people across an invisible membrane that holds in tension the difference between this fictive world and the one outside.

There are many itineraries that flow through the quarter; Nanjing people busy with their everyday routine or intent on a major shopping trip will patronize the shops found here. Trousseau items are purchased here, the "soft goods" required by the bride's family for marital exchanges—the quilts, bedding, and wardrobe of the new bride—drawing peasant families in a celebratory mood from a wide area. Along with this flow of everyday visitors, there are families with out-of-town visitors brought to see the "sights" of the city, poorer cousins from Subei, or wealthy relatives from Taiwan.[25] International tourists arrive in buses that disembark outside certain shops that cater especially to them; the higher prices and demand for foreign exchange of these shops mark their interiors as extraterritorial space. Chinese tourist groups also visit in large numbers, drawn to the splendid re-creation of the temple precincts now a center for recreation, dance halls, *kala-OK* (karaoke bars), and other amusements.

The groups of local tourists do not follow an aimless trajectory through the quarter (as might an independent foreign tourist in search of local "color") but a very specific itinerary, heavily inscribed with meanings not immediately obvious to a foreign visitor but powerful enough to arrest one's movement and obligate the taking of a photograph. The focal point of these photographs is the subject herself or himself, or a group shot, posing front and center, with the site serving as a backdrop, taken either by a fellow traveler or by a professional photographer whose tiny booth on-site lays claim to the custom of the photo "op" for that spot. The most famous of these is without question the Wende Bridge spanning the Qinhuai River, where pleasure boats and courtesans ply the waters once again, re-creating a scene described in the Qing dynasty drama *Taohuashan* (The peach blossom fan). The re-creation of this riverside tableau has been accomplished at great expense, entailing no less than a major cleanup for the Qinhuai River, badly polluted by industrial wastes upstream (Figure 5).

Figure 5.   The view from the Wende Bridge. (*China Pictorial*, November 1991)

The photo "op," which is always conventionally selected, is easily recognized by the line of people waiting their turn to pose and be photographed. The location promises a carefully selected frame for the camera into which the modern city does not intrude or does so only minimally so that a motivated gaze can easily edit out what it does not wish to see. The view from the Wende Bridge has as its far background the rooflines of a residential neighborhood that borders onto the south bank of the river. The walls immediately fronting the river have been whitewashed and rebuilt in keeping with the Ming dynasty aspect of the old town area. Behind these lies a maze of "alleys" winding through housing that dates from the late Qing period. This neighborhood is noted for its antique color and flavor, and the old town renovation is slowly expanding to incorporate the area immediately south of the river. Closer at hand, however, the noticeable absence of indoor plumbing is what invariably gets commented on while traveling the winding streets that lead out from this side of Fuzimiao proper. There are, apparently, two sides to the "antique" as a sensory experience.

While Fuzimiao is unequivocally a working commercial area—the stucco buildings open into quite ordinary modern shop interiors—it is a place of excursion, what Susan Stewart describes as a movement "from the zone of production to the zone of consumption . . . from work to play, from utility to aesthetics, from ends to means," a holiday from labor marked as such by its "superfluity of signification. . . . Understanding is sacrificed to being in context . . . a material allusion to a text which is no longer available to us, or which, because of its fictiveness, never was available to us except through a second-order fictive world."[26] However, this juxtaposition of a nostalgia for a historical past with the commodity is not accidental: the desire for one excites the desire for the other.

One goes to Fuzimiao to be enclosed by its atmosphere; one actively participates by buying something. The items for sale range from the practical to the surreal fetishism of kitsch. Vendors ply all manner of small items, sewing notions, the minutiae of everyday life, often in carts with tubs full of tiny objects, snaps and zippers, miniature folding shears, hardware, and plastic items in an assortment organized by a logic alien to a merchandising rationality. But Fuzimiao also caters to a nostalgia that is special to it, a revived urban cult of the rustic, with a section reserved for the sale of caged songbirds along with all the objects necessary for their care, goldfish in a bewildering array of special breeds, and the full complement of tiny items for cultivating miniature landscapes. The concentration of "handicraft items" (*gongyi pin*) in the shops demarcates this particular area as a place of excursion, as a place devoted to a love of looking as leisurely pastime. Of minimal "practical" value, these items are strictly for display, their value measured in terms of whether they are "good for play" (*haowan*). Despite their being referred to as handicraft objects, gongyi pin are frequently mass-produced with some hand labor in finishing. Most of this class of objects in the Fuzimiao market are produced in the rural areas of the Jiangnan, frequently for export, the seconds or overstock appearing in local markets such as this. This accounts for the heavy representation of "Christmas ornaments" intended for the international market. Their localized character as products "distinctive to the place" (*techan*) therefore has as much to do with global capital flows as it does with local "tradition."

People go to the Fuzimiao market as much out of a love of looking at these frothy commodities as out of desire to be immersed in the atmosphere of the place. It is easily the largest and most colorful of any market in Nanjing, as much a spectacle as it is a place of consumption and production, the heady reclamation of something "lost" during the austere years of Maoism.

The Collection

An excursion to Fuzimiao or other holiday sites is not completed merely by moving through the space it offers—it must also be collected. The photograph is the most obvious means of doing so, a practice that arrests one's movement at specific places that offer as background the distinctive features that announce the site. The purchase of a souvenir must also be ideally a small handicraft or natural object strongly associated with the locale. In addition to *gongyi pin*, the obvious choice in Nanjing is *yuhuashi*, small, colorful agates found on the slopes of the revolutionary martyrs' shrine outside the south gate of the old city wall, formerly the Guomindang execution grounds during the 1930s. Street peddlers hawk small assortments of these stones at every corner. An exhibition of these is housed in the renovated Confucian temple in the heart of the market.

However, the collection is not necessarily limited to the circuit of the commodity, or it may select objects that lie on the very border between what is a commodity and what is not. The ticket stub (*menpiao*) qualifies very well for this ambiguous status. The ticket stub is the ubiquitous residue of the imposed conditions for entering the enclosed spaces of representation. One buys a ticket at a window and delivers it a few feet away to the gatekeeper, who then returns half of it back to the bearer. The site is therefore "collected" before one actually enters the door. The extremely brief duration of its "functional" life marks the ticket stub as ephemera; it is in its "afterlife" that this object acquires its added weight of signification as the metonymic marker of a place. Fuzimiao itself does not require a ticket for admission: it is designed for urban life to flow through it. But there are many enclosed spaces within that larger whole that require one to enact this ritual of crossing a boundary, of stepping over a raised threshold that announces the special character of the space within, a sense of moving inward governed by rules of access.

The collectomania (*shoucangre*) that has swept China in the last decade is not necessarily a new phenomenon, but it would perhaps be exemplary to track how these practices are changing as China enters into an expanding circuit of commodity exchange. The objects that are marked as "collectible" in any society may well provide an interesting parallel or counterdiscourse on the social life of things. In China, as elsewhere, collectibles are often the detritus of the commodity form—such as empty cigarette packets—things that have no market value except in the special zone of desire marked by this curious "enthusiasm," a word that to be properly understood in this context must be taken back to the root of its meaning, the state of "being possessed" by the desire to possess what apparently has no value except, perhaps, to remember the excitement of something already consumed.

Walking through a public park in Kunshan City, I encountered one of these enthusiasts, who had mounted, at his own expense, an elaborate exhibition of his ticket stubs, all framed under glass, classified in groups according to the kind of site collected—temples, museums, parks, gardens—but also arranged in a temporal order that traced a history visually moving from the crude printing and rough paper of the Maoist era to the sophisticated graphics and glossy paper of the present. The ticket stub collects a place not only through the magic of the name of the site printed there but also by means of its miniaturized image graphically reproduced on it. Once again, the miniature condenses a much larger weight of signification, but its value as a collection is enhanced by its nostalgic inclusion of the Mao years, with its selection of sites mapping out a rather different itinerary to symbolize the nation-space. What comes to mind here are the epic journeys made by young Red Guards during the Cultural Revolution for the purpose of "exchanging revolutionary experiences" (*chuan-lian*), a phenomenon which took on a life of its own as a symbolic accumulation of revolutionary sites that metonymically stood for the nation but which also ritually embellished one's identity as a revolutionary successor (*geming houdai*). The ways in which these souvenirs, such as Mao buttons, ticket stubs, and so on, incorporated the site into one's identity to become a form of talismanic protection against political misfortune anticipated the refetishization of these objects in the 1990s. The collection amassed and displayed in this fashion offers yet another miniature nationscape, one that doubly marks a boundary between what lies inside and outside the circuit of the commodity, as well as marking the many crossings into the defined spaces of representation and outward again. It marks a tremulous space lying between social memory and the ability of the market to mobilize nostalgia as a commodity for sale.

The Internal Object

If the nationscape described in the beginning of this chapter suggests a concentrated virtual space of representation in the larger space of Shenzhen, it is indisputably a miniature within its larger frame. However, there is a sense in which it is also "monumental" as public spectacle, the viewing of which is a commodity available for purchase. This monumentality is perhaps most apparent when compared with another kind of miniature that takes its form in the documentation of personal memory.

A friend's diary from her youth during the Cultural Revolution reveals a series of miniature drawings rendered with pen and ink, so tiny that one must look very carefully to capture the exquisite detail of Mao's portrait, the Great Hall of the People, the pagoda at Yan'an. Every drawing is a painstaking recreation of conventional icons similar to those still used in the graphic design of official newspapers, such as the *People's Daily.* Technically designated in English as the "standing sig," these images are meant to work indexically, pointing the reader toward content of a specific kind. Throughout the Maoist period and

Figure 6.   "Standing sigs." (*Zhongguo gongren*, August 1959, p. 11, and *Fazhi ribao*, circa 1991)

beyond, what these images all point toward is the nation and by extension to the prescribed role of the media in the production of a national culture (Figure 6).[27]

My friend explains, as she displays this cherished object, that during the time she kept this diary there was nothing but time—an infinity of time that could be extravagantly expended in the solitary reverie of drawing the national icons so that they matched perfectly the finely etched lines of the engraver's plate. But the "look" of these miniature nationscapes is quite different from one that could be assembled with the repertoire of images used today. Their stylistic conventions evoke the socialist realist aesthetic of the Cultural Revolution and its totalitarian fantasies of massive national mobilizations, awakening memories of being caught in the grip of something that totally absorbed the self into the project of national purpose. These images that occupy a small notebook, wrapped in cloth, kept in a drawer in my friend's cramped apartment, suggest multiple layers of interiority, a space within a space, the most apt analogy for which Stewart suggests is "the locket or the secret recesses of the heart: center within center, within within within."[28] Yet when we penetrate the many layers in which these artifacts are secreted, we find not the essential private truth of the self but something so "public" as the nation.

I do not intend to suggest a point of difference here. Rather, I wish to destabilize any essentializing construction of the "individual" as what Caren Kaplan has critiqued as the "enclosed space of the modern ego, exiled by the world."[29] Indeed, as Lydia Liu has suggested, the Western notion of the individual is embedded within constructions of nation, state, and society. She quotes Anthony Cascardi: "The culture of modernity is given shape as a divided whole that can only be unified through the powers of an abstract subject or its political analog, the autonomous State."[30] This puts rather an interesting twist on May Fourth discussions of how the "interiority" of the subject was something lacking in Chinese constructions of the self, perhaps expressing the desperate search for that stable center around which the fragmenting modern subjectivity could organize itself, the "truth" that makes one whole. In this spirit, Benedict Anderson's point about how the "real power of the state" becomes revealed in the "infinite quotidian reproducibility of its regalia" takes on added significance when envisioned as moving beyond the scope of mass media into the innermost recesses of the self.[31] In the present economic upheaval, does not this contemplative act of my friend in search of her prior self betray a nostalgia for a wholeness no longer felt, indeed, rendered impossible by the fragmentation and dispersal that exceeds all state efforts to harness national subjects for its own ends? Dare I even begin to explore how her nostalgia intersects strangely with my own? My own emotion is perhaps best caught by Tom Nairn's hopeful suggestion, made in 1977, that the flight of socialism to the "Third World" as a therapy for uneven development meant, ironically, that "capitalism could not, finally, unify the world in its own image."[32] Is this why I am so motivated to "read" her diary as a space beyond commodification, when I know that nothing, really, is by nature exempt from its reach?

The motions of her hands in retrieving this object betray an act often repeated; the pages of the diary, tired from frequent handling, suggest their endlessly consumed "use value" as the means to contemplate a prior self, now perhaps graspable only through the mediation of this object. In the present commodification of everything, the guilty mementos of the Mao cult—the buttons bearing his likeness on the body and the miniature red books that conveyed his words into the intimate recesses of daily life—have acquired a market value as collectibles. Once gathered in symbolic itineraries that traversed a national landscape marked by a revolutionary history that had, apparently, irrevocably ruptured the past, these objects had once moved as a form of "protocommodity" in a circuit of symbolic exchanges.[33] How uncanny is this return of Mao—now dehistoricized, transformed into fetish both as commodity and as magical charm. The likeness of his corpse lying in state in his glass-enclosed sarcophagus has been discovered in a mountain range in Xinjiang now renamed in his honor. This discovery reverses the transformation of national sites into images that circulate. Mao Zedong Mountain is where the circulation of images comes to rest in a site that must be traveled to. It is, therefore, a gigantic analog of what Splendid China does in miniature. In the most contested periphery of the national space, we see Mao's figure expanding exponentially in inverse relation to his diminishing physical remains moldering in his Beijing mausoleum. He has become transubstantiated as a geographical feature of the national landscape in hopes of luring tourist dollars, in the process kicking off yet another round of images that circulate.[34]

In contrast, the status of the diary as an internal object is all the more marked by its remaining, for the present, "outside" commodification. Its replication by hand of a process of mechanical reproduction conveys a very particular kind of aura, one that condenses the immensity of the nation-space as it was individually experienced within a very different "time" of the nation. This moment captures evocatively Homi Bhabha's insistence on temporality as a way of breaking up the solidity of the nation as a coherent subject moving through history: "The focus on temporality resists the transparent linear equivalence of event and idea that historicism proposes; it provides a perspective on the disjunctive forms of representation that signify a people, a nation, or a national culture."[35]

This "temporality" is what underlies the "aura" of the diary as the embodiment of one's lived relation to the nation in a moment that is now relegated to the past, to the place of memory. The subject's access to this prior self is "by way of" this object rendered in her own hand. The process of reproduction here inverts Walter Benjamin's notion of what is lacking in the auratic quality of the mechanically reproduced work of art, namely, "its presence in time and space, its unique existence at the place where it happens to be."[36] The subtle differences that mark the reproduced image "in her own hand" from the mechanically reproduced "original" evoke the very act of drawing an image already solidified as a national icon. This connection between icon and the intense labor of internalizing its image by way of "one's own hand" is what ties the subject to the image as if "in the presence" of a prior self in another time and place.

Now a rising star in the academic establishment, my friend is caught up in the struggle to make even philosophy profitable, "responsible for its own profits and losses." What was once an "escape" from nonlabor into labor now offers an excursion in quite the opposite direction!

NOTES

Unless otherwise noted, all translations are mine.

1 The Chinese term *wenhua re* can be alternatively translated as "culture craze" or "culture fever." For a discussion of the 1980s "culture craze," see Richard Bodman, "From History to Allegory to Art: A Personal Search for Interpretation," in *Death-song of the River: A Reader's Guide to the Chinese TV Series, "Heshang"*, ed. Richard Bodman and Pin P. Wan (Ithaca: Cornell University Press, 1991), pp. 1–61.

2 For examples of extended discussions on this discourse of generations, see Yang Fan, *Gongheguo disandai* [The third generation of the People's Republic of China], in *Kuashiji congshu* [Across the century series] (Chengdu: Sichuan renmin chu-banshe, 1991), and also Zhang Yongjie and Cheng Yuanzhong, *Disidairen* [The fourth generation] (Hong Kong: Zhonghua shuju, 1989). See, for example, Wang Luxiang's characterization of the first four generations, cited in Bodman and Wan, *Deathsong*, pp. 74–75. One newspaper commentary that I read in an obscure newsletter for propaganda workers called *Jingshen wenming bao* [the *Spiritual civilization gazette*] (Sichuan, n.d.) contrasted an elderly grandmother with her son and his wife, all of whom went shopping for shoes. The grandmother searched exhaustively for the best value with the least expenditure, while her grandchild is taken by the parents for an equally exhaustive search for a prestige brand of shoes costing many times more. The values of frugality and a certain imperviousness to the lure of the commodity reside in an older generation, tempered by the experi-ence of extreme privation and an ideology of national autonomy. These values can no longer be reproduced in the next generation, who have a vastly different rela-tionship to the commodity form, suggesting simultaneously the triumphant affir-mation of putting privation behind while lamenting the passing of the "socialist" values of frugality and self-sacrifice.

3 See, for example, Etienne Balibar, "The Nation Form: History and Ideology," in Etienne Balibar and Immanuel Wallerstein, *Race, Nation, Class: Ambiguous Identi-ties* (London: Verso, 1991), pp. 86–106, and Homi K. Bhabha, ed., *Nation and Narration* (London: Routledge, 1990).

4   For the tension between the universal and particular aspects of the modern national form, see Partha Chatterjee, *Nationalist Thought and the Colonial World: A Derivative Discourse* (Tokyo: Zed, 1986), and Naoki Sakai, "Modernity and Its Critique: The Problem of Universalism and Particularism," *South Atlantic Quarterly* (1988): 93–122.

5   Chatterjee, *Nationalist Thought*, p. 50. Benedict Anderson, in his seminal *Imagined Communities: Reflections on the Origin and Spread of Nationalism* (2d ed.) (London: Verso, 1991), suggests the spread of nationalist models as the necessary stimulus for the imagining of national communities in Europe and elsewhere.

6   See Timothy Mitchell, *Colonizing Egypt* (Berkeley: University of California Press, 1988), pp. 109–110, for a mention of how Japan's military successes were interpreted in Egypt as deriving from their superior capability of modernizing without losing a sense of national identity.

7   See Homi K. Bhabha, "DissemiNation: Time, Narrative, and the Margins of the Modern Nation," in *Nation and Narration*, ed. Bhabha, pp. 291–322.

8   For a discussion of how this notion of "national subject" was integral to the construction of Chinese intellectuals during the May Fourth period, see Tani Barlow, "*Zhishifenzi* [Chinese Intellectuals] and Power," *Dialectical Anthropology* 16 (1991): 214. For a discussion of how the question, Who speaks for the nation? was debated among viewers of a popular television series, see Lisa Rofel, "*Yearnings*: Televisual Love and Melodramatic Politics in Contemporary China," *American Ethnologist* 21, 4 (1994): 700–722.

9   Michel Foucault, "Nietzsche, Genealogy, History," in *Language, Counter-Memory, Practice: Selected Essays and Interviews*, ed. Donald F. Bouchard (Ithaca: Cornell University Press, 1977), p. 140. Foucault reminds us at the outset of this essay that "the world of speech and desires has known invasions, struggles, plundering, disguises, ploys" (p. 138)—everything, in short, that disrupts the attempt to construct a coherent narrative of evolutionary unfolding in human cultural history.

10 Chatterjee, *Nationalist Thought*, pp. 50–52. One must also note the pessimism of this perspective, which assumes the universal triumph of capitalism, although Chatterjee's emphasis on contingency suggests the possibility of unpredictable arenas of contestation.

11 David Harvey is perhaps the most influential theorist of post-Fordist capital. See David Harvey, *The Condition of Postmodernity* (London: Blackwell, 1989).

12 Alongside this narrative, of course, is another running parallel to it in which Chinese "culture" is renarrativized from being an impediment to the development of capitalism to become an uncannily perfect "match" for the dynamic of post-Fordist capital, with its emphasis on flexible labor pools organized in small-scale, "mafia-like" or "familist" enterprises. What better describes the stunning takeoff of the township and village enterprises that have fueled a good part of China's economic growth beginning in the mid-1980s?

13 See Claude Lefort, *The Political Forms of Modern Society: Bureaucracy, Democracy, Totalitarianism* (Cambridge: MIT Press, 1986), p. 205.

14 See Jing Wang, "Romancing the Subject: Utopian Moments in the Chinese Aesthetics of the 1980s," *Discourse social/Social Discourse* [Special issue, "The Non-Cartesian Subjects East and West"] 6, 1–2 (Winter/Spring 1994): 115–142, for a fascinating critique of how this desire for cultural subjectivity played out in the cultural politics of the 1980s.

15 Marston Anderson, *The Limits of Realism: Chinese Fiction in the Revolutionary Period* (Berkeley: University of California Press, 1990).

16 In recent years, the use of prolepsis is most striking in the scholarly search for a civil society that hopes to anticipate its actual emergence in a liberated economic sphere. The most explicit statement of such a project is Mayfair Hei-hui Yang, *Gifts, Favors, and Banquets: The Art of Social Relationships in China* (Berkeley: University of California Press, 1994), p. 288.

17 See Yuan-tsung Chen, *The Dragon's Village: An Autobiographical Novel of Revolutionary China* (New York: Penguin, 1981), for a riveting account of a group of writers and artists who joined the land reform. In her narrative, "the wheels of history" was a repeating figure (for instance, pp. 149 and 165).

18 Lu Xun himself was elevated as a revolutionary icon, so that the critical edge of his radical doubt was effaced. For a discussion of how the film was used as recently as 1981 as a vehicle for reproducing party hegemony, see Ann Anagnost, "The Transformation of Gender in Modern China," in *Gender and Anthropology: Critical Reviews for Research and Teaching*, ed. Sandra Morgan (Amherst: Project on Gender and the Curriculum sponsored by the American Anthropological Association, 1989), p. 313.

19 See Mao Tsetung, "Report on an Investigation of the Peasant Movement in Hunan," in *Selected Readings from the Works of Mao Tsetung* (Peking: Foreign Languages Press, 1971), p. 27.

20 See Bhabha, "DissemiNation," p. 297, for a discussion of this distinction between the pedagogical and the performative in the discourse of nationalism.

21 Myron Cohen, "Cultural and Political Conventions in Modern China: The Case of the Chinese Peasant," in *China in Transformation*, ed. Weiming Tu (Cambridge: Harvard University Press, 1994), 151–170.

22 Prasenjit Duara, *Rescuing History from the Nation: Questioning the Narratives of Modern China* (Chicago: University of Chicago Press, 1995), p. 32.

23 Ibid.

24 Jacques Derrida, *Of Grammatology* (Baltimore: Johns Hopkins University Press, 1976), p. 155. For a more extended discussion of how this discursive maneuver manifests itself in historiographic discussions of the "origins" of the village compact, see Ann Anagnost, "Constructing the Civilized Community," in *Culture and State in Chinese History: Conventions, Conflicts, and Accommodations*, ed. R. Bin Wong, Theodore Huters, and Pauline Yu (Stanford: Stanford University Press, in press).

1   *Making History Speak*

1   Lu Xun, "Literature of a Revolutionary Period," in *Selected Works*, trans. Yang
     Xianyi and Gladys Yang, 4 vols. (Beijing: Foreign Languages Press, 1980), 2:420. Lu
     Xun delivered this comment in an address to the cadets of the Whampoa Military
     Academy just prior to the defeat of the revolution in 1927. He wished to deflate
     what he felt was an overly optimistic assessment of the importance of literature in
     revolutionary practice, expressing the Trotskyite notion that literature travels in the
     wake of real events and is never itself the motor of social change. See Paul G.
     Pickowicz, *Marxist Literary Thought in China: The Influence of Ch'ü Ch'iu-pai*
     (Berkeley: University of California Press, 1981), pp. 132–133.
2   Marston Anderson, *The Limits of Realism: Chinese Fiction in the Revolutionary
     Period* (Berkeley: University of California Press, 1990), pp. 124–125.
3   The word "subaltern" has attained great currency in historiographical debates
     because of the Subaltern Studies Group, which has extended its influence well
     beyond the sphere of South Asian studies. For these scholars, the subaltern repre-
     sents the "silenced" in history whose presence must be read symptomatically from
     the texts of colonial administrators. The subaltern is therefore no more than a trace
     that an insurgent historiography struggles to "make present" by insistently reading
     the colonial archives "otherwise." As Gayatri Chakravorty Spivak suggests, when
     the "subaltern speaks," "she" is no longer subaltern. The voicing of the class subject
     in Chinese revolutionary narrative presents us with a case in which the subaltern's
     speaking is flagrantly made "present" and thus raises important issues about voic-
     ing and the effects of power, so that a subaltern identity is here an effect of discourse
     that must be carefully understood as producing a speaking subject by producing an
     identifiable place from which to speak. See Ranajit Guha and Gayatri Chakravorty
     Spivak, eds.,. *Selected Subaltern Studies* (New York: Oxford University Press, 1988),
     and Gayatri Chakravorty Spivak, "Can the Subaltern Speak?" in *Marxism and the
     Interpretation of Cultures*, ed. Cary Nelson and Lawrence Grossberg (Urbana: Uni-
     versity of Illinois Press, 1988), pp. 271–313. See also Gail Hershatter, "The Subaltern
     Talks Back: Reflections on Subaltern Theory and Chinese History," *positions* 1, 1
     (Spring 1993): 103–130, for an important discussion of the issue of voicing in
     Chinese revolutionary narrative.
4   See Tani Barlow, "Theorizing Woman: *Funu, Guojia, Jiating* [Chinese Woman,
     Chinese State, Chinese Family]," *Genders* 10 (Spring 1991): 132–160, for how she
     puts this idea of Nietzsche to work in a genealogy of "woman" in modern China.
5   Tani Barlow, "*Zhishifenzi* [Chinese Intellectuals] and Power," *Dialectical Anthropol-
     ogy* 16 (1991): 211.
6   I use "political culture" here as defined by Elizabeth J. Perry (following historian
     Lynn Hunt and others) as the play of discourse and language in politics and not in
     its more established usage in sinology and modernization theory, in which it refers
     to the socialization practices that produce value consensus and a homogenous

cultural worldview. See Elizabeth J. Perry, "Chinese Political Culture Revisited," in *Popular Protest and Political Culture in Modern China: Learning from 1989*, ed. Jeffrey N. Wasserstrom and Elizabeth J. Perry (Boulder, Colo.: Westview, 1992), p. 5.

7   M. Anderson, *Limits of Realism*, p. 17.

8   The use of hyphenated words in my text is specifically intended to draw attention to the multiplicity of the meaning conveyed. Here, the sense of "realized" refers not only to the sense of producing an outcome but also to the sense of putting the agent in direct touch with a reality apparently unmediated by writing.

9   Many of the dilemmas surrounding the "coming to voice" of this subject were actively explored in fictional contexts written concurrently with the party's early experiments in peasant organization. Marxist experiments in organizing peasant unions date from the early 1920s. But, as is well known, the central leadership of the party did not recognize the peasants as the motive force of revolution until well after the abortive revolution of 1927.

10   I am indebted to Barlow's model of how *funu*, as "national woman," is a category inscribed by a revolutionary discourse that "unleashes" the very subjectivity it constitutes. See Barlow, "Theorizing Woman."

11   I am freely interpreting the third term from her inclusion of "national culture" as the third term of this relationship. Rey Chow, "Male Narcissism and National Culture: Subjectivity in Chen Kaige's *King of the Children*," *Camera Obscura* 25/26 (1991): 12. Theodore Huters refers to this representation of the bourgeois subject as the "hypertrophied self" in his "Blossoms in the Snow: Lu Xun and the Dilemma of Modern Chinese Literature," *Modern China* 10, 1 (1984): 53. He makes a similar argument by pointing toward the fraught relationship between this self and its "others."

12   Chow, "Male Narcissism," p. 36.

13   Here I bear in mind the multiple meanings of the English word "representation," in which a "portrait" is made and by this means a "proxy" calls itself into being. See Spivak, "Can the Subaltern Speak?" for an extended discussion on this dual meaning.

14   I follow Marston Anderson's practice of putting the real in scare quotes to draw our attention to how the real is mediated through representation. See his *Limits of Realism*.

15   Such an approach is now firmly established in the literature of nationalism, which looks at the realist novel as a critical means by which a national community is imagined into being. See Benedict Anderson, *Imagined Communities*, and the essays in Homi Bhabha, *Nation and Narration*. Theodore Huters calls for a more attentive exploration of the relationship between literature and political practice after May Fourth, suggesting that this relationship is not so much a case of means and ends, cause and effect, as a dialectical relationship in which both domains shared "an ideal of the powers of representation to bring imagined worlds into existence" that evolved via "a perpetual series of encounters and mutual interven-

tions." As Huters also notes, however, these worlds were imagined in a specific set of circumstances that overdetermined the categories out of which they were constructed. Huters, "Ideologies of Realism in Modern China: The Hard Imperatives of Imported Theory," in *Politics, Ideology, and Literary Discourse in Modern China*, ed. Liu Kang and Xiaobing Tang (Durham: Duke University Press, 1993), p. 161.

16 I take this notion of enframing from Timothy Mitchell, who uses it to show how "Western" ideas of rational order make "legible" what is "hidden, unknown, inaccessible." See Mitchell, *Colonizing Egypt*, p. 46.

17 For discussions developing the notion of colonial modernity, see the inaugural issue of *positions* 1, 1 (Spring 1993), especially the "Editor's Introduction," pp. v–vii, by Tani Barlow, and the essay by Lydia H. Liu, "Translingual Practice: The Discourse of Individualism between China and the West," pp. 160–193.

18 See Chatterjee, *Nationalist Thought*, for a discussion of how the nation form was overdetermined in the context of European colonial expansion without assuming the nation as a teleological product of history. See Huters, "Ideologies of Realism," for a discussion of how colonial modernity constituted a "trauma" for Chinese intellectuals as simultaneously the sign of their subjugation and the means of resistance to imperialist forces. See Prasenjit Duara, *Rescuing History*, where he argues that Enlightenment history became an important part of what propelled the unfolding of historical events in modern China.

19 See Huters, "Ideologies of Realism," for a discussion of the ironies inherent in the adoption of realism by Chinese intellectuals as the method for a "modern" social critique.

20 Jean-François Billeter, "The System of 'Class-Status,' " in *The Scope of State Power in China*, ed. Stuart R. Schram (London: School of Oriental and African Studies, 1985), p. 128.

21 Needless to say, this desire is reinscribed in the present as the search for a "civil society" as a zone of autonomy outside the oppressive order of the socialist state.

22 Alexander Woodside, *Community and Revolution in Modern Vietnam* (Boston: Houghton Mifflin, 1976), p. 54. Woodside reports that Japanese scholars went through about thirty different terms until the philosopher Nishi Amane hit on *shakai* (*shehui* in Chinese), a Sung dynasty term used by the philosopher Ch'eng Yi to refer to "communal religious meetings." Other terms, such as "civilization" (*wenming*), which will be treated in more detail in Chapter 3, shared this classicist sensibility for exhuming terms from an East Asian antiquity to designate modernist categories of analysis. This motivated pursuit of historical antecedents to the categories of the modern attests to nationalism's internal paradox of representing itself both as a rupture of the radically new *and* an evolutionary development of the selfsame. See Duara, *Rescuing History*, for a discussion of this aporia in the "time" of the nation. We need more of a history of these complex trajectories in the formation of modernities in East Asia to see how the dialectical interplay of colonial modernities within the region are in some cases more important than the

relationship between "East" and "West." See Liu, "Translingual Practice," for a genealogy of the category "Individual," and Barlow, "Theorizing Woman," for "Woman."

23 See Woodside, *Community and Revolution*, and James Pusey, *China and Charles Darwin* (Cambridge: Harvard University Press, 1983), pp. 195–196.

24 On this imagery of escape, see Huters, "Blossoms in the Snow," p. 55, and Rey Chow, *Woman and Chinese Modernity: The Politics of Reading West and East* (Minneapolis: University of Minnesota Press, 1991). See also Barlow, "Theorizing Woman."

25 See Barlow, "Theorizing Woman," for an extended discussion of how this social space ultimately reorganized kin relations around the sign of *funu*, signifying the "displacement" of Confucian hierarchies and kin ties by a modern, urban society.

26 Woodside, *Community and Revolution*, p. 54, and M. Anderson, *Limits of Realism*. See also B. Anderson, *Imagined Communities*, and Duara, *Rescuing History*, on the construction of the notion of a "people nation."

27 In 1917, Chen Duxiu identified "society" as one of the building blocks of a new national identity in May Fourth discourse. See M. Anderson, *Limits of Realism*, p. 28.

28 Cited in ibid. Marston Anderson suggests that social realism exploited the "exclusion of the other from writing to ensure the substantiality of the real" (ibid., p. 177).

29 See Bruce Robbins, "Telescopic Philanthropy: Professionalism and Responsibility in *Bleak House*," in *Nation and Narration*, ed. Bhabha, p. 215. Robbins's essay describes how a politics of presence in the form of moral responsibility for charity at home displaces the consciousness of imperialism that appears distant and marginal to the concerns of Dickens's novel. My point here is merely how this telescopy may be reversed in the colonies, so that the local becomes the means through which the global is "made present" as an anticolonial political practice.

30 Here I must acknowledge a rich body of readings that have unquestionably inspired my own. See in particular Huters, "Blossoms in the Snow," and Chow, *Woman and Chinese Modernity.*

31 Lu Xun, "The New Year's Sacrifice," in *Selected Stories of Lu Hsun*, trans. Yang Hsien-yi and Gladys Yang (Beijing: Foreign Languages Press, 1960), p. 127.

32 M. Anderson has discussed similar passages in other Lu Xun stories as cathartic moments in which the "weighty sense of identification" between narrator and victim is "exorcised"—the word is especially apt in the reading below. And yet the narrator's sense of "lightness" is not shared by the reader because of the undermining of the narrator's perspective by the story itself. See Anderson, *Limits of Realism*, p. 90.

33 Her answer focuses on the "impenetrability" of the other as a hardened object that deflects all access to her subjectivity. In my reading I do not contest this but want to heighten the uncanny pairing between the narrator and his other. Chow, *Woman and Chinese Modernity*, p. 110.

34 "From his solemn expression I suddenly suspected that he looked on me as choosing not earlier nor later but just this time to come and trouble him, and I was also a bad character." Lu Xun, "New Year's Sacrifice," pp. 129–130.

35 M. Anderson, *Limits of Realism*, p. 89. My thanks to Ted Huters for reminding me of this aspect of Anderson's reading.

36 B. Anderson, *Imagined Communities*, pp. 24–28. He is speaking of the novel here, yet I would suggest that it is equally true of any fictional genre in the realist style.

37 I am clearly indebted here to Huters, who demonstrates beautifully how Lu Xun's story unsettles the space "outside," rendering spurious the claim of objective social critique and forcing the realization of how implicated that space "outside" is within the very order from which it seeks to distance itself. See Huters, "Blossoms in the Snow," p. 69. To use Johannes Fabian's vocabulary, Lu Xun is asserting the "coevalness" of the rural homeplace with the urban milieu that defines itself as a space of the "modern," a move that unsettles the "allochronic" narrative practices that set the space of the modern as the radical other of "tradition." See Fabian, *Time and the Other: How Anthropology Makes Its Object* (New York: Columbia University Press, 1983).

38 See Huters, "Ideologies of Realism," for an eloquent discussion of how European models of literary realism held out this promise to Chinese writers in the 1920s.

39 Jacques Derrida, "Signature Event Context," in *Margins of Philosophy* (Chicago: University of Chicago Press, 1982), p. 318.

40 Similarly, Duara, *Rescuing History*, argues most convincingly for how history in the Hegelian sense becomes part of what propels historical events in early-twentieth-century China.

41 See Woodside, *Community and Revolution*, p. 87, for the suggestion of the propaganda function of literature. Indeed, in the debate on national forms in the late 1930s, the focus on literary reception did move literary production more in the direction of its instrumental application for national salvation.

42 Mitchell, *Colonizing Egypt*, pp. 126–127.

43 "What kind of society are we living in?" is Mao Dun's own question raised by a character early in the novel. "You can find an answer in the next room. There you have a successful financier and a captain of industry. That little drawing-room is Chinese society in miniature." Shen Yen-ping [Mao Dun], *Midnight* [Ziye] (Hong Kong: C & W, 1976), p. 29.

44 Shen Yen-ping [Mao Dun], *"Spring Silkworms" and Other Stories* (1933; reprint, Peking: Foreign Languages Press, 1956).

45 M. Anderson, *Limits of Realism*, charts this transformation in literary representation in the late 1920s and early 1930s.

46 Huters, "Ideologies of Realism," p. 167. I am also indebted to him for comments on an earlier version of this chapter that urged taking up the question of the Party's agency at this point in my argument.

47 William Hinton, *Fanshen: A Documentary of Revolution in a Chinese Village* (New York: Vintage, 1966).

48 Indeed, rereading this violence in the wake of 1989 compels us to reevaluate its place in the revolutionary process. This section was partly inspired by the pedagogical imperative of having to explain to students the importance of reading *Fanshen* in a post-1989 moment.

49 Arif Dirlik, "The Predicament of Marxist Revolutionary Consciousness: Mao Zedong, Antonio Gramsci, and the Reformulation of Marxist Revolutionary Theory," *Modern China* 9, 2 (April 1983), p. 190. See Pierre Bourdieu, *Outline for a Theory of Practice* (Cambridge: Cambridge University Press, 1977), for an elaboration of what he calls "doxa," the universe of "what goes without saying."

50 The quoted phrase is from Barlow, "Theorizing Woman," p. 133.

51 The quoted phrase is from James H. Kavanaugh, "Ideology," in *Critical Terms for Literary Study*, ed. Frank Lentricchia and Thomas McLaughlin (Chicago: University of Chicago Press, 1990), p. 310.

52 See Martin Jay, *Downcast Eyes: The Denigration of Vision in Twentieth-Century French Thought* (Berkeley: University of California Press, 1994), for a discussion of visuality in theoretical discourse. Also, see Bourdieu, *Outline*, pp. 191–197, for a discussion of how social relations are "enchanted" in their masking of exploitation as reciprocity and obligation structured within unquestioned primordial loyalties of kinship and patronage.

53 Dirlik, "Predicament," p. 196.

54 Most of the events that I have personally witnessed have been the venting of wives against husbands. Similarly, Margery Wolf has described the power of the women's community in Taiwanese villages as a forum in which women can report abusive behavior to a gossip network that threatens to damage the "face" of abusive husbands and mothers-in-law. See Wolf, *Women and the Family in Rural Taiwan* (Stanford: Stanford University Press, 1972).

55 Yet even the irresolvable antagonisms of class enmity can be cast in the terms of an ideal of retributive justice already in place in village conceptions of the moral order.

56 In their characterization of a Confucian tradition, Esherick and Wasserstrom noted that Confucian bureaucrats preferred the authority of the written word, mistrusting clever speech, and that this privileging of the written text accounted for the lack of a rhetorical tradition of public speaking and rational-critical debate in China, leading instead to the elaboration of a ritualized political theater. It did strike me, in a way that it had not really occurred to me before, how curious it was that Chinese revolutionary practice hung so heavily on what was essentially a speech act. I do not want to enter the debate as to whether Chinese metaphysics rests on the idea of presence but will perhaps note how speaking bitterness is necessarily a hybridized product of a Chinese practice of public plaint and a metaphysics intrinsic to the discourse of social science and Marxist critique. See Joseph W. Esherick and Jeffrey N. Wasserstrom, "Acting Out Democracy: Political Theater in Modern China," in

Popular Protest and Political Culture in Modern China: Learning from 1989, ed. Jeffrey N. Wasserstrom and Elizabeth J. Perry (Boulder, Colo.: Westview, 1992), p. 44 and again on pp. 56–57.

57   See Teresa de Lauretis, *Alice Doesn't: Feminism, Semiotics, Cinema* (Bloomington: Indiana University Press, 1984), p. 106, for the notion of the "cogs" of narrative. I am grateful to Barlow, "Theorizing Woman," p. 153, for pointing out this metaphor.

58   Barlow talks of how "woman" (*funu*), like "class," was a category that presumed to represent the interests it had itself constituted. But class, like funu, became redefined in the context of local practice and began to look quite different from its "universal" aspect. See Barlow, "Theorizing Woman." The classic story of "Goldflower" in Jack Belden, *China Shakes the World* (New York: Monthly Review, 1970), if read as an example of speaking bitterness narrative, shows how this metaphysics of presence worked in the creation of *funu*, the reinscribed, gendered subject.

59   See Dirlik, "Predicament," pp. 198–199. In Chapter 6 I explore how this trope of merging consciousness has not disappeared in the post-Maoist tropes of the party's rhetoric; it continues as an intrinsic part of the party's self-representation, but in terms of a rupturing of the relationship between party and masses (*dangqun guanxi*) that must be redressed.

60   Belden, *China Shakes the World*. Marc Blecher uses this same passage to demonstrate a closely related argument on the coexistence of statist with participatory politics in socialist China. See Blecher, "Structural Change and the Political Articulation of Social Interest in Revolutionary and Socialist China," in *Marxism and the Chinese Experience*, ed. Arif Dirlik and Maurice Meisner (Armonk, N.Y.: M. E. Sharpe, 1989).

61   Anita Chan, Richard Madsen, and Jonathan Unger, *Chen Village: The Recent History of a Peasant Community in Mao's China* (Berkeley: University of California Press, 1984), p. 79.

62   Raymond Williams, *Marxism and Literature* (New York: Oxford University Press, 1977), p. 132.

63   Here I wish to note how tears and emotion still remain a prominent feature of the party's self-representation. The narratives that describe an alteration in the consciousness of the subject in response to party tutelage often include the shedding of tears, but in the post-Mao context, these are tears of gratitude or shame, rather than sorrow and loss, a change that reflects quite profoundly the reconceptualization of the relationship between the party and the masses.

64   Barthes, *Rustle of Language*, p. 152.

65   Ernesto Laclau, *New Reflections on the Revolution of Our Time* (London: Verso, 1990), pp. 9–10.

66   George E. Marcus, "Contemporary Problems of Ethnography in the Modern World System," in *Writing Culture: The Poetics and Politics of Ethnography*, ed. James Clifford and George E. Marcus (Berkeley: University of California Press, 1986), p. 189.

67   Sidney L. Greenblatt, ed., *The People of Taihang: An Anthology of Family Histories* (White Plains, N.Y.: International Arts and Sciences Press, 1976), pp. xvii–xviii.

68   Siu-lun Wong, *Sociology and Socialism in Contemporary China* (London: Routledge and Kegan Paul, 1979), p. 96.

69   Sidney Greenblatt, *People of Taihang*, p. xix.

70   I first became acquainted with this local history writing during my field research in Yixing County in 1982. Yixing's rural artisans and pottery workers represented a proto-proletariat, closely tied to its agricultural base, whose class consciousness emerged out of a history of labor struggles. Among the titles produced there were "Taodu gongren huiyilu" (Worker recollections of the pottery capital), "Yixing taoye jinxi" (New dawn of the Yixing pottery industry), and "Yixing taoci gongye de fasheng, fazhan yu gaizao" (The origin, development, and transformation of the Yixing pottery industry), all in mimeograph versions, dated 1959. "Yixing taoci shi caogao" (History of Yixing pottery) was a manuscript of over 600 pages compiled by a worker-soldier-peasant team and dated 1975, and finally, "Yixing taoci jianshi" (A short history of the Yixing pottery industry) was a photocopied manuscript dated 1978. Copies were placed in the archives of the participating collective factories, the research archives of the Yixing Pottery and Porcelain Company, the Nanjing University History Department, and elsewhere. Embedded within them were not only speaking bitterness texts but also depictions of speaking bitterness performances in the political campaigns of the 1950s and 1960s.

71   This is true for several of the stories in Sidney Greenblatt, *People of Taihang*.

72   For extended discussion of some of the forms taken by this representational process, see Billeter, "System of 'Class-Status' "; Lowell Dittmer, "Radical Ideology and Chinese Political Culture: An Analysis of the Revolutionary *Yangbangxi*," in *Moral Behavior in Chinese Society*, ed. Richard W. Wilson, Sidney L. Greenblatt, and Amy Auerbacher Wilson (New York: Praeger, 1981), pp. 126–151; and Sidney Greenblatt's fine introduction to *People of Taihang*. The canon of socialist realism in artistic production is perhaps the most obvious case of something much more encompassing. One thinks of the famous tableau *Rent Collection Courtyard*, a direct translation of speaking bitterness into three-dimensional form. For a photo documentary of this installation in Dayi County, Sichuan, see *"Rent Collection Courtyard": Sculptures of Oppression and Revolt* (Peking: Foreign Languages Press, 1970).

73   Shoshona Felman, *The Literary Speech Act: Don Juan with J. L. Austin, or Seduction in Two Languages* (Ithaca: Cornell University Press, 1983), p. 19.

74   Emile Benveniste, *Problems in General Linguistics* (Coral Gables, Fla.: University of Miami Press, 1971), pp. 219–220.

75   See Sidney Greenblatt's introduction to *People of Taihang*, pp. xxxiv–xxxv.

76   I hope my critique of Billeter, "The System of 'Class-Status,' " does not obscure my indebtedness to what has been one of the most thoughtful discussions of Chinese political culture to date.

77   Billeter, "The System of 'Class-Status,' " pp. 129 and 138.

78   Ibid., p. 151.

79   The phrase in quotes is from Dittmer, "Radical Ideology," p. 135.

80   Chapter 2 explores in more detail the distinction between tactic and strategy in de Certeau's elaboration of a theory of practice. Michel de Certeau, *The Practice of Everyday Life* (Berkeley: University of California Press, 1984).

81   Claude Lefort, "Outline of the Genesis of Ideology in Modern Societies," in *The Political Forms of Modern Society: Bureaucracy, Democracy, Totalitarianism* (Cambridge: MIT Press, 1986), p. 194.

82   See Michel Foucault, *The History of Sexuality*, Vol. 1, *An Introduction*, trans. Robert Hurley (New York: Vintage, 1980).

83   Lefort, "Outline of the Genesis of Ideology," p. 205. As Lefort suggests, bourgeois ideology reveals itself as a text written in capital letters.

84   Lu Xun, "New Year's Sacrifice," p. 140.

85   Chan, Madsen, and Unger, *Chen Village*.

86   See Rofel, *"Yearnings,"* for an example of how issues of class continue to figure in contestations over who, or what class, can best speak for the nation.

87   Steven Mosher's *China Misperceived: American Illusions and Chinese Reality* (New York: Basic, 1990) is perhaps the most blatant expression of this characterization of the Chinese socialist state as driven by a blind will to power.

88   Partha Chatterjee, *The Nation and Its Fragments* (Princeton: Princeton University Press, 1993).

2   The Mimesis of Power

1   The "backdoor" refers to the use of "pull" in Chinese bureaucratic affairs.

2   *Guanxixue* is best translated as the "study" or "art" of social relationships in which the exchange of gifts or favors can be deployed to obtain special favor from powerful individuals. Mayfair Mei-hui Yang, "The Gift Economy and State Power in China," *Comparative Studies in Society and History* 31, 1 (January 1989): 25–54, is perhaps the best account of how *guanxi* works in the post-Mao period.

3   See Geremie Barmé, "A Word for the Imposter—Introducing the Drama of Sha Yexin," *Renditions*, nos. 19–20 (1983): 319–332, for an account of the politics surrounding the play's unofficial suppression and the writer Ba Jin's defense of the play. The principal author Sha Yexin has continued to write for the stage but found himself in trouble again with his drama *The Secret Life of Karl Marx*, which was condemned in the Spiritual Pollution Campaign in late 1983. See Barmé, "Word for the Imposter," p. 332.

4   For the Chinese text, see Sha Yexin, Li Shoucheng, and Yao Mingde, *Jiaru wo shi zhende* [If only I were real], *Qishi niandai* [The seventies] (January 1980): 76–96. For English translations, see Sha Yexin, Li Shoucheng, and Yao Mingde, *If Only I Were for Real*, trans. Janice Wickeri, in *The New Realism*, ed. Lee Yee (New York: Hippocrene, 1983), pp. 261–321, and Sha Yexin, Li Shoucheng, and Yao Mingde, *The Imposter (If I Were Real)*, trans. Daniel Kane, *Renditions*, nos. 19–20 (1983): 333–369.

5   My use of "the gift" here refers generally to the manifold ways in which reciprocity shapes the informal structures of everyday life in socialist China through the creation of networks of obligation and influence.

6   See Felman, *Literary Speech Act*, pp. 145–150.

7   My discussion of the performative aspect of the gift and its ability to create a self-referential reality has been inspired by Shoshona Felman's positive reappraisal of performative linguistics and the work of the speech act philosopher J. L. Austin. His discussion of such speech acts as promising, Felman claims, enacts the same sort of performance that his theory is meant to explain. The performative is a reality that constitutes itself. As such, it offers an interesting perspective from which to analyze an "art" of imposture. See ibid.

8   Chongming is a county north of the city which is within the Shanghai Municipality and to which many Shanghai youths had been rusticated. It is a luxury assignment, as far as rustication goes, being close enough to Shanghai to allow weekend visits to one's family.

9   Shanghai is China's most sophisticated and cosmopolitan city. Its young people are among the best dressed in the country. Zhang's garb, on the other hand, represents the values that were glorified in the party during the War of Resistance against the Japanese in the 1930s and 1940s: self-denial, self-reliance, and making do with what one has. These values continued to characterize the political style of the People's Liberation Army long after Liberation.

10   The gifts that accompany a betrothal theoretically flow in both directions between the two families. But the difficulty in finding a bride in China has led to an unequal balance in matrimonial exchange in favor of the bride and her family. The gift of a watch is a popular engagement present to the bride. In this case, however, it was given to the prospective groom. The fact that the gift is traveling in the "wrong" direction has perhaps a lot to say about the relative power positions in this particular matrimonial contract: the son of an old revolutionary cadre and the daughter of a former capitalist.

11   As the "son" of a high-ranking official, Zhang would have had access to goods not ordinarily available to the rest of the population. These people were enlisting Zhang as their agent by giving him money to buy them things at special shops that catered exclusively to officials and their families. Such shops have a ready supply of commodities that are unavailable or of poor quality elsewhere.

12   The revolutionary charisma of Zhang's putative "father" serves here as a potent antidote to the bad class background of the prospective bride. Zhang's appearance at the factory unit on behalf of one of these brothers had an almost magical effect. The factory leadership immediately began to regard their now apparently well-connected employee with new respect and planned to promote him from manual laborer to the position of secretary to the head engineer (*Wenhui bao*, September 11, 1979).

13   The expression used to describe this scene in the *Jiefang ribao* (September 11, 1979) was *renhuan cheming*, which means literally "the cheers of the crowd and the

honking of car horns." It is a sardonic turn on the classical phrase *renhuan majiao*, "the cheers of the crowd and the neighing of horses." Both versions are a figure for an impressive assemblage. Traveling by private automobile is definitely a statement of power in China, where most people are limited to bicycles or overcrowded public transportation. The horn is used not only as a sensing device (to alert others to your passage) but also as a form of self-advertisement. Traveling by car, therefore, lends one a casual arrogance of the road in which the constant use of the horn commands deference from more pedestrian modes of transportation. The borrowing of vehicles by Zhang represents much more than mere convenience by the accession to power. Ironically, it was the conspicuousness of his coming and going by car at his girlfriend's house that tipped off the local neighborhood committee and led them to investigate the true identity of the stranger (*Jiefang ribao*, September 12, 1979). At that time, only cadres grade seven or below were allowed a limousine for their exclusive use.

14   With so many young people awaiting employment in cities like Shanghai, the state was at that time encouraging young people to organize small collective enterprises in the city, mostly service enterprises. However, employment in a collective, especially a small one, is definitely second-rate as compared with working in a state-owned enterprise. One's job security is not assured, and usually a small collective cannot distribute equivalent benefits in health care, housing, and pensions. This inequality of prospects is especially evident in searching for a mate. A young man employed in a small collective would find it difficult to find a bride willing to put up with the insecurities of his future employment. Zhang's girlfriend would obviously benefit by being transferred into a state-run organization. But she could transfer only by going "through the back door" (going through pull) or by succeeding to such a job on a parent's retirement (in this case, given her parents' class background, out of the question). Since the time of our story, the state has de-emphasized the organization of these small collectives in favor of small family-managed enterprises (*geti hu*), and the "iron ricebowl" (*tie fanwan*) of job security in state-owned enterprises has been undermined in the extension of the responsibility system into industry.

15   See Stephen Greenblatt, *Renaissance Self-Fashioning: From More to Shakespeare* (Chicago: University of Chicago Press, 1980), p. 13. Greenblatt himself does not relate his work on Tudor England to his experiences as a visitor in China, but I feel that such a relationship is implicit in his uncanny comprehension of the presentation of self in China on the basis of such a short visit. See his "China: Visiting Rites," *Raritan* (Spring 1983): 1–23.

16   Andrew Kipnis, " 'Face': An Adaptable Discourse of Social Surfaces," *positions* 3, 1 (Spring 1995): 119–148.

17   See, for example, the classic article by Hsien-chin Hu, "The Chinese Concept of 'Face,' " *American Anthropologist* 46, 1 (1944): 45–64.

18   Kipnis, " 'Face,' " p. 21.

19   Ibid., p. 129.

20   Ibid., p. 18. Kipnis suggests that from the context *yanmian* can refer here to aspects of both *lian* and *mian*.

21   Dittmer, "Radical Ideology," p. 146; Mark Selden, "Cooperation and Conflict: Co-operative and Collective Formation in China's Countryside," in *The Transition to Socialism in China*, ed. Mark Selden and Victor Lippit (Armonk, N.Y.: M. E. Sharpe, 1982), p. 81.

22   See, for example, the story of the "10,000-pig farm" in William Hinton, *Shenfan: The Continuing Revolution in a Chinese Village* (New York: Vintage, 1983), pp. 243–244.

23   Xu Xiaotong, a doctoral student in the University of Illinois Department of An-thropology, has researched the construction of credit worthiness in Subei.

24   Dittmer deals briefly with this issue of imposture in the form of the "apparently reformed individual," which he does not call imposture but a spy tactic. I prefer the image of the imposter because he or she assumes an extraordinary identity; the spy, on the contrary, assumes the guise of ordinariness, the erasure of any distinguish-ing marks that separate him or her from the mass. In the example presented by Dittmer, the imposture clearly takes the form of hypercoherence with a designated ideal of behavior. The individual stigmatized by a bad class background has to be "redder than red" to escape the arbitrary power of class background to define moral worth. See Dittmer, "Radical Ideology," pp. 146–147.

25   The Dazhai model was promoted nationally during the late 1960s and 1970s as a model heavily dependent on moral incentives and greater centralization of ac-counting as a spur to productivity. The irony of Gu Hua's novella is produced by the awareness that the economic heterodoxy of Pagoda Ridge is composed of the decentralizing practices of the economic reform, the parceling out of land and production contracts to individual households in the "responsibility system" (*bao-chan daohu*). However, Pagoda Ridge was ten years too early, and its team leader was arrested and sent to labor reform camp for setting up "an independent king-dom." Gu Hua, *Pagoda Ridge*, in *"Pagoda Ridge" and Other Stories*, trans. Gladys Yang (Beijing: Panda Books, 1985).

26   See, for example, collections of this sort of reportage in Ren Qun et al., *Pian: Shijiu qi zhapian an de zhenxiang* [Swindles: The truth behind nineteen case histories of fraud] (Hebei: Guangming ribao chubanshe, 1989), which combines a public ser-vice mission of educating the public with the thrill of audacious exploits.

27   Michael Taussig, *Mimesis and Alterity: A Particular History of the Senses* (New York: Routledge, 1993), p. 255.

28   Felman, *Literary Speech Act*, pp. 9–12.

29   Ibid., p. 27. I owe immeasurable gratitude to Christopher Roberts Davis, who first drew my attention to Felman's text. She saw in a moment its implication for this project, an implication that took me years to figure out!

30   Emile Benveniste, "Analytical Philosophy and Language," in *Problems in General Linguistics*, p. 236. See also ibid., p. 98.

31 Pierre Bourdieu, "The Economics of Linguistic Exchanges," *Social Science Information* 16 (1977): 645–668.

32 Derrida's side of his debate with John R. Searle has been collected in *Limited Inc*, trans. Samuel Weber (Evanston, Ill.: Northwestern University Press, 1988).

33 See Felman, *Literary Speech Act*, p. 19 and p. 16 n. 2.

34 Here I am thinking through Felman's text paraphrastically. "If Don Juan subverts the uniqueness of the promise by repeating precisely the promise of uniqueness . . . it is in order to ruin not the performance of language, but its *authority*." Ibid., p. 50.

35 Ibid., p. 39.

36 *Confucian Analects* 12.11, cited in Lisa Raphals, *Knowing Words: Wisdom and Cunning in the Classical Traditions of China and Greece* (Ithaca: Cornell University Press, 1992), p. 29.

37 Felman, *Literary Speech Act*, pp. 31–32.

38 Ibid., p. 77.

39 Ibid., p. 93. Thereby, identity itself becomes a kind of performative excess; see also p. 81.

40 See ibid., p. 11, for this distinction. In this case, abuse stems from the imposter's own sense of heresy; see ibid., p. 32.

41 Such a gift is de rigueur in meeting with cadres to ensure their cooperation in resolving difficulties. If no such gift is forthcoming, then the response would be that the matter required further "study" (*yanjiu*) as a way of communicating this lapse. *Yanjiu* is a pun on "wine and cigarettes." The flow of gifts to cadres resembles a form of "feudal tribute," and it appears that way in cartoons that lampoon the practice (see, for example, *Fengci yu youmo*, December 20, 1982, p. 4).

42 Chiao Chien, "Chinese Strategic Behavior: Continuity and Change," paper delivered at the 1985 Annual Meetings of the American Anthropological Association. The sage is cited on page 19.

43 See Mayfair Mei-hui Yang, "The Gift Economy," p. 42, for discussion of how the gift works to incorporate another's substance.

44 See Felman, *Literary Speech Act*, p. 43, for a hint of how the teaching of rupture can lead toward the issue of corruption with which the practices of guanxi are often associated.

45 I transcribed the following segment from the NBC television special *Journey to the Heart of China* shown in 1984.

46 As purely anecdotal evidence, in 1981 my husband had wheeled an injured friend on a hospital gurney through the night streets of Nanjing to be greeted at the hospital gates by a man claiming to be Zhou Enlai.

47 De Certeau, *Practice of Everyday Life*, p. xx.

48 Ibid., pp. 22–24.

49 Raphals, *Knowing Words*, pp. 16–17.

50 See Deng Tuo, "Sanshiliu ji" [The thirty-six stratagems], in *Deng Tuo shi wen xuan*

[Selected works] (Beijing: Renmin ribao, 1986), pp. 104–107, and Gao Yuan, *Born Red* (Stanford: Stanford University Press, 1987), pp. 30–38.

51   All three authors were Beijing municipal officials. Wu Han, most famous as the author of the play *Hai Rui Dismissed from Office*, a historic drama that criticized Mao's Great Leap Forward, was a vice-mayor. Liao Mosha was a writer who also worked in the Beijing City propaganda department. Deng Tuo had been a former editor of the *Renmin ribao* and was then chief editor of the *Beijing Wanbao*, in which his *Yanshan ye hua* [Evening chats] had appeared. The *San jia cun* [Three-family village] had appeared in the Beijing Party Committee's monthly journal, *Frontline*, beginning in 1961. See Gao, *Born Red*, p. 36.

52   Gao, *Born Red*, p. 38.

53   De Certeau, *Practice of Everyday Life*, p. 35.

54   Ibid., p. 37.

55   See ibid., p. xix.

56   My thanks to Barlow, "Theorizing Woman," p. 144, for this phrase.

57   See, for example, Li Bingyan, ed., *Sanshiliuji xinbian* [A new edition of the thirty-six stratagems] (Beijing: People's Liberation Army Press, 1981). There are many more editions of this sort, which suggest that this literature, along with the growth of consumption of books of divination and magic in the 1980s, has a business application in the recently liberated marketplace. Likewise, for some time we have seen the repackaging of Sunzi's *Art of War* by American publishers as a guide for doing business. The logic of late-twentieth-century capitalism adopts tactics formerly identified with military practice so that they can be applied in the strategies of multinational corporations that wish to engage the emerging bureaucratic capitalisms of the East.

58   For an account of how Malaysian Chinese use epigrammatic images from a mythic history to address contemporary dilemmas of identity, see Jean DeBernardi, "Historical Allusion and the Defense of Identity: Malaysian Chinese Popular Religion," in *Asian Visions of Authority*, ed. Charles Keyes, Laurel Kendall, and Helen Hardacre (Honolulu: University of Hawaii Press, 1994), pp. 117–140.

59   A fox, the very image of cunning, impresses the tiger when the animals flee at the sight of them walking together in the forest.

60   Chiao Chien, "Chinese Strategic Behavior," p. 23.

61   This drawing appeared in the *Wenhui bao*, September 11, 1979.

62   See Hinton, *Shenfan*, p. xxxviii, for the case of "whiskers" Shen. See *Funu*, March 1985, pp. 15–16, for the story of a young man who registered himself as a matrimonially minded son of a cadre at several marriage bureaus in Shanghai.

63   See a story in the weekly edition of the *Zhongguo qingnianbao*, October 20, 1985, p. 5, for a story of this imposture.

64   Marcel Mauss, *The Gift: Forms and Functions of Exchange in Archaic Societies* (New York: Norton, 1967), pp. 8–9.

65   De Certeau, *Practice of Everyday Life*, p. 23.

3   Constructions of Civility in the Age
of Flexible Accumulation

1   For a discussion on *youhuan yishi*, see Su Xiaokang, "My Views on 'A Sense of Mission,'" *Qiushi* [Seeking facts], no. 2 (1988): 47–48. See also Bodman, "From History to Allegory to Art," pp. 40–43, for a discussion of that essay.

2   See Chapter 6 for a more extended treatment of official and popular discussions of population quality (*renmin suzhi*).

3   Flexible accumulation (or post-Fordist capitalism) is how David Harvey characterizes the global reorganization of capitalism that began in the mid-1970s in which a new flexibility with respect to labor processes and labor control is made possible by global flows of capital and labor. Harvey suggests that the regressive norms of labor practices in rapidly developing areas of the world are reimported back into the metropole to undercut the power of organized labor. What will become striking for the issues developed in my argument will be the global nature of the discourses that evaluate the "quality" of labor in terms of its discipline and docility. Harvey, *Condition of Postmodernity*, p. 147.

4   My first reaction to this inquiry was that it portended a new level of escalating expectations in the quid pro quo that structures the working of instrumental relationships in reform-era China. And, indeed, who knows what novel forms of production might have emerged from such an intimate intertwining of ethnographic praxis with capital logic? Other foreign scholars doing research in the Chinese countryside have also reported to me similar encounters with local power holders.

5   The township has a long history extending back to the Maoist era of being represented as a model, perhaps having more to do with its suburban location outside a major transportation hub rather than with any moral claim to superior spiritual resources.

6   Investment from overseas Chinese in Taiwan, Hong Kong, and Southeast Asia is perhaps the most significant source of foreign investment in China's rural industrial zones.

7   The quoted phrase is from Ranajit Guha, "On Some Aspects of the Historiography of Colonial India," in *Selected Subaltern Studies*, ed. Ranajit Guha and Gayatri Chakravorty Spivak (New York: Oxford University Press, 1988), p. 43 (emphasis in original), in discussing the angst of nationalist intellectuals in India. This sense of angst was pervasive among the educated classes in China in 1991, the year of my field study.

8   Prakash asserts "second sight" is not just another mode of colonization but as the very means by which modernizing elites could exercise their subjectivity and agency. See Gyan Prakash, "Science 'Goes Native' in India," *Representations* (Winter 1992): 163–164.

9   See James L. Hevia, *Cherishing Men from Afar: Qing Guest Ritual and the Macartney*

Embassy of 1793 (Durham: Duke University Press, 1995), for a stunning discussion of missionary constructions of the Chinese national character. Sun Yatsen's description of the Chinese people as a tray of sand is only one example of how these national characteristics were already present in the thinking of earlier modernizing elites.

10   See Chapter 6 for a more extended discussion of this articulatory practice.

11   See Rofel, "*Yearnings*," for an excellent discussion of the ambiguous position intellectuals hold in the national imaginary.

12   See Duara, *Rescuing History*, p. 32.

13   In the post-Mao period this uneasy positioning between the past and the future is omnipresent in people's consciousness as well as in the often contradictory policies of policing the cultural realm. The post-Mao period has seen the recuperation of a tradition that re-creates a glorious past that is in some way directly connected to the present. Tradition becomes a commodity that constructs the glory of the national past, but one that must be "reinvented" in opposition to the Maoist narratives of the unmitigated darkness of the feudal past, sanitized and channeled for the promotion of internal tourism and foreign investment. See Chapter 7 for a more extended discussion of the material forms this nostalgia has taken since the 1980s.

14   Bhabha, "Sly Civility," *October* 34 (1985): 75.

15   Chatterjee, *Nationalist Thought*.

16   Weng Qiyin, *Wenming gujintan* [Civilization: Discussions old and new] (Fuzhou: Fujian renmin chubanshe, 1985), p. 1. Reference is also frequently made to a passage in the *Shujing* [The book of history]. See, for instance, Sun Meiyao, ed., *Xuanchuan gongzuo shiyong shouce* [A practical guide to propaganda work] (Beijing: Hongqi chubanshe, 1988), p. 178.

17   The passage by Li Yu was cited in the dictionary entry for *wenming* in *Cihai* (Shanghai: Shanghai cishu Press, 1979), p. 1534.

18   Sun Meiyao, *Xuanchuan gongzuo shiyong shouce*, p. 178.

19   See, for instance, Carol Gluck, *Japan's Modern Myths: Ideology in the Late Meiji Period* (Princeton: Princeton University Press, 1985), p. 18. For more specific accounts of how the early modernizing states in East Asia pursued the reform of ritual practices, see Takeshi Fujitani, "Inventing, Forgetting, Remembering: Toward a Historical Ethnography of the Nation-State," in *Cultural Nationalism in East Asia: Representation and Identity*, ed. Harumi Befu, Research Papers and Policy Studies, no. 39 (Berkeley: Institute of East Asian Studies, University of California, 1993), pp. 77–106, for Japan; and for China, see Prasenjit Duara, "Knowledge and Power in the Discourse of Modernity: The Campaigns against Popular Religion in Early Twentieth-Century China," *Journal of Asian Studies* 50, 1 (1991): 67–83.

20   The only examples given are "civilized marriage" (*wenming jiehun*), walking sticks (*wenming kun'er*), and a form of improvisational theater popular in Shanghai in the early twentieth century (*wenming xi*). See *Xiandai hanyu cidian* [Dictionary of contemporary Chinese] (Beijing: Shangwu yinshuguan, 1990), p. 1204.

21   Tang Daiwang, "Woguo shi shei zuizao lunshu 'liangge wenming' de guanxi?"
       [Who was the first in China to theorize the relationship between the "two civiliza-
       tions"?], in *Shehui zhuyi jingshen wenming ziliao suoyin* [Index to materials on
       socialist spiritual civilization], vol. 2, ed. Lanzhou daxue tushuguan (Lanzhou:
       Gansu renmin chubanshe, 1985), pp. 52–53. This essay had previously appeared in
       Qiusuo, no. 4 (1984), and in *Xinhua wenzhai*, no. 10 (1984). The essay by Gong Fazi
       from which Tang cites extensively was entitled "Wuzhi wenming de biyao" [The
       indispensability of material civilization]. It appeared in the journal *Yishu huibian*
       [Collected translations], ed. Hu Yingmin, 1, 11 (1902): 105.

22   However, the deployment of wenming in the stage theory of human development
       had perhaps much more political salience for minority groups, which found their
       contemporary identities defined by the stage of development assigned to them by
       Marxist historians and social scientists.

23   For a discussion of this possibility, see Michael Rustin, "No Exit from Capitalism?"
       New Left Review 193 (May/June 1992): 96–107.

24   The "American dream" has become eminently consumable in the circulation of
       narratives about instant wealth for Chinese émigrés in the United States. In the
       novel *Beijing ren zai Niu Yue* [Beijing people in New York], the sweatshop economy
       in the immigrant community in New York City exemplifies Harvey's point about
       how post-Fordist modes of accumulation have led to "a convergence between 'third
       world' and advanced capitalist labor systems" (*Condition of Postmodernity*, p. 152).
       According to this account, the American dream is for Chinese to come to America
       to exploit other Chinese in a novelistic world almost devoid of non-Chinese. The
       book was made into an enormously successful television series that was the first
       Chinese television program to be filmed in the United States. However, the TV
       series shifted its emphasis from the novel's hermetically sealed émigré world to
       focus on the duel-to-death struggle between the Chinese male hero and his Ameri-
       can competitor in love and business. It stimulated a storm of debate about the
       "spiritual" degradation of Chinese who lose their spiritual values in the relentless
       pursuit of wealth in the United States. The novel has been translated into English;
       see Glen Cao, *Beijinger in New York*, trans. Ted Wang (San Francisco: Cypress Book
       Company, 1993).

25   See Rustin, "No Exit from Capitalism?"

26   And yet the agents of capital may themselves be blind to this conjuncture of forces.
       One expatriate American factory manager I knew in Nanjing had no idea if his
       workers participated in these civilizing disciplines, nor could he tell me whether his
       factory had a Party organization. Moreover, despite repeated promises by him to
       inquire, he never did, which leads me to suspect a certain level of "willed igno-
       rance" on his part. It was not his role to discipline his workers—that was in other
       hands. His workers were "delivered" as an already finished product. At the same
       time, there is a developing discussion of "enterprise culture" (*qiye wenhua*) pre-
       sumably based on foreign "corporate" models. This is another side of the con-
       juncture that I have not yet had a chance to explore fully.

27 This gaze is not exclusively "Western" but is exemplified by the remarks of a Japanese prime minister about the "low" quality of American labor as accounting for the economic decline of the United States.

28 The "five-good family" has a much longer history as a model than the "civilized household" status, but it has been reprised in the post-Mao period as a status that varies in its significance from one administrative area to another.

29 See Chapter 6 for a discussion on the discourse of population in post-Mao China.

30 For a more detailed discussion of this set of categories, see Ann Anagnost, "Prosperity and Counter-Prosperity: The Moral Discourse on Wealth in Post-Mao China," in *Marxism and the Chinese Experience*, ed. Arif Dirlik and Maurice Meisner (Armonk, N.Y.: M. E. Sharpe, 1989), pp. 210–234.

31 This account is translated from the *Nongmin ribao* [Peasant gazette], January 15, 1987, p. 1.

32 The first five-year campaign to promulgate legal knowledge (*pufa huodong*) began in 1986. A second five-year campaign was kicked off in 1991. These initiatives are closely related to social order concerns that have grown in the reform years, along with concerns of how to handle interpersonal disputes, failure to meet contracts, and the problems of tax collection.

33 The principle of mutual responsibility as a means of surveillance has an ancient history in China. In the post-Mao period this sort of small group is but one part of the total net (*wangluo*) of organizational practices promoted by the party's ideological apparatuses to ensure a complete "coverage" of party-led activities over all society in the wake of the dissolution of collective structures from the Maoist period.

34 What is needed here is an ethnography of weeping and tears and how they are made to signify in such texts as these. Such an ethnography would open out into a discussion of "interiority" in the constitution of the modern subject and May Fourth longing for a religion that touches on the inner soul of the subject, what Foucault discusses as the "pastoral mode." Tears here communicate shame, obligation, and a concern with face. They suggest the strongly interpersonal constitution of the subject and a consciousness of a social gaze that is discretely different from the silent, invisible technologies of the subject that Foucault describes.

35 My interlocutor here was a graduate student from China who had spent ten years in the remote countryside of the northwest during the Cultural Revolution and its aftermath.

36 The mirror plaque is an honorary marker, always bestowed from above by an official organ of the party to individuals, households, or units (*danwei*). For instance, the local government might issue them to peasant households that have members away in the army at New Years. The mirror background is a sign of elegance and splendor.

37 Václav Havel, cited in Jacques Rupnik, "Totalitarianism Revisited," in *Civil Society and the State: New European Perspectives*, ed. John Keane (London: Verso, 1988), p. 271.

38   Achille Mbembe, "Prosaics of Servitude and Authoritarian Civilities," *Public Culture* 5, 1 (Fall 1992): 132.

4   The Politicized Body

1   *Hong gaoliang*, dir. Zhang Yimou, Shaanxi Film Studio, 1987.

2   This reading of the film is indebted to Yingjin Zhang, "Ideology of the Body in *Red Sorghum*: National Allegory, National Roots, and Third Cinema," *East-West Film Journal* (June 1990): 38–53.

3   It is all too common in much of the social science literature on China to see ideology merely as a manipulative tool of the state rather than something which suffuses all of society, which structures what Václav Havel calls "the panorama of everyday life," and within which the leadership are themselves enveloped. See Havel, "The Power of the Powerless," in *Václav Havel, or Living in Truth*, ed. Jan Vladislav (London: Faber and Faber, 1986), p. 50.

4   This account is translated from *Nongmin ribao* [Peasant gazette], August 7, 1987, p. 2.

5   Indeed, in this highly stylized account, his comment may be the only "authentic" voice in the story. My thanks to Carolyn Wakeman for this insight. The irony lies in that the inclusion of such authentic elements both constructs and deconstructs the verisimilitude of the story. While it may heighten the drama of Zhou's struggle for recognition, it also interrupts the text with the possibility of a counterdiscourse, outside the party, about the lack of power of these ritual makers to signify anything of value.

6   I talk elsewhere of how these categories operate in the post-Mao moral discourse on wealth and in the context of the one-child family policy. See Ann Anagnost, "Family Violence and Magical Violence: The 'Woman-as-Victim' in China's One-Child Family Policy," *Women and Language* 1, 2 (1988): 16–22, and Anagnost, "Prosperity." In both these contexts the household is opened to the panoptic gaze of the state, but the deployment of economic and other sanctions is made possible through the process of specification and judgment to induce a reformation of social practices.

7   Havel, "Power of the Powerless," p. 42.

8   The criteria for assigning the status of "law-abiding household" may vary from place to place but assume compliance both with state law and with locally drafted regulations. In the post-Mao period, these latter will often take the form of a "village compact" (*xianggui minyue*) that addresses local concerns of social order and interpersonal conflicts. A common complaint by higher-level authorities is that these local charters may, in some cases, contradict national law or the policy concerns of the central government. See Chapter 6 for a more extended discussion of these compacts.

9   See Mayfair Mei-hui Yang, "The Modernity of Power in the Chinese Socialist Order," *Cultural Anthropology* 3, 4 (November 1988): 414–415.

10   Chad Hansen, "Punishment and Dignity in China," in *Individualism and Holism:*

Studies in Confucian and Taoist Values, ed. Donald Munro (Ann Arbor: University of Michigan Press, 1985), p. 366.

11   My thanks to Angela Zito for making this point. It is perhaps one of the ironies of history that this concern with correct practice became manifested in Maoism as a concern with how ideology is situated in practice, a basic premise underlying the concept of cultural revolution, which in turn has had a rather significant impact on Western Marxisms since Louis Althusser and which now contributes to critical attempts to understand the society that Mao helped to create.

12   This issue of his (rarely her) political subjectivity is one that could easily become a lengthy discussion in itself. As an agent of the party-state, he represents its interests in the local community; but as a member of that small community, his social being is to a certain extent defined by a network of relations of obligation and influence that structures social life. The current wisdom that frames our understanding of the interests and motivations of the local official is this: In the early years of the socialist state, his commitment to the party and its ideals and projects, for the most part, outweighed his social obligations within the community—that is, he identified himself more as an agent of the party than as a member of the village. Increasingly during the last two decades, he has taken a more defensive posture vis-à-vis the state to protect local interests from the arbitrary demands of a state that did not take local needs or circumstances into sufficient account. At the level of ideology this shift is understood as one that negotiates a relatively idealistic period of Chinese socialism in its early years to a more pragmatic, cynical worldview that presumes an end to ideology. However, we should not assume this split within the local official between his official and social selves to be a clean one. To do so would oversimplify a conception of the subject. Rather, I would suggest that the local-level official is a fragmented subject, a complex assemblage of opportunistic self-interest, conviction, social vision, and desire for power. Furthermore, I would posit that this cynical disavowal of ideology expressed privately, if not publicly, is not necessarily a total rejection of socialist ideals for self-interested goals but rather a kind of despair. Detailed portraits of local Party leaders by both Richard Madsen, *Power and Morality in a Chinese Village* (Berkeley: University of California Press, 1984), and Shumin Huang, *The Spiral Road: Change in a Chinese Village through the Eyes of a Communist Party Leader* (Boulder, Colo.: Westview, 1989), communicate some of the complexities of their political subjectivity.

13   Mayfair Mei-hui Yang attributes the necessity for these oppositions to the party's self-definition as a universal and transcendent authority. She contrasts this totalizing tendency to the more subterranean influence of a relational ethics based on personal ties of kinship, reciprocity, or common identities. See Yang, "Modernity of Power," p. 415.

14   See Billeter, "System of 'Class-Status.'"

15   Although counterrevolutionaries are not, strictly speaking, a specific class in the Marxist sense, they do compose one of the categories in the class-status system of the Maoist era that falls on the side of "class enemies."

16   This distinction between "contradictions among the people" and the contradictions of class was made by Mao in his classic essay "On the Correct Handling of Contradictions among the People" (1957), reprinted in *Selected Readings from the Works of Mao Tsetung* (Peking: Foreign Languages Press, 1971), pp. 432–479.

17   See Katerina Clark, *The Soviet Novel: History as Ritual* (Chicago: University of Chicago Press, 1985).

18   See Mikhail Bakhtin, *Rabelais and His World*, trans. Hélène Iswolsky (Bloomington: Indiana University Press, 1984). And yet these activities are precisely where power most deconstructs itself, as they mark the corrupt official, who has always existed as "the other within" the party, subject to its disciplinary rituals, but who has increasingly become the popular image of power rather than the hagiographic representations of model party secretaries.

19   Fengcheng County in Liaoning Province instituted the above-mentioned "village people's educational activities group" at the village level, as reported in the *Nongcun gongzuo tongxun* [Rural work report], July 1988, pp. 42–43. These committees are composed of three to five members who take decimal units of ten households each as the object of their educational activities. The group members are elected by the people at large or are selected by the party branch in consultation with the masses. They tend to fall into six categories of persons: party members, young league members, retired village cadres, people of high moral character, women "heads of household" (*nüdangjia*), and individuals of known ability (*nengren*). These small groups are intended to carry out propaganda and educational activities, mobilize the masses for public works, resolve conflicts, transmit information, provide mediation services, and other functions. Their primary means are supposed to be limited to persuasion and the exertion of personal influence. The *shehui daode pingyi hui* is to be found in Wei County, Hebei Province (*Nongmin ribao*, July 15, 1987); a similar organization in Hunan Province was named "small group for the public discussion of ethics" (*daode gongyi xiaozu*) (*Nongmin ribao*, May 9, 1987, p. 1). The *hongbai xishi lishihui* was reported in the *Nongmin ribao* (July 15, 1987, p. 2), and the *wenming zu*, in *Renmin ribao* (May 27, 1986, p. 5).

20   The language used to elicit such an emotionally charged response would be interesting to examine. Unfortunately, the published examples of this "heart talk" (*tanxin*) are too fragmentary to explore the subtleties of its operation. One can imagine a parallel in José María Arguedas's *Deep Rivers*, in which the Catholic priest subdues an Indian revolt by addressing the rioters as wayward children who are humbled by the highly emotional expression of concern for them. There is no alternative for them but to occupy a disempowered and debased position within this discourse that "hails" them as children or beasts of the field. See Arguedas, *Deep Rivers*, trans. Frances Horning Barraclough (Austin: University of Texas Press, 1978). The emotive power of these rituals must necessarily draw our attention to the symbolic power relations embedded within discourse. As Pierre Bourdieu suggests, "Competence [eloquence, the power to move one's auditors] implies the power to

impose reception." Bourdieu, "Economics of Linguistic Exchanges," p. 648. In this sense, the language of tanxin is both a part of everyday discourse and alien to it as something imposed from above. Although they are not completely autonomous from the state, as they are often constructed in opposition to official language, underground or popular discourses offer powerful counterdiscourses to officially defined realities. The novels of Wang Shuo come to mind, along with the emergence of hooligan literature in the post-Mao period. See selections translated in Geremie Barmé, *New Ghosts, Old Dreams* (New York: Farrar, Straus and Giroux, 1990). See also a piece of reportage by Jia Lusheng, "Hei hua" [Black (unofficial) talk], *Baogao wenxue*, no. 1 (January 1989): 16–25, 76. These examples are perhaps the closest we can get to an ethnography of unofficial speech. Evidence of this heteroglossia also makes a controlled appearance in official texts when it is "ventriloquized" for calculated effects. Note the reference to farting in the story of Zhou Yixiang. Its function in the narrative is discussed in the next section of this chapter.

21   In Fengcheng County, Liaoning Province, these sorts of organizational innovations were praised for their efficacy in "resensitizing the deadened nerve endings" (*mamude "shenjing moshao" you lingminle*) of the social body and restoring avenues of communication between party organizations and the masses—can we assume between the head and the body? See *Nongcun gongzuo tongxun*, July 1988.

22   de Certeau, *Practice of Everyday Life*, p. 130.

23   Bourdieu, "Economics of Linguistic Exchanges."

24   For example, according to a lengthy discussion of the goals and methods for building spiritual civilization in the countryside, "The great mass of peasants have created [*chuangzaole*] in practice a number of excellent forms for the construction of spiritual civilization in the countryside based on the special characteristics of rural social life." See Fan Zuogang et al., comps., *Nongcun jingshen wenming jianshe xintan* [New explorations into building rural spiritual civilization] (Beijing: Nongye chubanshe, 1987), p. 6.

25   I am adapting a "specular logic" borrowed from feminist film theory—specifically, from Kaja Silverman's discussion of suture. See Silverman, *The Subject of Semiotics* (New York: Oxford University Press, 1983).

26   Lefort, *Political Forms of Modern Society*, p. 298.

27   Michel Pêcheux, *Language, Semantics, and Ideology* (New York: St. Martin's, 1982), p. 108.

28   Pierre Bourdieu, "Delegation and Political Fetishism," *Thesis Eleven*, no. 10/11 (1984/85): 56–57; emphasis in original.

29   Michel Pêcheux, "Are the Masses an Inanimate Object?" in *Linguistic Variation: Models and Methods*, ed. David Sankoff (New York: Academic Press, 1978), pp. 251–266.

30   Bourdieu, "Delegation," p. 63; emphasis in original. This discussion resembles, in some respects, Lefort's discussion of the Egocrat. See Lefort, *Political Forms of Modern Society*.

31   Havel, "Power of the Powerless," pp. 46–47.

32   In reading the text in this way, I found Barthes's five semiotic codes—semic, pro-airetic, hermeneutic, symbolic, and cultural—to be a useful tool of analysis. See Roland Barthes, *S/Z*, trans. Richard Miller (New York: Hill and Wang, 1974). I have also been guided by Silverman, *Subject of Semiotics*, and Seymour Chatman, *Story and Discourse: Narrative Structure in Fiction and Film* (Ithaca: Cornell University Press, 1978), along with discussions with Elena Feder on the narratological dimensions of the story. The issue of whether one can legitimately apply a method of reading the realist text to the socialist-realist text will be addressed later in the chapter.

33   Silverman, *Subject of Semiotics*, p. 255.

34   Ibid., p. 254.

35   Ibid., p. 263.

36   Ibid., p. 262.

37   Barthes, *S/Z*, p. 27.

38   Silverman, *Subject of Semiotics*, p. 270.

39   Phrases in quotes are from Barthes, *S/Z*, p. 216.

40   The "law-abiding household" competition is itself a part of this quasi-democratic discourse.

41   Havel, "Power of the Powerless." We could point in the more recent literature to at least one example where this limit to power went unrecognized. In *The Spiral Road*, Party Secretary Ye describes his alienation from the party bureaucracy and his own struggle to maintain socialist ideals in the face of the pressure to decollectivize. In 1984, a delegation came to his village to promote the construction of socialist spiritual civilization. They did nothing but criticize local conditions: the unpaved roads, the poultry running loose, the uncovered sewage ditches and stinky latrines. "I was furious. Who did they think we were? A bunch of rich overseas Chinese building a retirement compound in the countryside? . . . After they ate our good food and smoked our special cigarettes, they slapped our faces for being filthy peasants." Huang, *Spiral Road*, pp. 168–169. The next day he called a meeting to organize the division of the brigade.

42   One could also argue, however, that narratological theory was founded on Vladimir Propp's structural analysis of the folktale, which claims a more universal application. See Clark, *The Soviet Novel*, for her adaptation of the structural analysis of narrative to Soviet socialist-realist literature.

43   Foucault, *History of Sexuality*, pp. 140–144.

44   See Michel Foucault, *Discipline and Punish: The Birth of the Prison*, trans. Alan Sheridan (New York: Vintage, 1979), pp. 94–103, for this notion of "semiotechnique."

5   Neo-Malthusian Fantasy and National Transcendence

1   From author's field notes, May 5, 1991.

2   From author's field notes, July 14, 1991.

3   The ubiquity of population as a catchall explanation for the frustrations of every-
     day life was brought home to me after my experience with a small bureaucratic
     matter that quickly grew to be hopelessly complex. Instead of dwelling on the
     problems of bureaucratism (another important discourse in Chinese social life), I
     was stunned when friends provided explanations that all related to population as
     the principal problem (China's massive bureaucracy is necessary to keep everyone
     employed; China's population is so great, it has desensitized bureaucrats to the
     everyday frustrations of the people; and so forth).

4   In 1991, in a speech marking the seventieth anniversary of the founding of the
     Chinese Communist Party, Jiang Zeming cited it as the most pressing task, along-
     side economic and technological development, and every party cadre I interviewed
     gave it the same priority.

5   Bo Yang (Guo Yidong), *Choulou de Zhongguoren* [The ugly Chinaman] (Hong
     Kong: Yiwen tushu gongsi, 1988).

6   See Richard Bodman and Pin P. Wan, eds., *Deathsong of the River: A Reader's Guide
     to the Chinese TV Series, "Heshang"* (Ithaca: Cornell University Press, 1991). Among
     the cultural factors cited were a slavish attitude toward authority, an overly cen-
     tralized polity, and self-enclosure against foreign influences.

7   Wang Xiaoqiang and Bai Nanfeng, *Furaode pinkun: Zhongguo luohou diqude jingji
     kaocha* [The poverty of wealth: An economic investigation of China's backward
     areas] (Chengdu: Sichuan renmin chubanshe, 1986).

8   Stevan Harrell reports that the Yi people he does research with in Sichuan Province
     see the issue of China's internal "uneven development" as one that is funded by the
     unchecked exploitation of the backward periphery by the more advanced core.

9   Foucault, *History of Sexuality*, 1:146. For a discussion of how population figures in
     the rationality of the modern state, see also Michel Foucault, "Governmentality,"
     Ideology and Consciousness 6 (Autumn 1979): 5–21, reprinted in *The Foucault Effect:
     Studies in Governmental Rationality*, ed. Graham Burchell et al. (Chicago: Univer-
     sity of Chicago Press, 1991).

10   Michel Foucault, "Governmentality," p. 14.

11   *Zhongguo renkou bao* [China population gazette], June 1, 1991, pp. 1–2.

12   This attribution is extremely ironic given Mao's strongly pronatalist stance during
     the 1950s and his persecution during the antirightist campaign of 1957 of the noted
     demographer Ma Yinchu for advocating birth control. It suggests, along with other
     signs, a rehabilitation of Mao's reputation in an era of renewed concern for social
     stability and central control within the party.

13   I found this curious not only because most of the Chinese children I knew looked
     to be both healthy and well cared for but also because of the gentle criticism we
     encountered about the way we cared for our children. We were always doing the
     wrong things—dressing them inappropriately for the weather, feeding them the
     wrong foods, allowing our infant son to walk too early. And yet I never found this
     comparison expressed in genetic terms or in any specific domain of practice, with
     perhaps the exception of nutrition. Instead, it seemed to derive as the imagined

sum total of the advantages of a more advanced stage of "development" and the superior conditions (*tiaojian*) for childbearing and -rearing. Presumably Western childrearing practices were inappropriate for the *tiaojian* of a Chinese dormitory.

14   Indeed, these practices by parents of China's middle class force us to look at transnational processes that in some respects make them resonate with practices elsewhere in Asia and in the United States. See Ann Anagnost, "The Child as the Site of National Transcendence in Modern China," in *Constructing China*, ed. Ernest Young (Ann Arbor: University of Michigan Press, in press).

15   For instance, Frank Dikötter notes that the work of Pan Guangdan, a prominent eugenicist from the 1920s and 1930s, has been republished in the 1980s. "Pan called for the 'citizenization' (*gongminhua*) of the movement, as eugenics could not be considered the responsibility of scientists alone: race improvement was closely related to the politics of the state. The emergence of the nation coalesced with the rise of the race." See Dikötter, *The Concept of Race in Modern China* (Stanford: Stanford University Press, 1992), p. 175.

16   Ibid., p. 172.

17   Havel, "Power of the Powerless."

18   See Chapter 3 for a more detailed discussion of the producing body.

19   Shen Maotang, ed., *Rang renkou jingzhong changming* [Let the population alarm bell continue to ring: Reflections on the fourth population survey] (Nanjing: Nanjing Press, 1991), p. 64.

20   Foucault, *History of Sexuality*, 1:138. Although the "one-child" family is still the ideal, in many rural areas two or more are commonly permitted when the first child is a girl. See, for instance, John A. Jowitt, "Mainland China: A National One-Child Program Does Not Exist," parts 1 and 2, *Issues and Studies* 25, 9 (September 1989): 48–70; 10 (October 1989): 71–97. Susan Greenhalgh's research suggests that having two children (one of each sex) has become the ideal for most peasant families in the context of the policy. Her conclusions suggest that despite a preference for male births, female births are also highly valued. See Greenhalgh, "The Peasantization of the One-Child Policy in Shaanxi," in *Chinese Families in the Post-Mao Era*, ed. Deborah Davis and Stevan Harrell (Berkeley: University of California Press, 1993), p. 230. And yet it can also be argued that the policy sets up a complex set of unequal exchanges that have devastating effects on women: the abduction and sale of women and abusive domestic situations for women who produce girl babies. Although some practice of female infanticide exists, it is difficult to determine its actual incidence. To some extent, sex ratio imbalances can also be accounted for by the multiple ways in which female births fail to be registered. See Anagnost, "Family Violence," for a discussion of the issue of wife abuse and its reappropriation by the state to promote its population policies.

21   Susan Champagne has recently completed a dissertation on this aspect of the interconnections between childhood intelligence and *yousheng youyu*. Champagne, "Producing the Intelligent Child: Intelligence and the Child Rearing Discourse in the People's Republic of China" (Ph.D. diss., Stanford University, 1992).

22 Foucault, *History of Sexuality*, 1:150.

23 *Zhongguo renkou bao*, May 27, 1991, p. 4. Susan Greenhalgh (personal communication) suggests that I underplay the importance of "blood" in the Chinese eugenics discourse, which she recognizes in a concern for cultivating physical perfection rather than racial purity. This is clearly apparent in the eugenics laws, which promote the abortion of defective fetuses and prevent genetically inferior individuals from marrying or bearing children.

24 Stevan Harrell (personal communication) suggests that cross-cousin marriage, a powerful ethnic marker for many minority groups, is often cited by Han scholars and officials as the culprit of inbreeding among these populations.

25 See Shen Maotang, *Rang renkou jingzhong*. There is a current rage for applying Piaget's intelligence tests to minority populations, presumably to measure the degree to which a backward culture inhibits movement through the normal developmental stages of the maturing individual. An interesting counterpoint to this fascination with scientific measurement of the capacity for "civility" is the appropriation of "colorful" minority cultures by intellectuals and artists as a potential reservoir of cultural vitality to reinvigorate the national culture that has been impoverished by socialism.

26 In the same year, laws protecting the rights of those with disabilities were also drafted. These facts, together, help to explain the hypnotic appeal of a Taiwanese family drama that was aired in the Shanghai area that autumn about the deaf mute wife of the son of an elite family in the early republican period. The dramatic narrative hinged on the husband's brutal forcing of an abortifacient down his wife's throat because he could not bear the thought of her bearing a child who might be similarly disabled. This drama of forced abortion and fears of weakening the race, along with concerns for the rights of the person, played directly to contemporary concerns and provoked much discussion of the male protagonist's moral "weakness" among women viewers. See Rofel, "*Yearnings*," for another example of how women's bodies allegorize the nation in contemporary Chinese popular culture.

27 This remark is taken from my fieldnotes, September 12, 1991. I discuss this repositioning of the locus of control at greater length in Anagnost, "Family Violence."

28 These statistics were cited to me as the surplus births, defined by projected rates of "natural" population growth, that were successfully "prevented" by the birth policy. What is hidden in these statistics, of course, is the termination or prevention of actual pregnancies by abortion and sterilization, not to mention the possibility of female infanticide, that was necessary to deliver these "success" rates.

29 *Zhongguo renkoubao*, June 24, 1991, p. 1.

30 The "Sunan model" (*Sunan moshi*) characterizes the very prosperous region south of the lower Yangzi River. Its defining characteristic is the persistence of a strong collective economy despite the decentralization of production elsewhere, combined with a lively enterprise economy. A strong collective economy implies a strong collective leadership for meeting birth quotas. This article appeared in *Zhongguo renkoubao* [China Population Gazette], July 5, 1991, p. 1.

31 This story, "Ta yu tianxia diyinan" [She and the most difficult task under heaven], appeared in the *Nongmin ribao* [Peasant's daily], July 16, 1991, p. 2.

32 See Huang, *The Spiral Road*, for an illustration of how official impartiality and personal connections can be accommodated in the allocation of permission to carry a pregnancy to term.

33 Barlow, "Theorizing Woman," p. 146.

34 "Dahe zhi hun" [The soul of the big river], in *Zhongguo renkoubao*, May 13, 1991, pp. 1–2.

35 The phrase in quotation marks is taken from my fieldnotes, September 15, 1991.

36 Catherine Gallagher, "The Body versus the Social Body in the Works of Thomas Malthus and Henry Mayhew," *Representations* 14 (Spring 1986): 92.

37 See Guha, "Historiography of Colonial India," p. 43, for a discussion of the obsession of nationalist historiography in India to account for the failure of the nation "to come into its own." Rofel, "*Yearnings*," reveals how the trope of self-sacrifice works through gendered categories in popular debates that allegorize the nation in a popular television series. Her essay bears far too many implications for the examples here for me to present.

38 Catherine Gallagher, "The Bio-Economics of *Our Mutual Friend*," *Zone* 5 (1989): 345–365, discusses this opposition borrowed from Ruskin's critique of Malthus. But this construction was not always uncontested and stands in marked contrast to Mao's pronatalist stance early in the post-Liberation period.

39 I am indebted to Lisa Rofel (personal communication) for a most emphatic reminder of this basic point, even to the felicitous wording offered here.

40 Xie Zhihong and Lusheng Jia, *Gulaode zui'e: Quanguo funu da guaimai jishi* [An age-old crime: An on-the-spot record of the nation-wide abduction and sale of women] (Zhejiang: Zhejiang wenyi chubanshe, 1989).

41 This sensational display perhaps accounts for a story that appeared in the Western press about the sale of women, which noted that in some rural marketplaces women "had been observed" for sale in cages, dressed only in their underwear with price placards hung around their necks. This event raises issues about how the discourse of social disorder within China itself gets picked up in an international press eager to display these markers of China's backwardness and internal disarray. The scandal of women being bought and sold is only one of a number of regularly recurring stories that expose these scandals as if they were really "news," in the sense of being a "novel" discovery. For instance, without any apparent awareness of their staged nature, the pictures promoting Xie and Jia's book on this subject were later reprinted in Nicholas D. Kristof and Sheryl WuDunn, *China Wakes: The Struggle for the Soul of a Rising Power* (New York: Random House/Times, 1994), p. 211.

42 Wu Ying, "Renfanzi yu yeman de hunyin" [The human peddler and a barbaric marriage], *Baogao wenxue* [Reportage literature] 1 (1989): 60–65. The journal *Baogao wenxue* was discontinued soon after the Tiananmen crackdown. "Reportage literature," which flowered in the post-Mao period, is a genre that blurs the line

between fiction and reportage in its literary narrativization of events, reconstruction of dialogue, and use of composite characters. The category also tends to bridge the line between work of recognized literary merit and writing that verges on the sensational or pornographic, especially in its depiction of violent crime. This literature, in its focus on the ills of society, is intended as a literature of exposure, which accounts for its suppression after 1989. But in the form it takes in legal pictorials, it vividly documents the dangers of social disorder in ways that restore popular support for a strong, centralized leadership.

43   "Baoying," in *Nongmin ribao*, July 4, 1991, p. 3. Women are not the only commodity moved by this traffic. Children are also stolen, bought, and sold. Kidnappers operating in Jiangsu Province, where I lived, stole children and then posed as peasants on the run who had decided to sell their out-of-plan children so they could return home. *Minzhu yu fazhi* [Democracy and law], May 21, 1991, p. 1.

44   It also suggests a potent (and, one would suspect, deeply felt) marker of class differentiation.

45   See *Xincun* [New village], July 1990.

46   Jean Comaroff and John Comaroff, *Of Revelation and Revolution: Christianity, Colonialism, and Consciousness in South Africa*, vol. 1 (Chicago: University of Chicago Press, 1991), p. 5.

6   Chili Pepper Politics

1   The film was released in 1991. It was based on a story by Chen Yuanbin, "Wanjia sugong" [The Wan family lawsuit]. The screenplay can be found in Liu Heng, *Liu Heng yingshi zuopinji* [The collected screenplays of Liu Heng] (Beijing: Zhongguo shehui kexue chubanshe, 1993). This discussion of Zhang Yimou's film is indebted to many fruitful discussions with Heh-Rahn Park, who may, however, find my reading entirely too optimistic.

2   This quote is from an interview with Zhang Yimou by an anonymous interviewer as reported in the China News Digest, Books and Journals Review, April 25, 1993, on the World Wide Web (http://www.cnd.org:8010/). The dictionary pronunciation is *shuofa*. Zhang Yimou may have been responding to the English-language subtitles which translate *shuafa* as "apology."

3   Louis Althusser, "Ideology and Ideological State Apparatuses," in *Lenin and Philosophy* (New York: Monthly Review Press, 1971), p. 170.

4   For a more detailed discussion of the village compacts in reform-era China and a brief history of their earlier prototypes during the Maoist era, see Ann Anagnost "Socialist Ethics and the Legal System," in *Popular Protest and Political Culture in Modern China*, ed. Jeffrey N. Wasserstrom and Elizabeth J. Perry (Boulder, Colo.: Westview, 1992), pp. 177–205, and Anagnost, "Constructing the Civilized Community." See also Timothy Cheek, "Contracts and Ideological Control in Village Administration: Tensions in the 'Village Covenant System' in Late Imperial China"

(paper presented at the annual meeting of the Association of Asian Studies, Washington, D.C., March 1984), for a discussion of the presocialist antecedents of these compacts in late imperial statecraft and in Liang Shumin's village reform movement.

5   Indeed, the official discourse on the compacts effectively confuses Homi Bhabha's distinction between the pedagogical and performative aspects of subjectivity. Bhabha's formulation replicates at the level of a national body Foucault's dual sense of the subject, both as "subject to" a heteronomous rule and as an agent "tied to his [sic] own identity by a conscience or self-knowledge." What Bhabha calls the "pedagogical" refers to a set of practices and discourses that calls into being a subjective identification of individuals with a national body, a citizenry. See Bhabha, "DissemiNation," p. 297, and Michel Foucault, "The Subject and Power," afterword to *Michel Foucault: Beyond Structuralism and Hermeneutics*, ed. Hubert L. Dreyfus and Paul Rabinow (Chicago: University of Chicago Press, 1983), p. 212.

6   See Duara, *Rescuing History*. For a similar discussion of the recursivity of political representation more generally, see Spivak, "Can the Subaltern Speak?" and Bourdieu, "Delegation."

7   I owe this felicitous wording to Myron Cohen from his comments on an earlier draft of this paper.

8   The compacts are supposed to be drafted by the people themselves or by the newly constituted village committees (*cunwei*), but the process is usually initiated and implemented under the leadership of local party organizations and personnel. In Jiangdong Township (outside Nanjing), where I interviewed in 1991, the compact was first drafted in 1983 by various bureaus within the local government in response to the most urgent needs, identified as the implementation of the birth policy and the handling of civil disputes. The compact was revised at the township level in 1990 by the local People's Congress (*renda*). Huang mentions village compacts as part of the normal functioning of local government. The party secretary himself wrote the local laws and ordinances, as well as presiding over litigations and dispensing justice. See Huang, *The Spiral Road*, p. 107.

9   These are, of course, idealized locations. Subjectivity never lies on one side or the other but in an uncertain, oscillating space between the pedagogical and the performative, between being made subject to a heteronomous order of meaning and the seizing upon one's subject position as a place of agency.

10   See Mayfair Mei-hui Yang, "Of Gender, State Censorship, and Overseas Capital: An Interview with Director Zhang Yimou," *Public Culture* 5, 2 (Winter 1993): 299.

11   See Anagnost, "Prosperity and Counter-Prosperity," for a discussion of the early 1980s when local party secretaries still faithful to a Maoist egalitarian ethic acted as a significant constraint on peasant enterprises. Local officials may also drag their heels on granting permits if the application fails to be accompanied by a gift or bribe. In 1991, the janitor in my building at Nanjing University had pulled her labor from her family's chicken-processing business precisely because of the fear of too much prosperity. However, she did not take too well to the subservient position

required by her status as a "temporary worker" (*linshigong*) of an urban work unit, which led to many noisy altercations with the building manager. Not surprisingly, she soon left her job for the more glamorous business of plucking chickens, declaring that charring was no job for a "beautiful person" (*meiren*) like herself.

12 For instance, the compact for Jiangdong Township revised in 1990 has an entire section regarding the rules for housing construction, the second article of which stipulates: "Land conservation and management is a basic national policy. . . . Villagers, wishing to build, must obtain permission from the village government first before approaching the township land management office for a permit."

13 See Anagnost, "Family Violence," for a discussion of how the state's rhetoric of this "victimization" of women operates as a disavowal of the violence generated by its own policies.

14 See Huang, *The Spiral Road*, for a chilling account of the complex calculus between the impersonal exercise of power and personal obligations to kin and family that comes into play when the birth quota dictates that not all pregnancies be allowed to come to term.

15 This point beckons toward Zhang Yimou's observations about the lack of avenues of appeal: "[*The Story of Qiu Ju*] is a very ordinary story that happens all the time in China. One never knows who to talk to, what to do, where to go. Most problems are not so bad to start with, they only become so because of the workings of the bureaucratic system and the ordeals you have to go through." See the interview with Zhang Yimou, *China News Digest*.

16 For instance, Section 1, Article 6 of the 1990 revision of the compact for Jiangdong Township requires all citizens to assist and support the cadres in charge of mediation, to report all civil disputes promptly, and not to resort to suicide as a mode of protest or escalation of the conflict.

17 My use of how the dual senses of "the supplement" cover over the internal contradictions of power is clearly inspired by Derrida, *Of Grammatology*.

18 The discouragement of "unhealthy practices" (such as feudal superstition, gambling), the adherence to national policies (land use, birth limitation, the fulfillment of state contracts), and social order issues (family quarrels, interpersonal disputes, vandalism, and petty theft) all fall within the domain of the compact.

19 See Chapter 5 for a discussion of this notion of "euphemization" in the context of the birth policy.

20 The attribution of *renzhi*, as opposed to *fazhi* (the abstract and impersonal "rule by law"), as a deeply rooted pattern in the Chinese national character was central to the cultural critique of the late 1980s. While recognizing the necessity for oppositional intellectuals in China to clothe their political critique in the guise of a cultural one, we all too easily use the same argument, which lapses into an orientalizing discourse that doesn't properly undertake the project of how renzhi is actively reconstituted under the conditions of late-twentieth-century capitalism. The village compact, as a model for community reform, lies at the heart of the issues concerning popular sovereignty and history in the post-Mao period. Al-

though the compacts bear some resemblance to the *xiangyue* of the late imperial period, the question of this historical identity is a vexed one and must be put into the context of the "heated" culture debates of the late 1980s. The compact is, therefore, a "split" object, simultaneously old and new, a quintessentially "Chinese" approach to the social order *and* a novel instrument of "democratic reform." This splitness suggests the working of ideology, the masking of an undecidable contradiction within the party's own discourse. See Anagnost, "Constructing the Civilized Community," for a more extended discussion of the problem of history in the context of the village compacts.

21   See Bourdieu, "Economics of Linguistic Exchanges," on how language operates as symbolic capital and symbolic violence.

22   *Diao* means "artful," "tricky," "sly." It can also refer to people who like to make things difficult. See Lianjiang Li and Kevin O'Brien, "Chinese Villagers and Popular Resistance" (paper presented at the Twenty-Fourth Sino-American Conference on Contemporary China, Washington, D.C., June 1995), for *diaomin* strategies dealing with the arbitrary power of local officials. I thank the authors for allowing me to cite their unpublished work.

23   One might note the Chinese expression "running into a nail" (*peng dingzi*) for encountering an obstacle in achieving one's goal. A *dingzihu* ("nail household") therefore is a "problem household" that refuses to comply with state policy. On this category, see ibid. See Anagnost, "Prosperity and Counter-Prosperity," on the general practice of constituting categories of social analysis as objects of control by means of the nominalizer *hu* ("household"), and Anagnost, "Family Violence," for a discussion of dingzihu as a designation in the implementation of the birth policy. Indeed, many of the examples of dingzihu violence cited by Li and O'Brien seem to have occurred in the context of challenges to the birth policy.

24   Li and O'Brien, "Chinese Villagers and Popular Resistance," discuss the social colorations of these terms.

25   See Chapters 3 and 4 on how the category "law-abiding household" (*zunji shoufa hu*) operates in the state's rituals of subjectification.

26   This speculation is explored by Li and O'Brien, "Chinese Villagers and Popular Resistance," pp. 23–25.

27   See Sylvia Chan, "A Bird-Cage Culture: How Big Was the Cage?" in *China Review*, ed. Joseph Yu-shek Cheng and Maurice Brosseau (Hong Kong: Chinese University Press, 1993), p. 19.

28   See Chapter 5 for a discussion of how financial penalties in birth policy implementation might operate as a marker of class difference.

29   Gong Li told her director during filming: "I myself still can't understand why Qiu Ju keeps on pursuing this matter, even though she's received formal monetary reparations from the cadres. You need to make the reason clearer to the audience, otherwise they will think this woman is being unreasonable, pestering people endlessly." Zhang Yimou assures her that the village chief's imperious manner will

make the audience side with Qiu Ju. See Mayfair Mei-hui Yang, "Of Gender, State Censorship, and Overseas Capital," p. 304.

30   Interview with Zhang Yimou, *China News Digest*.

31   See, for instance, Barlow, "Theorizing Woman," on the "women's association" (*fulian*) as a state apparatus that enters the domestic sphere, bearing the state's solicitous concern for women's reproductive health.

32   Meng Yue, "Female Images and National Myth," in *Gender Politics in Modern China: Writing and Feminism*, ed. Tani Barlow, pp. 119–136 (Durham: Duke University Press, 1993).

33   It would be a mistake, however, to reduce Qiu Ju's sense of injury entirely to the register of sexuality, given the way in which concerns of male potency in Chinese medical practice are fully integrated into the overall health of male bodies and how concerns about reproduction and labor power are intensified by the economic reforms.

34   See Chapters 1 and 5, respectively, for elaborations of these two modes of embodiment.

35   Many of these films, in particular *Yellow Earth* [*Huang tudi*] (dir. Chen Kaige), *Old Well* [*Lao jing*] (dir. Wu Tianming, 1987), and *Red Sorghum* [*Hong gaoliang*] (dir. Zhang Yimou, 1987), were made by the "fifth generation" directors from the Shaanxi Film Studio. For a discussion of how this nostalgic retrieval of folk culture influenced popular music, see Andrew F. Jones, *Like a Knife: Ideology and Genre in Contemporary Chinese Popular Music* (Ithaca: Cornell East Asia Institute, 1992), p. 55.

36   For a brilliant critique of xungen literature, see Jing Wang, "Romancing the Subject," pp. 115–142.

37   Lisa Rofel, "Liberation Nostalgia and a Yearning for Modernity," in *Engendering China: Women, Culture, and the State*, ed. Christina K. Gilmartin, Gail Hershatter, Lisa Rofel, and Tyrene White (Cambridge: Harvard University Press, 1994).

38   This phrase was suggested by Ted Huters (personal communication).

39   See Chapter 5 for a discussion of how this film fits into a more general theme of party work as a form of "consuming labor."

40   My comments on the psychological effects of the film's camerawork are indebted to observations made by Shawn Brixley, professor of film at the University of Washington, in a seminar on Chinese film taught by Jerome Silbergeld. Lucien Jamey, one of the students in this course, wrote a fascinating seminar paper in which he detailed the aspects of the camerawork that employed an optic of surveillance that contributed to the documentary feel of the film but also captured, perhaps for a Chinese audience, the reality of living in a surveillance state.

41   See Chapter 5 for a discussion of how the trade in women's bodies becomes a potent signifier of the distance between the country and the city.

42   Here I must regretfully note the absence in my analysis of an ethnography of reception, which could have documented how this film was in fact received by its intended audience.

43   That Zhang Yimou himself is aware of how *The Story of Qiu Ju* may be read as an allegory of how the bans on his films were removed in China is clear from the interview in the *China News Digest*: "It does not matter whether I am Qiu Ju or whether her story is like mine since this is a very ordinary story that happens all the time in China. . . . The films [*Judou* and *Raise the Red Lantern*] were never released and nobody ever gave me a '*shuafa*' [*sic*] about the ban."

44   Lydia Liu, "Translingual Practice," 184–186.

45   Taussig, *Mimesis and Alterity*, p. xvii.

46   See Chapter 5 for a discussion of how the market commodifies women as a scarce resource and becomes, thereby, a source of unfreedom for them.

47   For de Certeau's notion of tactics in the context of modern China, see Chapter 2.

48   Quoted passages are from Jing Wang, "*Heshang* and the Paradoxes of Chinese Enlightenment," *Bulletin of Concerned Asian Scholars* 23, 3 (1991): 24.

49   Harvey, *Condition of Postmodernity*.

50   Jing Wang, "*Heshang* and the Paradoxes of Chinese Enlightenment," p. 29.

7   The Nationscape

1   Splendid China first opened to the public in the fall of 1989. This theme park has its analogs in Asia and elsewhere. Indeed, we can see its origins in the great exhibitions of the nineteenth century as described by Mitchell, *Colonizing Egypt*. See John Pemberton, *On the Subject of "Java"* (Ithaca: Cornell University Press, 1994), for a compelling reading of Indonesia's Mini, which must be one of the earliest of these miniature "national" parks, having opened in 1975.

2   Susan Stewart, *On Longing: Narratives of the Miniature, the Gigantic, the Souvenir, the Collection* (1984; reprint, Durham: Duke University Press, 1993), p. 43.

3   Ibid., p. 45.

4   This photograph records the making of the miniature display in Teng County, Shandong, that is similar to the one in Shenzhen but modeled on a smaller scale and funded by an overseas Chinese company.

5   Benedict Anderson, *Imagined Communities*, p. 172.

6   Ibid., pp. 184–185. This representation of the nation-space is akin to Anderson's idea of the nation as a logo, in which it is lifted out of its geographic context like a puzzle piece in the map of the world (personal communication).

7   Geoffrey Bennington, "Postal Politics and the Institution of the Nation," in *Nation and Narration*, ed. Homi K. Bhabha (London: Routledge, 1990), p. 121. Of course, the notion of Shenzhen as the center or as the fast-forward projection into the future of the nation is something that is actively contested. See note 8 below.

8   However, Splendid China is by no means the only tourist attraction in Shenzhen to display the panoply of "recognized" ethnicities constituting the "imagined community" of the Chinese multiethnic nation-state. The Folk Cultural Village in Shenzhen was set up by the end of August 1992. Due to "limited space," it includes

hamlets or villages of only twenty-one Chinese minority nationalities and covers forty-six hectares. By October 1992 it reported more than five million admissions.

9   Compare Benedict Anderson's discussion of the secularization of sacred sites as the necessary precondition to their becoming part of the "regalia" of the modern nation-state. Anderson, *Imagined Communities*, p. 182. The inclusion of the Potala Palace in the Chinese-financed sister park in Florida that replicates Splendid China sparked a chain of demonstrations by those who protest China's occupation of Tibet. See *New York Times*, January 1994. This more recent production deserves a commentary of its own that examines China's new national assertiveness that has grown along with the staggering increase in its economic growth since the Tiananmen crackdown.

10   See Chapter 3 for a discussion of how this multiplicity of alternatives becomes the language by which the various factions within the party now argue about China's proper course of modernization. This heteroglossia is in marked contrast to the Maoist tendency toward a totalitarian "one cut of the knife" in which all regions were subject to the same developmental model regardless of local conditions.

11   Deng's sobriquet as "the Whirlwind" appeared in the *Beijing Review* and is an appellation that heightens the ironic contrast between a dynamic natural force and the declining physical powers of the aging leader. However, the designation of his journey as a "southern progress," in its evocation of the ritual progressions of the Qing emperors, draws attention to the ritual efficacy of Deng's physical presence as the one figure (emperor/god/national leader) with sufficient prestige to successfully affirm China's economic opening to the outside. See James L. Hevia, *Cherishing Men from Afar: Qing Guest Ritual and the Macartney Embassy of 1793* (Durham: Duke University Press, 1995), for a discussion of the constitutive nature of Chinese ritual.

12   Benedict Anderson, *Imagined Communities*, and Bhabha, "DissemiNation." See Duara, *Rescuing History*, for a discussion of the aporias within early-twentieth-century discourses of Chinese nationalism.

13   For this image, see Tom Nairn, "The Modern Janus," in *The Breakup of Britain* (London: New Left Books, 1977), pp. 329–363, and its later elaboration in Benedict Anderson, *Imagined Communities*, and Bhabha, "DissemiNation."

14   My thanks to Marilyn Young for reminding me of this one exception. It is exemplary here in the sense that Sun Yatsen, as the "father" of the Chinese nation, becomes the last link represented before the phenomenon of Shenzhen itself, which suggests a refusal to recognize the socialist era as enabling China to progress in history. Sun also represents the former unity of the national movement before its split into two warring parties; therefore he operates as a wishful political rapprochement between Taiwan and the mainland that would parallel the increasing economic ties between them.

15   Bennington, "Postal Politics," p. 120.

16   My thanks to Angus Lockyer for suggesting this possibility. Likewise, Benedict

Anderson suggests that the nation must be narrated to conceal the ruptures that disturb the desired presence of a seamless continuity. Anderson, *Imagined Communities*, pp. 204–205.

17 My reading here takes this diminished and re-sited representation of Zhongnanhai quite seriously in part because of the very real competition between the two places in the realm of representation. An attraction that mimics Shenzhen's Folk Cultural Village, called the Nationalities Culture Center, is in construction outside Beijing with a projected cost of $120 million U.S. dollars. It plans to be more inclusive, representing all fifty-six of China's officially recognized national minorities and covering 280 hectares, and more authentic, avoiding some of the "inaccuracies" of the Shenzhen park. The number of visitors to this new park is expected to surpass the one in Shenzhen quickly because of its more "comprehensive elucidation of all the nationalities in China" (*Beijing Review*, October 19, 1992, p. 33). We might well read this expression of intent as a reassertion of the power of the center to "represent" the nation more authoritatively, in the two senses of the word that Spivak notes, as portrait *and* proxy. See Spivak, "Can the Subaltern Speak?" p. 276. Meanwhile, not to be outdone, Shenzhen is planning two new parks, Five Thousand Years of China and the Cultural City of Ancient China. Various shopping venues will be available in a series of palaces built in the successive dynastic styles (*Beijing Review*, August 10, 1992, p. 35).

18 Mitchell, *Colonizing Egypt*, p. xiii. This book offers an exemplary discussion of how a national or cultural "tradition" becomes retrospectively "enframed" and how this enframement colludes with the simultaneous construction of "modernity."

19 Ibid., p. 19.

20 Ibid., p. 11. Once again, I am indebted to Mitchell for the importance of distance in enframing tradition.

21 See Susan Willis, *A Primer for Daily Life* (London: Routledge, 1991), p. 4.

22 Indeed, one could focus on travelogue, a genre that figures prominently in Chinese television, as yet another leisurely pastime in the visual consumption of the national space. Even so, it was Su Xiaokang's involvement in the making of a documentary film on the Yellow River that inspired him to blast open the problem of history in "River Elegy" (*Heshang*). See Bodman, "From History to Allegory to Art," p. 15.

23 Among the first of these was the renovation of the Temple of the City God (Chenghuang miao) in Shanghai into a shopping "mall" and Liulichang, an alley of curiosity shops in Beijing, which in the early 1980s was "renovated" to re-create the look of the city in late imperial times.

24 Stewart, *On Longing*, p. 66.

25 Nanjing was the capital of the Guomintang (KMT) government that fled to Taiwan in 1949; many of the government bureaucrats who left still have relatives living in the city.

26 Stewart, *On Longing* pp. 59–60. Hence the importance of the literary referent of *The Peach Blossom Fan* to evoke the ambience of the past of this place.

27 These images collectively make up what Benedict Anderson calls a "pictorial cen-
    sus" of the state's patrimony, its official "regalia," a process of "logoization" that is
    only one step away from the market. See Anderson, *Imagined Communities*, p. 182.
    What comes immediately to mind as the logo that most represents the nation is, of
    course, the Great Wall, an "antique" production that acquires its significance as
    national sign only in retrospect. See Arthur Waldron, "Representing China: The
    Great Wall and Cultural Nationalism in the Twentieth Century," in *Cultural Na-
    tionalism in East Asia: Representation and Identity*, ed. Harumi Befu (Berkeley:
    Institute of East Asian Studies, University of California, 1993), pp. 107–138, for a
    discussion of the complex significations that have condensed there in the post-Mao
    period.

28 Stewart, *On Longing*, p. 61.

29 Caren Kaplan, "Deterritorializations: The Rewriting of Home and Exile in Western
    Feminist Discourse," *Cultural Critique* 6 (Spring 1987): 197.

30 Cascardi cited in Lydia Liu, "Translingual Practice," p. 171, and Anthony J. Cascardi,
    The Subject of Modernity (Cambridge: Cambridge University Press, 1992), p. 179.

31 Benedict Anderson, *Imagined Communities*, p. 183. However, my friend's practice
    of drawing the national icons was not necessarily restricted to the private realm of
    reverie but was, in her career as a young propagandist for the local party commit-
    tee, put to public use in embellishing "blackboard newspapers" and propaganda
    materials, the latter crudely dittoed by inscribing a film with a stylus and then using
    a flexible scraper to spread the ink onto paper by hand, a mode of reproduction
    that can best be described as semimechanical. Her activities as a propagandist
    marked her, moreover, as one securely in possession of the status of "revolutionary
    successor" to be groomed for party membership.

32 Nairn, *Breakup of Britain*, p. 357. See Rey Chow, *Writing Diaspora: Tactics of Inter-
    vention in Contemporary Cultural Studies* (Bloomington: Indiana University Press,
    1992), for her critical examination of the "Maoist (she)" as a particular kind of
    China scholar who mourns the loss of "socialist" China as an idealized object of
    desire and who cannot bear the thought of China's "capitulation" to a capitalist
    modernity. Although this reading is not totally inaccurate, it does ignore the posi-
    tionality of those China scholars entering the field during the Vietnam War era who
    saw their scholarship as a necessary intervention into U.S. cold war imperialism.

33 Feng Jicai's acerbic short story "The Mao Button" comments on the status antago-
    nism provoked by such objects during the Cultural Revolution. Feng Jicai, "The
    Mao Button," in *"Chrysanthemums" and Other Stories*, trans. Susan Wilf Chen
    (New York: Harcourt Brace Jovanovich, 1985), pp. 14–29. These mementos of the
    Cultural Revolution had acquired, by the early 1980s, a status equivalent to nuclear
    waste as guilty reminders of past participation in political violence, causing many
    to divest themselves of their collections, often passing them into the hands of
    foreign students who were all too eager to acquire them, thus these objects entered
    into a global circuit of symbolic exchanges.

34 This mountain is located near Tacheng City in an ethnic Uighur area. The local

tourist bureau reports that every part of Mao's body lies in proportion, the features of his face being especially clear. This mountain site is expected to draw an influx of tourists caught up in the current "Mao craze," intensified by the observance this year of his birth one hundred years ago. Reported by UPI, July 13, 1993, as posted in the China News Digest—Global News, July 14, 1993, on the World Wide Web (http://www.cnd.org:8010/). The use of Mao images as talismans against traffic accidents by taxi drivers in Guangdong is frequently cited in the international media as evidence for the "rebirth" of a "Mao cult." See Geremie Barmé, *Shades of Mao: The Posthumous Cult of the Great Leader* (Armonk, N.Y.: M. E. Sharpe, 1996), for an encyclopedic accounting of the Mao cult of the 1990s.

35   Bhabha, "DissemiNation," p. 292.

36   Walter Benjamin, "The Work of Art in the Age of Mechanical Reproduction," in *Illuminations*, trans. Harry Zohn (New York: Schocken, 1969), p. 220.

BIBLIOGRAPHY

Althusser, Louis. "Ideology and Ideological State Apparatuses." In *Lenin and Philosophy*, pp. 127–186. New York: Monthly Review Press, 1971.

Anagnost, Ann. "The Child as the Site of National Transcendence in Modern China." In *Constructing China*, ed. Ernest Young. Ann Arbor: University of Michigan Press, in press.

——. "Constructing the Civilized Community." In *Culture and State in Chinese History: Conventions, Conflicts, and Accommodations*, ed. R. Bin Wong, Theodore Huters, and Pauline Yu. Stanford: Stanford University Press, in press.

——. "Family Violence and Magical Violence: The 'Woman-as-Victim' in China's One-Child Family Policy." *Women and Language* 1, 2 (1988): 16–22.

——. "Prosperity and Counter-Prosperity: The Moral Discourse on Wealth in Post-Mao China." In *Marxism and the Chinese Experience*, ed. Arif Dirlik and Maurice Meisner, pp. 210–234. Armonk, N.Y.: M. E. Sharpe, 1989.

——. "Socialist Ethics and the Legal System." In *Popular Protest and Political Culture in Modern China*, ed. Jeffrey N. Wasserstrom and Elizabeth J. Perry, pp. 177–205. Boulder, Colo.: Westview, 1992.

——. "The Transformation of Gender in Modern China." In *Gender and Anthropology: Critical Reviews for Research and Teaching*, ed. Sandra Morgan, pp. 313–329. Amherst: Project on Gender and the Curriculum sponsored by the American Anthropological Association, 1989.

Anderson, Benedict. *Imagined Communities: Reflections on the Origin and Spread of Nationalism.* 2d ed. London: Verso, 1991.

Anderson, Marston. *The Limits of Realism: Chinese Fiction in the Revolutionary Period.* Berkeley: University of California Press, 1990.

Arguedas, José María. *Deep Rivers.* Trans. Frances Horning Barraclough. Austin: University of Texas Press, 1978.

Austin, J. L. *Philosophical Papers.* Ed. J. O. Urmson and G. L. Warnock. New York: Oxford University Press, 1979.

Bakhtin, Mikhail. *Rabelais and His World.* Trans. Hélène Iswolsky. Bloomington: Indiana University Press, 1984.

Balibar, Etienne. "The Nation Form: History and Ideology." In Etienne Balibar and Immanuel Wallerstein, *Race, Nation, Class: Ambiguous Identities*, pp. 86–106. London: Verso, 1991.

Barlow, Tani. "Editor's Introduction." *positions* 1, 1 (Spring 1993): v–vii.

———. "Theorizing Woman: *Funu, Guojia, Jiating* [Chinese Woman, Chinese State, Chinese Family]." *Genders* 10 (Spring 1991): 132–160.

———. "*Zhishifenzi* [Chinese Intellectuals] and Power." *Dialectical Anthropology* 16 (1991): 209–232.

Barmé, Geremie. *Shades of Mao: The Posthumous Cult of the Great Leader* (Armonk, N.Y.: M. E. Sharpe, 1996).

———. "A Word for the Imposter—Introducing the Drama of Sha Yexin." *Renditions*, nos. 19–20 (1983): 319–332.

———, ed. *New Ghosts, Old Dreams*. New York: Farrar, Straus and Giroux, 1990.

Barthes, Roland. *The Rustle of Language*. New York: Hill and Wang, 1986.

———. *S/Z*. Trans. Richard Miller. New York: Hill and Wang, 1974.

Belden, Jack. *China Shakes the World*. New York: Monthly Review, 1970.

Benjamin, Walter. "The Work of Art in the Age of Mechanical Reproduction." In *Illuminations*, pp. 217–252. Trans. Harry Zohn. New York: Schocken, 1969.

Bennington, Geoffrey. "Postal Politics and the Institution of the Nation." In *Nation and Narration*, ed. Homi K. Bhabha, pp. 121–137. London: Routledge, 1990.

Benveniste, Emile. *Problems in General Linguistics*. Coral Gables, Fla.: University of Miami Press, 1971.

Bhabha, Homi K. "DissemiNation: Time, Narrative, and the Margins of the Modern Nation." In *Nation and Narration*, ed. Homi K. Bhabha, pp. 291–322. London: Routledge, 1990.

———. "Sly Civility." *October* 34 (1985): 71–80.

———, ed. *Nation and Narration*. London: Routledge, 1990.

Billeter, Jean-François. "The System of 'Class-Status.'" In *The Scope of State Power in China*, ed. Stuart R. Schram, pp. 127–169. London: School of Oriental and African Studies, 1985.

Blecher, Marc. "Structural Change and the Political Articulation of Social Interest in Revolutionary and Socialist China." In *Marxism and the Chinese Experience*, ed. Arif Dirlik and Maurice Meisner, pp. 190–209. Armonk, N.Y.: M. E. Sharpe, 1989.

Bodman, Richard. "From History to Allegory to Art: A Personal Search for Interpretation." In *Deathsong of the River: A Reader's Guide to the Chinese TV Series, "Heshang,"* ed. Richard Bodman and Pin P. Wan, pp. 1–61. Ithaca: Cornell University Press, 1991.

Bodman, Richard, and Pin P. Wan, eds. *Deathsong of the River: A Reader's Guide to the Chinese TV Series, "Heshang."* Ithaca: Cornell University Press, 1991.

Bourdieu, Pierre. "Delegation and Political Fetishism." *Thesis Eleven*, no. 10/11 (1984/85): 56–70.

———. "The Economics of Linguistic Exchanges." *Social Science Information* 16 (1977): 645–668.

——. *Outline for a Theory of Practice.* Cambridge: Cambridge University Press, 1977.

Bo Yang (Guo Yidong). *Choulou de Zhongguoren* [The ugly Chinaman]. Hong Kong: Yiwen tushu gongsi, 1988.

Cao, Glen. *Beijinger in New York.* Trans. Ted Wang. San Francisco: Cypress Book Company, 1993.

Cascardi, Anthony J. *The Subject of Modernity.* Cambridge: Cambridge University Press, 1992.

Champagne, Susan. "Producing the Intelligent Child: Intelligence and the Child Rearing Discourse in the People's Republic of China" (Ph.D. diss., Stanford University, 1992).

Chan, Anita, Richard Madsen, and Jonathan Unger. *Chen Village: The Recent History of a Peasant Community in Mao's China.* Berkeley: University of California Press, 1984.

Chan, Sylvia. "A Bird-Cage Culture: How Big Was the Cage?" In *China Review*, ed. Joseph Yu-shek Cheng and Maurice Brosseau. Hong Kong: Chinese University Press, 1993.

Chatman, Seymour. *Story and Discourse: Narrative Structure in Fiction and Film.* Ithaca: Cornell University Press, 1978.

Chatterjee, Partha. *Nationalist Thought and the Colonial World: A Derivative Discourse.* Tokyo: Zed, 1986.

——. *The Nation and Its Fragments.* Princeton: Princeton University Press, 1993.

Cheek, Timothy. "Contracts and Ideological Control in Village Administration: Tensions in the 'Village Covenant System' in Late Imperial China." Paper presented at the annual meeting of the Association of Asian Studies, Washington, D.C., March 1984.

Chen, Yuan-tsung. *The Dragon's Village: An Autobiographical Novel of Revolutionary China.* New York: Penguin, 1981.

Chiao Chien. "Chinese Strategic Behavior: Continuity and Change." Paper delivered at the 1985 Annual Meetings of the American Anthropological Association.

Chow, Rey. "Male Narcissism and National Culture: Subjectivity in Chen Kaige's *King of the Children.*" *Camera Obscura* 25/26 (1991): 9–39.

——. *Woman and Chinese Modernity: The Politics of Reading West and East.* Minneapolis: University of Minnesota Press, 1991.

——. *Writing Diaspora: Tactics of Intervention in Contemporary Cultural Studies.* Bloomington: Indiana University Press, 1992.

Clark, Katerina. *The Soviet Novel: History as Ritual.* Chicago: University of Chicago Press, 1985.

Cohen, Myron. "Cultural and Political Inventions in Modern China: The Case of the Chinese 'Peasant.'" In *China in Transformation*, ed. Weiming Tu, pp. 151–170. Cambridge: Harvard University Press, 1994.

Comaroff, Jean, and John Comaroff. *Of Revelation and Revolution: Christianity, Colonialism, and Consciousness in South Africa.* Vol. 1. Chicago: University of Chicago Press, 1991.

DeBernardi, Jean. "Historical Allusion and the Defense of Identity: Malaysian Chinese

Popular Religion." In *Asian Visions of Authority*, ed. Charles Keyes, Laurel Kendall, and Helen Hardacre, pp. 117–140. Honolulu: University of Hawaii Press, 1994.

de Certeau, Michel. "The Oppositional Practices of Everyday Life." *Social Text* 3 (Fall 1980): 3–43.

——. *The Practice of Everyday Life*. Berkeley: University of California Press, 1984.

de Lauretis, Teresa. *Alice Doesn't: Feminism, Semiotics, Cinema*. Bloomington: Indiana University Press, 1984.

Deng Tuo. "Sanshiliu ji" [The thirty-six stratagems], in *Deng Tuo shi wen xuan* [Selected works] (Beijing: Renmin ribao, 1986), pp. 104–107.

Derrida. Jacques. *Limited Inc*. Trans. Samuel Weber. Evanston, Ill.: Northwestern University Press, 1988.

——. *Of Grammatology*. Trans. Gayatri Chakravorty Spivak. Baltimore: Johns Hopkins University Press, 1976.

——. "Signature Event Context." Trans. Alan Bass. In *Margins of Philosophy*, pp. 307–330. Chicago: University of Chicago Press, 1982.

Detienne, Marcel, and Jean-Pierre Vernant. *Cunning Intelligence in Greek Culture and Society*. Atlantic Highlands, N.J.: Humanities Press, 1978.

Dikötter, Frank. *The Concept of Race in Modern China*. Stanford: Stanford University Press, 1992.

Dirlik, Arif. "The Predicament of Marxist Revolutionary Consciousness: Mao Zedong, Antonio Gramsci, and the Reformulation of Marxist Revolutionary Theory." *Modern China* 9, 2 (April 1983): 182–211.

Dittmer, Lowell. "Radical Ideology and Chinese Political Culture: An Analysis of the Revolutionary *Yangbangxi*." In *Moral Behavior in Chinese Society*, ed. Richard W. Wilson, Sidney L. Greenblatt, and Amy Auerbacher Wilson, pp. 126–151. New York: Praeger, 1981.

Duara, Prasenjit. "Knowledge and Power in the Discourse of Modernity: The Campaigns against Popular Religion in Early Twentieth-Century China." *Journal of Asian Studies* 50, 1 (1991): 67–83.

——. *Rescuing History from the Nation: Questioning the Narratives of Modern China*. Chicago: University of Chicago Press, 1995.

Esherick, Joseph W., and Jeffrey N. Wasserstrom. "Acting Out Democracy: Political Theater in Modern China." In *Popular Protest and Political Culture in Modern China: Learning from 1989*, ed. Jeffrey N. Wasserstrom and Elizabeth J. Perry, pp. 28–66. Boulder, Colo.: Westview, 1992.

Fabian, Johannes. *Time and the Other: How Anthropology Makes Its Object*. New York: Columbia University Press, 1983.

Fan Zuogang et al., comps. *Nongcun jingshen wenming jianshe xintan* [*New explorations into building rural spiritual civilization*]. Beijing: Nongye chubanshe, 1987.

Felman, Shoshona. *The Literary Speech Act: Don Juan with J. L. Austin, or Seduction in Two Languages*. Ithaca: Cornell University Press, 1983.

Feng Jicai. "The Mao Button." In *"Chrysanthemums" and Other Stories*. Trans. Susan Wilf Chen, pp. 14–29. New York: Harcourt Brace Jovanovich, 1985.

Foucault, Michel. *Discipline and Punish: The Birth of the Prison*. Trans. Alan Sheridan. New York: Vintage, 1979.

——. "Governmentality." *Ideology and Consciousness* 6 (Autumn 1979): 5–21. Reprinted in *The Foucault Effect: Studies in Governmental Rationality*, ed. Graham Burchell et al. Chicago: University of Chicago Press, 1991.

——. *The History of Sexuality*. Vol. 1, *An Introduction*. Trans. Robert Hurley. New York: Vintage, 1980.

——. "Nietzsche, Genealogy, History." In *Language, Counter-Memory, Practice: Selected Essays and Interviews*, ed. Donald F. Bouchard. Ithaca: Cornell University Press, 1977.

——. "The Subject and Power." Afterword to *Michel Foucault: Beyond Structuralism and Hermeneutics*, ed. Hubert L. Dreyfus and Paul Rabinow, pp. 208–226. Chicago: University of Chicago Press, 1983.

Fujitani, Takeshi. "Inventing, Forgetting, Remembering: Toward a Historical Ethnography of the Nation-State." In *Cultural Nationalism in East Asia: Representation and Identity*, ed. Harumi Befu, pp. 77–106. Research Papers and Policy Studies, no. 39. Berkeley: Institute of East Asian Studies, University of California, 1993.

Gallagher, Catherine. "The Bio-Economics of *Our Mutual Friend*." *Zone* 5 (1989): 345–365.

——. "The Body versus the Social Body in the Works of Thomas Malthus and Henry Mayhew." *Representations* 4 (Spring 1986): 83–106.

Gao Yuan. *Born Red*. Stanford: Stanford University Press, 1987.

Gluck, Carol. *Japan's Modern Myths: Ideology in the Late Meiji Period*. Princeton: Princeton University Press, 1985.

Greenblatt, Sidney L., ed. *The People of Taihang: An Anthology of Family Histories*. White Plains, N.Y.: International Arts and Sciences Press, 1976.

Greenblatt, Stephen. "China: Visiting Rites." *Raritan* (Spring 1983): 1–23.

——. *Renaissance Self-Fashioning: From More to Shakespeare*. Chicago: University of Chicago Press, 1980.

Greenhalgh, Susan. "The Peasantization of the One-Child Policy in Shaanxi." In *Chinese Families in the Post-Mao Era*, ed. Deborah Davis and Stevan Harrell, pp. 219–250. Berkeley: University of California Press, 1993.

Guha, Ranajit. "On Some Aspects of the Historiography of Colonial India." In *Selected Subaltern Studies*, ed. Ranajit Guha and Gayatri Chakravorty Spivak. New York: Oxford University Press, 1988.

Guha, Ranajit, and Gayatri Chakravorty Spivak, eds. *Selected Subaltern Studies*. New York: Oxford University Press, 1988.

Gu Hua. *Pagoda Ridge*. In *"Pagoda Ridge" and Other Stories*. Trans. Gladys Yang. Beijing: Panda Books, 1985.

——. *A Small Town Called Hibiscus*. Trans. Gladys Yang. Beijing: Panda Books, 1983.

Hansen, Chad. "Punishment and Dignity in China." In *Individualism and Holism: Studies in Confucian and Taoist Values*, ed. Donald Munro, pp. 359–382. Ann Arbor: University of Michigan Press, 1985.

Harvey, David. *The Condition of Postmodernity*. London: Blackwell, 1989.

Havel, Václav. "The Power of the Powerless." In *Václav Havel, or Living in Truth*, ed. Jan Vladislav, pp. 36–122. London: Faber and Faber, 1986.

Hershatter, Gail. "The Subaltern Talks Back: Reflections on Subaltern Theory and Chinese History." *positions* 1, 1 (Spring 1993): 103–130.

Hevia, James L. *Cherishing Men from Afar: Qing Guest Ritual and the McCartney Embassy of 1793*. Durham: Duke University Press, 1995.

———. *Making China Perfectly Equal*. Durham: Duke University Press, forthcoming.

Hinton, William. *Fanshen: A Documentary of Revolution in a Chinese Village*. New York: Vintage, 1966.

———. *Shenfan: The Continuing Revolution in a Chinese Village*. New York: Vintage, 1983.

Hu, Hsien-chin. "The Chinese Concept of 'Face.'" *American Anthropologist* 46, 1 (1944): 45–64.

Huang, Shu-min. *The Spiral Road: Change in a Chinese Village through the Eyes of a Communist Party Leader*. Boulder, Colo.: Westview, 1989.

Huters, Theodore. "Blossoms in the Snow: Lu Xun and the Dilemma of Modern Chinese Literature. *Modern China* 10, 1 (1984): 49–78.

———. "Ideologies of Realism in Modern China: The Hard Imperatives of Imported Theory." In *Politics, Ideology, and Literary Discourse in Modern China*, ed. Liu Kang and Xiaobing Tang, pp. 147–173. Durham: Duke University Press, 1993.

Jay, Martin. *Downcast Eyes: The Denigration of Vision in Twentieth-Century French Thought*. Berkeley: University of California Press, 1994.

Jones, Andrew. *Like a Knife: Ideology and Genre in Contemporary Chinese Popular Music*. Ithaca: Cornell East Asia Institute, 1992.

Jowitt, John A. "Mainland China: A National One-Child Program Does Not Exist." Parts 1 and 2. *Issues and Studies* 25, 9 (September 1989): 48–70; 10 (October 1989): 71–97.

Kaplan, Caren. "Deterritorializations: The Rewriting of Home and Exile in Western Feminist Discourse." *Cultural Critique* 6 (Spring 1987): 187–198.

Kavanaugh, James H. "Ideology." In *Critical Terms for Literary Study*, ed. Frank Lentricchia and Thomas McLaughlin, pp. 306–320. Chicago: University of Chicago Press, 1990.

Kipnis, Andrew. "'Face': An Adaptable Discourse of Social Surfaces." *positions* 3, 1 (Spring 1995): 119–148.

Kristof, Nicholas D., and Sheryl WuDunn. *China Wakes: The Struggle for the Soul of a Rising Power*. New York: Random House/Times, 1994.

Laclau, Ernesto. *New Reflections on the Revolution of Our Time*. London: Verso, 1990.

Lefort, Claude. *The Political Forms of Modern Society: Bureaucracy, Democracy, Totalitarianism*. Cambridge: MIT Press, 1986.

Li, Lianjiang, and Kevin O'Brien. "Chinese Villagers and Popular Resistance." Paper presented at the Twenty-Fourth Sino-American Conference on Contemporary China, Washington, D.C., June 1995.

Liang, Heng, as told to Judith Shapiro. *Son of the Revolution*. New York: Vintage, 1984.

Li Bingyan, ed. *Sanshiliuji xinbian* [A new edition of the thirty-six stratagems]. Beijing: People's Liberation Army Press, 1981.

Liu, Lydia H. "Translingual Practice: The Discourse of Individualism between China and the West." *positions* 1, 1 (Spring 1993): 160–193.

Liu Heng. *Liu Heng yingshi zuopinji* [The collected screenplays of Liu Heng]. Beijing: Zhongguo shehui kexue chubanshe, 1993.

Li Zhenxi and Bai Yukun, eds. *Zhongguo baokan ciyu* [New Chinese press terms]. Beijing: Huayu jiaoxue chubanshe, 1987.

Lu Xun [Lu Hsun]. "Literature of a Revolutionary Period." In *Selected Works*, 4 vols., trans. Yang Xianyi and Gladys Yang, 2:334–341. Beijing: Foreign Languages Press, 1980.

——. "The New Year's Sacrifice." In *Selected Stories of Lu Hsun*. Trans. Yang Hsien-yi and Gladys Yang. Beijing: Foreign Languages Press, 1960.

Madsen, Richard. *Power and Morality in a Chinese Village*. Berkeley: University of California Press, 1984.

Mao Tsetung. "On the Correct Handling of Contradictions among the People" (1957). In *Selected Readings from the Works of Mao Tsetung*, pp. 432–479. Peking: Foreign Languages Press, 1971 (pp. 432–479).

——. "Report on an Investigation of the Peasant Movement in Hunan" (1927). In *Selected Readings from the Works of Mao Tsetung*, pp. 23–39. Peking: Foreign Languages Press, 1971.

Marcus, George E. "Contemporary Problems of Ethnography in the Modern World System." In *Writing Culture: The Poetics and Politics of Ethnography*, ed. James Clifford and George E. Marcus, pp. 165–193. Berkeley: University of California Press, 1986.

Mauss, Marcel. *The Gift: Forms and Functions of Exchange in Archaic Societies*. New York: Norton, 1967.

Mbembe, Achille. "Prosaics of Servitude and Authoritarian Civilities." *Public Culture* 5, 1 (Fall 1992): 123–145.

Meng Yue. "Female Images and National Myth." In *Gender Politics in Modern China*, ed. Tani E. Barlow, pp. 119–136. Durham: Duke University Press, 1993.

Mitchell, Timothy. *Colonizing Egypt*. Berkeley: University of California Press, 1988.

Mosher, Steven. *China Misperceived: American Illusions and Chinese Reality*. New York: Basic, 1990.

Nairn, Tom. *The Breakup of Britain*. London: New Left Books, 1977.

Pêcheux, Michel. "Are the Masses an Inanimate Object?" In *Linguistic Variation: Models and Methods*, ed. David Sankoff, pp. 251–266. New York: Academic Press, 1978.

——. *Language, Semantics, and Ideology*. New York: St. Martin's, 1982.

Pemberton, John. *On the Subject of "Java."* Ithaca: Cornell University Press, 1994.

Perry, Elizabeth J. "Chinese Political Culture Revisited." In *Popular Protest and Political Culture in Modern China: Learning from 1989*, ed. Jeffrey N. Wasserstrom and Elizabeth J. Perry, pp. 1–13. Boulder, Colo.: Westview, 1992.

Pickowicz, Paul G. *Marxist Literary Thought in China: The Influence of Ch'ü Ch'iu-pai.* Berkeley: University of California Press, 1981.

Prakash, Gyan. "Science 'Goes Native' in India." *Representations* (Winter 1992): 153–178.

Pusey, James. *China and Charles Darwin.* Cambridge: Harvard University Press, 1983.

Raphals, Lisa. *Knowing Words: Wisdom and Cunning in the Classical Traditions of China and Greece.* Ithaca: Cornell University Press, 1992.

Ren Qun, ed. *Pian: Shijiu qi zhapian an de zhenxiang* [Swindles: The truth behind nineteen case histories of fraud]. Hebei: Guangming ribao chubanshe, 1989.

Robbins, Bruce. "Telescopic Philanthropy: Professionalism and Responsibility in *Bleak House.*" In *Nation and Narration,* ed. Homi K. Bhabha, pp. 213–230. London: Routledge, 1990.

Rofel, Lisa. "Liberation Nostalgia and a Yearning for Modernity." In *Engendering China: Women, Culture, and the State,* ed. Christina K. Gilmartin, Gail Hershatter, Lisa Rofel, and Tyrene White, pp. 226–249. Cambridge: Harvard University Press, 1994.

——. "*Yearnings:* Televisual Love and Melodramatic Politics in Contemporary China." *American Ethnologist* 21, 4 (1994): 700–722.

Rupnik, Jacques. "Totalitarianism Revisited." In *Civil Society and the State: New European Perspectives,* ed. John Keane, pp. 263–289. London: Verso, 1988.

Rustin, Michael. "No Exit from Capitalism?" *New Left Review* 193 (May/June 1992): 96–107.

Sakai, Naoki. "Modernity and Its Critique: The Problem of Universalism and Particularism." *South Atlantic Quarterly* (1988): 93–122.

Selden, Mark. "Cooperation and Conflict: Cooperative and Collective Formation in China's Countryside." In *The Transition to Socialism in China,* ed. Mark Selden and Victor Lippit, pp. 32–97. Armonk, N.Y.: M. E. Sharpe, 1982.

Sha Yexin, Li Shoucheng, and Yao Mingde. "If Only I Were for Real." Trans. Janice Wickeri. In *The New Realism,* ed. Lee Yee, pp. 261–322. New York: Hippocrene, 1983.

——. "The Imposter (If I Were Real)." Trans. Daniel Kane. *Renditions,* nos. 19–20 (1983): 333–369.

——. "Jiaru wo shi zhende" [If only I were real]. *Qishi niandai* (January 1980): 76–96.

Shen Maotang, ed. *Rang renkou jingzhong changming* [Let the population alarm bell continue to ring: Reflections on the fourth population survey]. Nanjing: Nanjing Press, 1991.

Shen Yen-ping [Mao Dun]. *Midnight* [Ziye]. Hong Kong. C & W, 1976.

——. "*Spring Silkworms*" *and Other Stories.* 1933. Reprint, Peking: Foreign Languages Press, 1956.

Silverman, Kaja. *The Subject of Semiotics.* New York: Oxford University Press, 1983.

Spivak, Gayatri Chakravorty. "Can the Subaltern Speak?" In *Marxism and the Interpretation of Cultures,* ed. Cary Nelson and Lawrence Grossberg, pp. 271–313. Urbana: University of Illinois Press, 1988.

Stewart, Susan. *On Longing: Narratives of the Miniature, the Gigantic, the Souvenir, the Collection.* 1984. Reprint, Durham: Duke University Press, 1993.

Sun Meiyao, ed. *Xuanchuan gongzuo shiyong shouce* [Practical guide to propaganda work]. Beijing: Hongqi chubanshe, 1988.

Su Xiaokang. "My Views on 'A Sense of Mission,' " *Qiushi* [Seeking facts], no. 2 (1988): 47–48.

Tang Daiwang. "Woguo shi shei zuizao lunshu 'liangge wenming' de guanxi?" [Who was the first in China to theorize the relationship between the "two civilizations"?]. In *Shehui zhuyi jingshen wenming ziliao suoyin* [Index to materials on socialist spiritual civilization], vol. 2, ed. Lanzhou daxue tushuguan, pp. 52–53. Lanzhou: Gansu renmin chubanshe, 1985.

Taussig, Michael. *Mimesis and Alterity: A Particular History of the Senses.* New York: Routledge, 1993.

Trinh Minh-ha. Introduction to "The Inappropriate/d Other." Special issue of *Discourse* 8 (Fall/Winter 1986/87): 3–10.

Waldron, Arthur. "Representing China: The Great Wall and Cultural Nationalism in the Twentieth Century." In *Cultural Nationalism in East Asia: Representation and Identity*, ed. Harumi Befu, pp. 107–138. Berkeley: Institute of East Asian Studies, University of California, 1993.

Wang, Jing. "*Heshang* and the Paradoxes of Chinese Enlightenment." *Bulletin of Concerned Asian Scholars* 23, 3 (1991): 23–32.

——. "Romancing the Subject: Utopian Moments in the Chinese Aesthetics of the 1980s." *Discourse social/Social Discourse* [Special issue, "The Non-Cartesian Subjects East and West"] 6, 1–2 (Winter/Spring 1994): 115–142.

Wang Xiaoqiang and Bai Nanfeng. *Furaode pinkun: Zhongguo luohou diqude jingji kaocha* [The poverty of wealth: An economic investigation of China's backward areas]. Chengdu: Sichuan renmin chubanshe, 1986.

Weng Qiyin. *Wenming gujintan* [Civilization: Discussions old and new]. Fuzhou: Fujian renmin chubanshe, 1985.

Williams, Raymond. *Marxism and Literature.* New York: Oxford University Press, 1977.

Willis, Susan. *A Primer for Daily Life.* London: Routledge, 1991.

Wolf, Margery. *Women and the Family in Rural Taiwan.* Stanford: Stanford University Press, 1972.

Wong, Siu-lun. *Sociology and Socialism in Contemporary China.* London: Routledge and Kegan Paul, 1979.

Woodside, Alexander. *Community and Revolution in Modern Vietnam.* Boston: Houghton Mifflin, 1976.

Wu Ying. "Renfanzi yu yeman de hunyin" [The human peddler and a barbaric marriage]. *Baogao wenxue* [Reportage Literature] 1 (1989): 60–65.

Xie Zhihong and Lusheng Jia. *Gulaode zui'e: Quanguo funu da guaimai jishi* [An age-old crime: An on-the-spot record of the nation-wide abduction and sale of women]. Zhejiang: Zhejiang wenyi chubanshe, 1989.

Yang Fan. *Gongheguo disandai* [The Third Generation of the People's Republic of China] in *Kuashiji congshu* [Across the century series]. Chengdu: Sichuan renmin chuban-she, 1991.

Yang, Mayfair Mei-hui. "The Gift Economy and State Power in China." *Comparative Studies in Society and History* 31, 1 (January 1989): 25–54.

———. *Gifts, Favors, and Banquets: The Art of Social Relationships in China.* Berkeley: University of California Press, 1994.

———. "The Modernity of Power in the Chinese Socialist Order." *Cultural Anthropology* 3, 4 (November 1988): 408–427.

———. "Of Gender, State Censorship, and Overseas Capital: An Interview with Director Zhang Yimou." *Public Culture* 5, 2 (Winter 1993): 297–317.

Zhang, Yingjin. "Ideology of the Body in *Red Sorghum*: National Allegory, National Roots, and Third Cinema." *East-West Film Journal* (June 1990): 38–53.

Zhang Yimou. "Interview." By anonymous interviewer. China News Digest, Books and Journals Review, April 25, 1993, on the World Wide Web (http://www.cnd.org.8010/).

Zhang Yongjie, and Cheng Yuanzhong. *Disidairen.* [The fourth generation]. Hong Kong: Zhonghua shuju, 1989. Originally published by the Renmin chubanshe.

INDEX

Ann Anagnost is Assistant Professor of Anthropology
at the University of Washington.

Library of Congress Cataloging-in-Publication Data
Anagnost, Ann.
National past-times : narrative, representation, and
power in modern China / by Ann Anagnost.
p.   cm. — (Body, commodity, text)
Includes bibliographical references and index.
ISBN 0-8223-1961-6 (alk. paper). — ISBN 0-8223-1969-1
(pbk. : alk. paper)
1. China—Civilization—1949–   2. China—Social
conditions—1976–   3. China—Politics and government—1976–   I. Title.   II. Series.
DS777.6.A43   1997   951.05—dc21   96-6609 CIP